Hiking Mississippi

HELP US KEEP THIS GUIDE UP TO DATE

Every effort has been made by the author and editors to make this guide as accurate and useful as possible. However, many things can change after a guide is published—trails are rerouted, regulations change, techniques evolve, facilities come under new management, and so on.

We would appreciate hearing from you concerning your experiences with this guide and how you feel it could be improved and kept up to date. While we may not be able to respond to all comments and suggestions, we'll take them to heart, and we'll also make certain to share them with the author. Please send your comments and suggestions to the following address:

GPP
Reader Response/Editorial Department
P.O. Box 480
Guilford, CT 06437

Or you may e-mail us at: editorial@GlobePequot.com

Thanks for your input, and happy trails!

Hiking Mississippi

A Guide to 50 of the State's
Greatest Hiking Adventures

Johnny Molloy

FALCONGUIDES

GUILFORD, CONNECTICUT
HELENA, MONTANA
AN IMPRINT OF GLOBE PEQUOT PRESS

FALCONGUIDES®

Copyright © 2009 by Morris Book Publishing, LLC

All interior photos by Johnny Molloy

Project editor: David Legere
Text design: Nancy Freeborn
Layout artist: Maggie Peterson
Maps: Trailhead Graphics © Morris Book
Publishing, LLC

Library of Congress Cataloging-in-Publication Data is
available on file.

ISBN 978-0-7627-1117-8

Printed in the United States of America

10 9 8 7 6 5 4 3 2 1

To the people of Water Valley, my grandfather's hometown.

Contents

TARGET
EXPECT MORE. PAY LESS.

NORTH JACKSON - 601-956-1150
12/26/2019 04:33 PM EXPIRES 03/25/20

GROCERY
212340113   MP RICE   FB $0.85

HEALTH-BEAUTY-COSMETICS
253035975   Bounty   T $9.99

SUBTOTAL		$10.84
T = MS TAX 8.0000% on $9.99		$0.80
B = MS TAX 7.0000% on $0.85		$0.06

TOTAL $11.70
CASH PAYMENT $20.00
CHANGE DUE $8.30

REC#2-9360-0754-0081-0976-2 VCD#752-289-945

Help make your Target Run better.
Take a 2 minute survey about today's trip:

informtarget.com
User ID: 7063 9924 6991
Password: 890 238

CUÉNTENOS EN ESPAÑOL

Please take this survey within 7 days.

or credit REDcard™. **Apply now** in store
or at target.com/REDcard.

Go to target.com/returns for full refund/exchange policy.

REDcard™

Everyday savings.
Exclusive extras.

Elevate your Target run with Target debit
or credit REDcard™. **Apply now** in store
or at target.com/REDcard.

Mississippi Overview

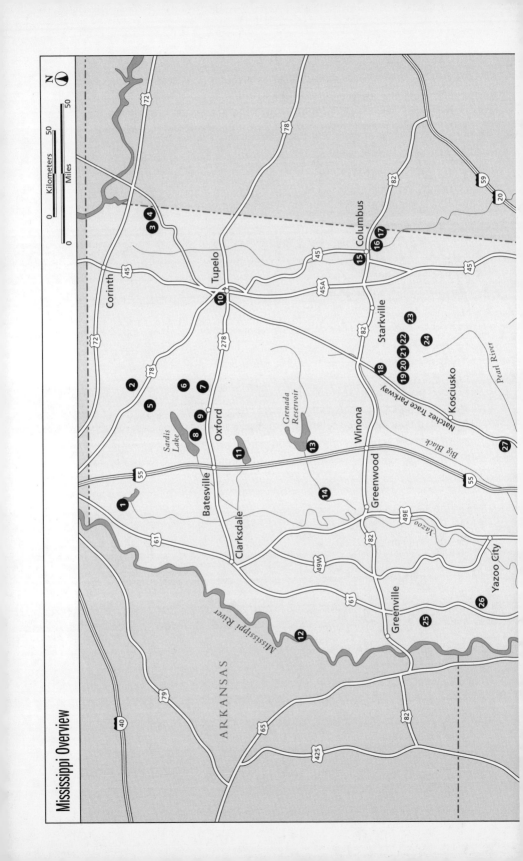

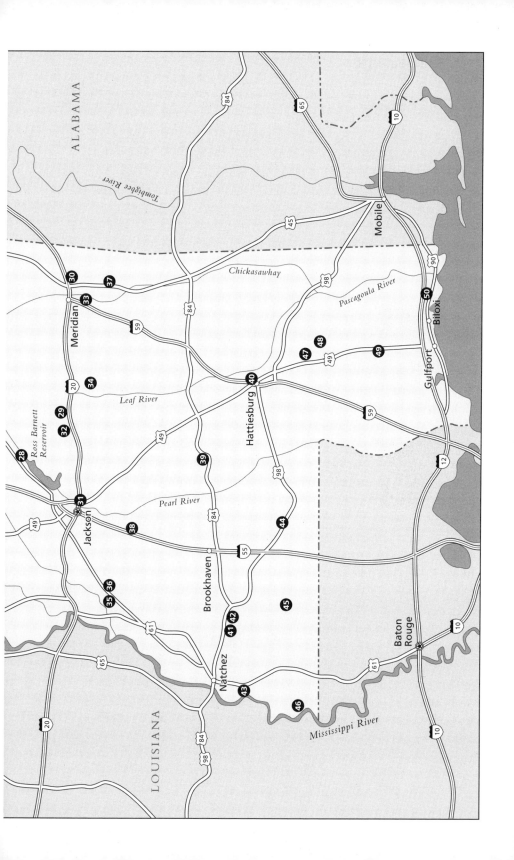

Acknowledgments

Thanks to the people of Mississippi who helped me every step of the way and to the land managers who answered my persistent questions. Thanks to DeLorme for use of the reliable Earthmate PN-20 and to Merrell for quality hiking shoes. Also a special thanks to Ernest Herndon for the sardine lunch and to Scott B. Williams, too. Specifically, I would like to thank the people who hiked with me: Pam Morgan, Wes Shepherd, and others. Thanks to my family in Memphis who housed me between research trips.

Introduction

I'm a lucky man to have had the privilege of writing this book. Being a native Memphian I had an idea of Mississippi's vast treasure of natural wonders. Over the years I had made forays into the Magnolia State, boating, fishing, backpacking, camping, and even grappling for catfish! But a trip along Black Creek down south demonstrated just what a beautiful and ecologically diverse place is Mississippi. The weeklong adventure just blew me away. First, we floated 41 miles down federally designated wild and scenic Black Creek, winding through the De Soto National Forest. Then, we strapped on backpacks and hiked our way on the Black Creek Trail back upriver for 40 miles. I'll never forget the nights spent camped on white sandbars, and the days cruising the river plain under big magnolias and widespread beeches, and standing on pine-topped bluffs that afforded sweeping views of the stream. It was then and there I realized Mississippi offered beauty from the Appalachian foothills to the Mississippi River to the Gulf Coast.

Inspired, I wrote this book, systematically exploring Mississippi for the best hikes. It was a real pleasure (most of the time) to travel the trails of Mississippi, from quiet Blue Lake Nature Trail in the Delta, to the busy Outcroppings Trail at Tishomingo State Park, to the wetlands of the Clear Springs Trail complex down Meadville way.

This book details fifty of the best hikes in Mississippi organized from north to south, from the Coldwater Nature Trail near the Tennessee state line to the boardwalks at Davis Bayou on the Gulf Coast and throughout the state between. Specific emphasis was placed on the most scenic destinations and unique places that make Mississippi so special, places like the rocky Bear Creek, the waterfalls of Clark Creek Natural Area, and the crest of Little Mountain.

Mississippi offers distinct regions in which to trek: the lake country of North Mississippi, the Delta and piney midlands of the Heart of Mississippi, and the coastal plain of South Mississippi. Hikes covering all three areas, of assorted lengths and difficulties, are included, and add to the variety of experiences. Many hikes take place in Mississippi's six national forests, covering 1.2 million acres spread about the state. These forests not only have hiking trails, but also campgrounds, waterways to float and fish, special scenic areas, botanical areas, hunting, and more. Mississippi state parks and forests also dot the land and are destinations for those who want to hike and explore. Wall Doxey State Park harbors innumerable springs. Lake Lowndes State Park offers recreation of all stripes, including, of course, hiking. Leroy Percy State Park has brooding swamp woods. These are but three examples of a fine state park system of which Mississippians should be proud. And don't forget the linear national park that extends 310 miles through the Magnolia State—the Natchez Trace Parkway. The Parkway functions as a corridor of protected land on which numerous hiking trails are found, including preserved sections of the historic Trace. No matter what entity manages the land, there is plenty to see in this state, from winding blackwater rivers to waterfalls framed in rich forests, to rock outcrops where overhangs provide trailside shelter, to dark swamps where nature's beasts find retreat.

Mississippi and its hiking destinations can be divided into three general regions. North Mississippi includes all points from its border with Tennessee to U.S. Highway 82 and an east-west line extending roughly from Greenville on the Big Muddy east to the Alabama line. This area is characterized by Appalachian foothills in the northeast, sloping southwesterly toward the Mississippi River. Army Corps of Engineers dams impound many area waterways and create recreational areas around them. North Mississippi also has several state parks, including what is regarded as Mississippi's finest hiking destination, Tishomingo State Park. This area is also home to the Holly Springs National Forest and the Tombigbee Waterway, both of which have hikes included along or near them. The Natchez Trace runs through this section on its way to the town of Natchez.

The Heart of Mississippi has the most hikes in it and is also the largest by size and population. This area ranges from US 82 south to approximately U.S. Highway 84, which stretches from the Louisiana border near Natchez, east to Waynesboro at the Alabama line. This vast heart encompasses a lot of Mississippi, ranging from classic Delta country to surprisingly hilly terrain in the east. This area holds four of Mississippi's national forests, multiple state parks, and the longest stretch of the Natchez Trace.

South Mississippi covers the most consistent terrain, which is the coastal plain. This land preserves state natural areas, national forests, and many state parks, as well as Davis Bayou, which is part of the Gulf Islands National Seashore. This is an area of vast pine forests cut by clear sand-bottomed streams and more vertical variation than the average person might expect. Clark Creek Natural Area, with its dense concentration of waterfalls, is an ideal example.

Each of these three regions adds to the variety and spice of the Mississippi hiking experience. Make sure and visit them all to see what the Magnolia State has to offer trail treaders.

You must reach these places by foot. The rewards increase with every footfall beneath stately pines on a sunny knoll or along a scenic lake. A respite into the "real" Mississippi will revitalize both mind and spirit. To wander through remote forests, to contemplate pioneer lives at an old homesite, or to peer into a cypress swamp will put our lives into perspective.

That is where this book will come into play. It will help you make every step count, whether you are leading the family on a brief day hike or undertaking a challenging backpack into the back of beyond. Because time is precious, this book distills the knowledge you'll need to make your outdoor experience the fullest.

With the joy of completing a book and the sadness of an adventure ended, I finished my research. But I will continue putting my lessons to work, enjoying more of Mississippi in future outdoor adventures. May this book help you get out and make some memories of your own, trekking the treasures of the Magnolia State.

Weather

Mississippi's climate offers good hiking conditions most of the year with high summer being the only time not conducive for hiking. During the long summer, highs regularly reach the 90s and a thunderstorm can come most any afternoon. Warm nights stay up in the 70s. Fall brings cooler nights and warm days. October is the driest month. Winter is variable. By the Gulf, highs push 60 degrees. Expect lows in the 40s, though subfreezing temperatures are the norm during cold snaps. Up north, winter highs are in the low 50s. No matter where you are in Mississippi, there are usually several mild days during each winter month. Precipitation comes in strong continental fronts, with persistent rains followed by sunny, cold days. Snow is uncommon, though not unheard of. The longer days of spring begin the warm-up process, even becoming hot, but temperatures can vary wildly. Spring will move north from the Gulf but is in full control of the entire state by mid-April. Using Jackson as a baseline, the rainiest months are from November through April. It is during this same span that highs average below 80, which are more favorable for hiking. However, you can still hike during the warmer months. Try to do your trekking in the mornings; that way you will also avoid most summer thunderstorms.

Flora and Fauna

Mississippi's topography ranges from the Appalachian foothills in the northeast to the Piney Hills to the enormous and wild Mississippi River bottoms to the Gulf Coast. Thus, the state's flora and fauna reflects this variety. Mississippi is a bit over 50 percent forested. The creeks and major river bottoms are covered in cypress, tupelo, and wetland oaks, as well as beech and the straight-trunked tulip tree. Shortleaf pine is king in the upland areas, along with its partners, the drier oaks—such as post oak, red oak, and mockernut hickory. Longleaf and slash pines are more common in central and southern Mississippi, with loblolly pines being in the moister areas of the south. Planted pine plantations extend throughout the state. Sweetgums seem to be everywhere.

Wildlife is abundant throughout the state. Raccoons, rabbits, and squirrels range widely. Deer are found in high numbers and are the mammal you are most likely to see. Kudzu—of which Mississippi has plenty—is an important browse food for deer, especially where they are in high numbers. Fawns use the dense vine cover of kudzu to stay hidden. Deer population estimates vary, with some ranging as high as a staggering 1.75 million of these four-legged creatures.

The black bear is making a comeback, but their numbers are limited to a few hundred. The state features two species: the American black bear and the endangered Louisiana black bear, each of which reach their greatest numbers in the Delta near Rolling Fork and all along the Mississippi River corridor from Louisiana to a couple of counties south of Memphis. Some are also found in the national forests in south Mississippi. A few are sighted every year in the northeast as well. Louisiana black bears are federally protected in Mississippi as a threatened subspecies.

The American alligator also ranges throughout south and central Mississippi, but sometimes can be found as far north as Lafayette County. Population estimates range around 35,000 spread out over 400,000 acres of alligator habitat. One-quarter of all the state's alligators live in Jackson County, home of the Pascagoula River. Another coastal county with a high population is Hancock.

The coastal component of Mississippi consists of marshes, beaches, dunes, and barrier islands. The saltwater-influenced environments are worlds unto themselves, with a variety of saltwater fish and mammals, including sharks and sea turtles. Pelicans, herons, egrets, skimmers, and other shorebirds occupy the Gulf Coast.

Zero Impact

We, as Mississippi trail users and advocates, must be especially vigilant to make sure our passage leaves no lasting mark. Here are some basic guidelines for preserving trails in the region:

- Pack out all your own trash, including biodegradable items like orange peels. You might also pack out garbage left by less considerate hikers.
- Don't approach or feed any wild creatures—the ground squirrel eyeing your snack food is best able to survive if it remains self-reliant.
- Don't pick wildflowers or gather rocks, antlers, feathers, and other treasures along the trail. Removing these items will only take away from the next hiker's experience.
- Avoid damaging trailside soils and plants by remaining on the established route. This is also a good rule of thumb for avoiding poison ivy and briars.
- Don't cut switchbacks, which can promote erosion.
- Be courteous by not making loud noises while hiking.
- Some of these trails are multiuse, which means you'll share them with other hikers, trail runners, mountain bikers, and equestrians. Familiarize yourself with the proper trail etiquette, yielding the trail when appropriate.
- Use outhouses at trailheads or along the trail.

How to Use This Guide

This guide is designed to be simple and easy to use. Each hike is described with a map and summary information that delivers the trail's vital statistics including distance, difficulty, fees and permits, schedule, canine compatibility, and trail contacts. Directions to the trailhead are also provided, along with a general description of what you'll see along the way. A detailed route finder (Miles and Directions) sets forth mileages between significant landmarks along the trail.

Hike Selection

This guide describes trails that are accessible to every hiker, whether visiting from out of state or someone lucky enough to live in Mississippi. The hikes range from 1 to over 20 miles, and a range of miles between, though most are less than 6 miles. They range in difficulty from flat excursions perfect for a family outing to more challenging treks in remote national forests. While these trails are among the best, keep in mind that nearby trails, often in the same park or preserve, may offer other options. I've sought to space hikes throughout the Magnolia State, so wherever your starting point, you'll find a great hike nearby.

Difficulty Ratings

To aid in the selection of a hike that suits particular needs and abilities, each is rated easy, moderate, or difficult. Bear in mind that even the most challenging routes can be made easy by hiking within your limits and taking rests when you need them.

- **Easy** hikes are generally short and flat, taking no longer than an hour to complete.
- **Moderate** hikes involve increased distance and relatively mild changes in elevation, and will take one to two hours to complete.
- **Difficult** hikes feature some steep stretches, greater distances, and generally take longer than two hours to complete.

These are completely subjective ratings—consider that what you think is easy is entirely dependent on your level of fitness and the adequacy of your gear (primarily shoes). If you are hiking with a group, you should select a hike with a rating that's appropriate for the least fit and prepared in your party.

Approximate hiking times are based on the assumption that on flat ground, most walkers average two miles per hour. Adjust that rate by the steepness of the terrain and your level of fitness (subtract time if you're an aerobic animal and add time if you're hiking with kids), and you have a ballpark hiking duration. Be sure to add more time if you plan to picnic or take part in other activities like bird watching or photography.

Trail Finder

Best Short Hikes
26 Blue Lake Nature Trail
34 Marathon Lake Loop
24 Legion State Park Loop
44 Bogue Chitto Water Park

Best Long Hikes
21 North Noxubee Hills Loop
22 Sheepranch Loop
29 Shockaloe Trail
49 Tuxachanie Trail

Best Hikes for History Lovers
35 Historic Trace near Rocky Springs
27 Natchez Trace at Choctaw Boundary
15 Double Loop at Plymouth Bluff
 2 Lakeshore Trail at Chewalla Lake

Best Hikes for Wildflowers
 1 Coldwater Nature Trails at Arkabutla Lake
48 Black Creek Trail from Janice Landing
31 Lefleur's Bluff State Park
13 Lost Bluffs Trail at Grenada Lake

Best Hikes for Bicyclers
 8 Clear Creek Loop at Sardis Lake
40 Longleaf Trace near Hattiesburg
39 Longleaf Trace near Prentiss
45 Ethel Vance Natural Area Trails

Best Hikes for Solitude Lovers
13 Lost Bluffs Trail at Grenada Lake
43 Magnolia Trail at Saint Catherine Creek National Wildlife Refuge
16 Lake Lowndes Horse and Bike Trail
41 Richardson Creek/Mills Branch Loop

Best Hikes for Backpackers
48 Black Creek Trail from Janice Landing
29 Shockaloe Trail
42 Tallys Creek Loop
49 Tuxachanie Trail

Best Hikes for Children
 6 Puskus Lake Interpretive Trail

Map Legend

Transportation

Interstate Highway	═══⟨55⟩═══
U.S. Highway	══⟨278⟩══
State Road	══⟨7⟩══
County/Forest Road	⊏CR 90⊐⊏FR 90⊐
Dirt Road	======
Railroad	┼─┼─┼─┼
Featured Trail	▬▬▬▬▬
Other Trail	─ ─ ─ ─ ─

Hydrology

Lake/Reservoir	
River/Creek	～
Intermittent Stream	~·~·~
Marsh/Swamp	
Sandbar	
Waterfall	⫽
Spring	⟳

Land Use

National Forest	
Local Park/State Park/ Wildlife Area	

Symbols

Trailhead (Start)	❶
Visitor Center	❓
Headquarters	🛈
Campground	⧋
Point of Interest/ Structure	■
Mountain/Peak	▲
Parking	🅿
Picnic Area	⛱
Restroom	🚻
Tower	🗼
Boat Launch	⛴
City/Town	○
Bridge	⌣
Viewpoint/ Overlook	⚐
Bench	▭
Gate	•—•
Steps	⦀⦀⦀

Scale	0 Kilometer 1 / 0 Mile 1

North Mississippi

1 Coldwater Nature Trails at Arkabutla Lake

This trail system explores the wooded bottomlands below Arkabutla Lake Dam in the Coldwater River drainage. Leave the well-developed recreation facilities situated in the general Outlet Channel area and follow a winding track, often paralleling old drainage canals in big woods. The final part of the hike travels the Big Oak Nature Trail along the Coldwater River.

Start: Outlet Channel Recreation Area
Distance: 4.9-mile loop
Approximate hiking time: 2.5 to 3.5 hours
Difficulty: Moderate
Trail surface: Dirt, leaves in varied woodlands
Seasons: Year-round
Other trail users: Mountain bicyclists
Canine compatibility: Leashed dogs permitted
Land status: Army Corps of Engineers property

Nearest town: Hernando
Fees and permits: No fees or permits required
Schedule: Open year-round
Maps: Coldwater River Nature Trail System; USGS maps: Banks, Frees Corner
Trail contacts: U.S. Army Corps of Engineers, 3905 Arkabutla Dam Road, Coldwater, MS 38618; (662) 562-6261; www.mvk.usace .army.mil/Lakes/ms/arkabutla

Finding the trailhead: From exit 280 on Interstate 55, Hernando/Commerce Street, take Highway 304 west 1.4 miles to the Hernando town square. Continue west on Highway 304 for 10.6 more miles, to the community of Eudora, and turn left at a four-way intersection, joining Highway 301 south, following signs for Arkabutla Lake Dam. Go for 4.1 miles, then turn left onto Pratt Road. Continue forward for 1.8 miles, then reach the base of the dam. Turn right toward Outlet Channel. Go for 0.8 mile, then turn right, following the road to Outlet Channel. Enter a circular drive and picnic area, reaching the trailhead near the Outlet Channel and covered pavilion. The trailhead has covered shelter, water, a shaded picnic area, and a playground. *DeLorme: Mississippi Atlas & Gazetteer:* Page 17 D10. GPS trailhead coordinates: N34 45' 37.28" / W90 7' 43.61".

The Hike

The Coldwater River Nature Trail System offers interconnected loops. This primarily bottomland circuit circles around old canals, elevated dikes, and irregular bottoms that are inundated for parts of the year. At times it drops off and on the dikes or comes along canals, long since overgrown, and that's when the trail undulates. Late summer and fall is when this trail will be its driest and its best. The sloughs and old canals are intermittent and will run nearly dry too, but almost always have a little water in them somewhere. You'll also notice the beaver dams here and there in these waterways. Mountain bikers enjoy the track as well. Bug spray is recommended during the warmer weather months.

This is the Five Mile Loop and is the longest loop in the system. It is blazed in red. To start the hike you will be tempted to head forward from the trailhead kiosk, bridging a small stream that flows into the Coldwater River. Don't! This is your return route. Instead, backtrack about 100 yards on the road on which you came. Then, as you near the restrooms, turn left and enter the forest.

The hike starts with some surprising undulation amid an imperious forest of paw paw, oaks, sweetgum, ash, and sycamore. Shagbark hickory and hackberry trees are easy to spot with their unusual bark. Shagbark looks like it is peeling and hackberry bark is gray with warty bumps on it. Huge vines swaddle bigger trees. The trail roughly follows a dug channel to the left. Pass a wildlife clearing bordered with bird nest boxes.

The track persists northeasterly to reach a trail junction. The Five Mile Loop stays right to shortly cross Pratt Road. Pines become more prevalent in this area—they were planted after the dam was built in the 1940s. The old roadbed penetrates a field bordered with pines, then veers right in pines and oaks. Climb a hill. You'll undoubtedly notice the hunting blinds. Disabled hunters use this area for a late fall deer hunt every year. Check with the Army Corps of Engineers office for the exact dates if you are hiking then.

This hike often follows a raised berm overlooking bottomland forest

Kudzu infiltrates the woods here. Go by the Dub Patton Day Use alternate trailhead, accessible via Arkabutla Lake Road. Travel the highest elevation of the trail system while circling the upper end of the watershed. The main creek and its tributaries were mostly canalized when the dam was built. Mature pine woods distinguish themselves from the bottomland hardwoods you traveled earlier. Begin meandering south back into bottomland to cross Pratt Road a second time, reaching a junction shortly thereafter. A left turn shortens the loop, but bear right to continue the described trail.

Continue forward, winding in rich bottomland forest, circling around a creek that you cross. Notice the river birch and cypress trees immediately along the stream. The Five Mile Loop journeys under tall and sturdy laurel oaks and water oaks before joining the main streambed flowing toward the Coldwater River. End up on a dike heading south-southwest. Land drops off on both sides of you, with water below in season.

Follow the high dike for a distance, then drift left just before reaching the parking area, and come to a trail junction with a bench. Turn right here onto the Big Oak Nature Trail. An accompanying handout, available at the trailhead or nearby corps office, enhances this part of the hike, which comes alongside the channelized Coldwater River. You can see a boat ramp across the water after coming alongside the river. Shortly reach the trailhead and cross a bridge to reach the parking area.

Miles and Directions

0.0 Start at Outlet Channel. Backtrack on the road entered, following it to leave left into the woods before the restrooms.

0.5 Pass around a wildlife clearing with bird boxes on its perimeter. The trail reenters woods.

1.3 Reach trail junction; Two Mile Loop and Three Mile Loop trails turn left here.

1.4 Cross paved Pratt Road. Trail follows the old roadbed. Pines increase in number.

1.6 Trail veers right as old roadbed continues straight ahead.

2.0 Reach alternate trailhead coming from Arkabutla Lake Road. Stay left.

2.9 Cross Pratt Road a second time, now southbound. Pass a trail junction and keep right for the longest loop.

3.5 Cross an unnamed creek. The Five Mile Loop continues circling streamside.

4.1 Trail junction. This loop turns right, south, as the other trail uses rock-elevated track to get over canal.

4.6 At a final trail junction, veer right onto Big Oak Nature Trail.

4.9 Cross a bridge over a streambed to arrive back at the trailhead.

More Information

Local Information

Desoto County Tourism Association, P.O. Box 147, Southaven, MS 38671; (662) 393-877; www.desotocountytourism.com.

Coldwater Nature Trails at Arkabutla Lake

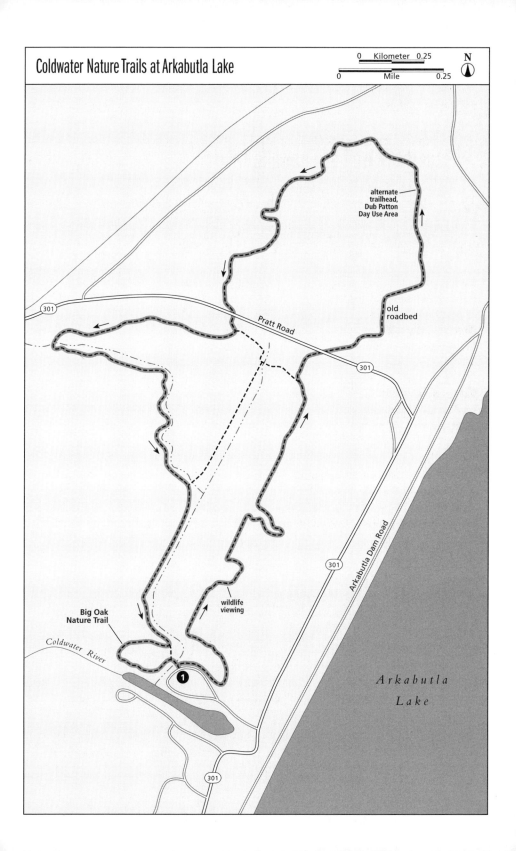

0   Kilometer   0.25

0   Mile   0.25

N

alternate
trailhead,
Dub Patton
Day Use Area

old
roadbed

301

Pratt Road

301

301

Arkabutla Dam Road

Big Oak
Nature Trail

Coldwater River

wildlife
viewing

1

301

*Arkabutla
Lake*

Local Events/Attractions

Tunica Casinos, www.tunica.com. The numerous casinos of Tunica, Mississippi, are located just southwest of Arkabutla Lake and Desoto County. Food and entertainment are part of the greater Tunica experience.

2 Lakeshore Trail at Chewalla Lake

This hike traces a winding track along the west shoreline of scenic 260-acre Chewalla Lake, traveling about the recreation area facilities and also by an old Indian mound. It continues curving among hills to reach the lake dam, which it crosses before ending.

Start: Chewalla Lake boat ramp
Distance: 3.4 miles out-and-back
Approximate hiking time: 1.5 to 2.5 hours
Difficulty: Moderate
Trail surface: Gravel, leaves, dirt
Seasons: Year-round
Other trail users: Hikers only
Canine compatibility: Leashed dogs permitted
Land status: National forest
Nearest town: Holly Springs

Fees and permits: Recreation area user fee required
Schedule: Open year-round
Maps: Holly Springs National Forest; USGS maps: Potts Camp
Trail contacts: Holly Springs National Forest, 1000 Front Street, Oxford, MS 38655; (662) 236-6550; www.fs.fed.us/r8/mississippi/hollysprings

Finding the trailhead: From the intersection of Highway 7 and U.S. Highway 78 on the south side of Holly Springs, take US 78 east for 6.9 miles to Lake Center, exit 37. Turn left to cross over US 78 and go for 0.3 mile, then turn left (west) on Highway 178 and follow it 0.7 mile to Higdon Road. Turn right on Higdon Road, then follow it 3.0 miles to Chewalla Lake Road, Forest Road 611. Turn right on Chewalla Lake Road and follow it to dead-end at the lake. Stay left toward the boat ramp. *DeLorme: Mississippi Atlas & Gazetteer:* Page 19 D8. GPS trailhead coordinates: N34 44' 5.3" / W89 20' 16.4".

The Hike

This hike is just one highlight of this fine North Mississippi recreation destination, which also offers fishing and camping. The 260-acre lake is named for its main feeder branch, Chewalla Creek. The Choctaw word "Chewalla" means Supreme Being, and refers to the Indian mound that is preserved as part of the recreation area. A quality twenty-seven-site campground, with hot showers, makes for a good base camp to enjoy this hiking trail as well as the swim beach, playground, and boat ramp for fishing.

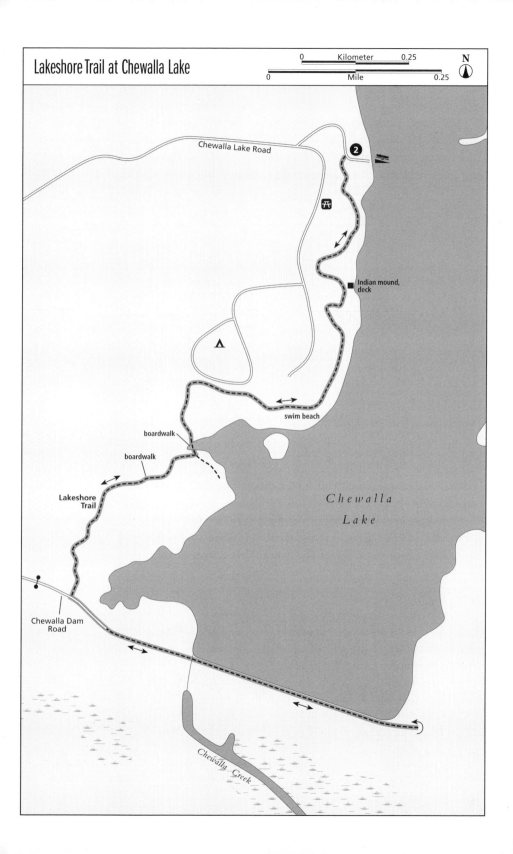

Lakeshore Trail at Chewalla Lake

0 Kilometer 0.25

0 Mile 0.25

N

Chewalla Lake Road

2

Indian mound, deck

swim beach

boardwalk

boardwalk

Lakeshore Trail

Chewalla Lake

Chewalla Dam Road

Chewalla Creek

As you face the boat ramp, the trail starts to your right through the opening of the split rail fence. The wide, pea gravel track enters the greater Chewalla Lake Recreation Area. The impoundment is to your left. Immediately span a small branch. Hills bordering the lake rise to your right. Picnic tables stand under tall trees. Circle around a small spring branch and enjoy a grand view of the lake. Bridge a second branch to reach two highlights at once—the Chewalla Indian Mound and an observation deck overlooking the lake. The high perch avails a superlative aquatic vista.

Mississippi has a surprisingly large number of Indian mounds. Archaeologists guess this particular mound was from the Middle Woodland Period, about 2,000 years ago. These early Mississippians, despite living in permanent or semi-permanent settlements, survived through hunting and gathering. The Chewalla Mound is typical of the Woodland Period mounds—roundish and dome shaped, ranging up to 18 feet in height and 100 feet in diameter. Often, high-ranking members of the settlement were buried in these mounds.

Beyond the mound, the path circles around intermittent drainages to reach the swim area. A spur trail uses a covered bridge to reach a small island. The main path shortly reverts to dirt, becoming more of a traditional hiking trail as it skirts behind the recreation area campground. Reach rich bottomland to bridge an arm of the lake. A long boardwalk crosses the swampy slough. Remain in thick trailside woodland, shortly crossing a wetland on another boardwalk. The trail then leaves the shoreline for hill country. Dogwoods, oaks, and tulip trees grace the hillside, along with the inevitable sweetgums. The terrain's steepness may astonish here.

After gaining the hilltop the Lakeshore Trail joins closed Chewalla Dam Road, a simple dirt track. Keep the lake to your left. Emerge onto the narrow, open, earthen dam. The outflow of the lake is clearly audible, and is the resumption of Chewalla Creek, which is the main branch feeding Chewalla Lake. A spur trail leads right, down to the rocky stream below the dam. This is a popular fishing spot. The dam crest reveals long-range views northward of the lake. The swim beach is clearly visible. Travel the arrow-straight length of the dam. Beyond the far side of the earthen structure, you can see where Chewalla Dam Road continues, while other spur trails head toward the lake, but all peter out before long. This is a good place to turn around.

Miles and Directions

0.0 Start at recreation area boat ramp. Walk through opening in split rail fence.

0.2 Reach Chewalla Indian Mound and the lake observation deck.

0.5 Pass the recreation area swim beach.

0.8 Bridge swampy slough on boardwalk. Trail splits ahead. Faint path goes left along lakeshore. Main path curves right.

1.1 Reach closed and gated Chewalla Dam Road. Stay left here.

1.7 Reach the end of the dam, turn around.

3.4 Arrive back at trailhead.

More Information

Local Information
Holly Springs Chamber of Commerce, 148 E. College Avenue, Holly Springs, MS 38635; (662) 252-2943; www.hollyspringsmschamberofcommerce.org.

Local Events/Attractions
Kudzu Festival, www.visithollysprings.org. Held on the square in fall, it offers a carnival, a gospel jamboree, a political rally, arts and crafts, a rodeo, and a barbecue cook-off.

Holly Springs Pilgrimage, www.visithollysprings.org. Tour all the historic antebellum homes of the city; a place spared the destruction of the Civil War.

3 Bear Creek Loop

Tishomingo State Park, 1,530 acres, is set among outlier foothills of the Appalachian Mountains and is Mississippi's high country. This hike travels along Bear Creek, with its stone outcrops towering over rapids, then turns away from the valley to pass a pioneer cabin. From here the trail travels the upper end of the Bear Creek Canyon, paralleling rockhouses, overhangs, and other stone features before returning to Bear Creek with its watery splendor.

Start: Picnic area near the park pool

Distance: 4.1-mile loop

Approximate hiking time: 2.5 to 3.5 hours

Difficulty: Somewhat difficult due to hills and rocky trail

Trail surface: Forested footpath, often rocky

Seasons: Year-round

Other trail users: Hikers only

Canine compatibility: Leashed dogs permitted

Land status: State park

Nearest town: Tishomingo

Fees and permits: Park entry fee required

Schedule: Open year-round

Maps: Tishomingo State Park trails; USGS maps: Belmont

Trail contacts: Tishomingo State Park, P.O. Box 880, Tishomingo, MS 38873; (662) 438-6914; http://home.mdwfp.com/parks.aspx

Finding the trailhead: From Tupelo, take the Natchez Parkway northeast to milepost 304 and an intersection. Turn left at the intersection and follow the paved road 0.5 mile, then turn right to reach the state park entrance station. Continue on the main park road and after 2.9 miles stay forward at an intersection, following signs for the Swinging Bridge and swimming pool. Follow the road until it ends near the swimming pool. *DeLorme: Mississippi Atlas & Gazetteer:* Page 21 F10. GPS trailhead coordinates: N34 36' 12.57" / W88 10' 50.00".

The Hike

This hike explores the human and natural history of Tishomingo State Park, a place considered to have the finest hiking in the Magnolia State. Be prepared for a rocky trek and take your time. Leave the park picnic area and follow a couple of disc golf holes that leave you wondering if you are on the right path. Nearby Bear Creek flows quietly, shaded by large beech trees. Beyond a 65-foot bridge spanning a tributary, the Bear Creek valley reveals mossy stones and ferns. The trail narrows, crossing intermittent feeder branches flowing into Bear Creek. Beard cane makes the lush valley even thicker. The creekside flats will be rich with wildflowers such as trillium and bloodroot in spring. Over 600 species of ferns and wildflowers have been identified in the park.

Lose sight of the creek to join an old roadbed. Look for an old exposed iron pipe. This was installed by the Civilian Conservation Corps (CCC) when they developed this park in the 1930s. The upper end of the pipe once led from a spring down to the park swimming pool. Nowadays, the park pool is fed through a public source and is chlorinated. How times have changed! Trace a rocky branch on your right then pop out onto the main park road. Just ahead is an 1840s pioneer cabin moved here from Prentiss County. Circle around the Lily Pond, also known as the CCC Pond, on a

Boulders line the trail in the Bear Creek Canyon

Bear Creek Loop

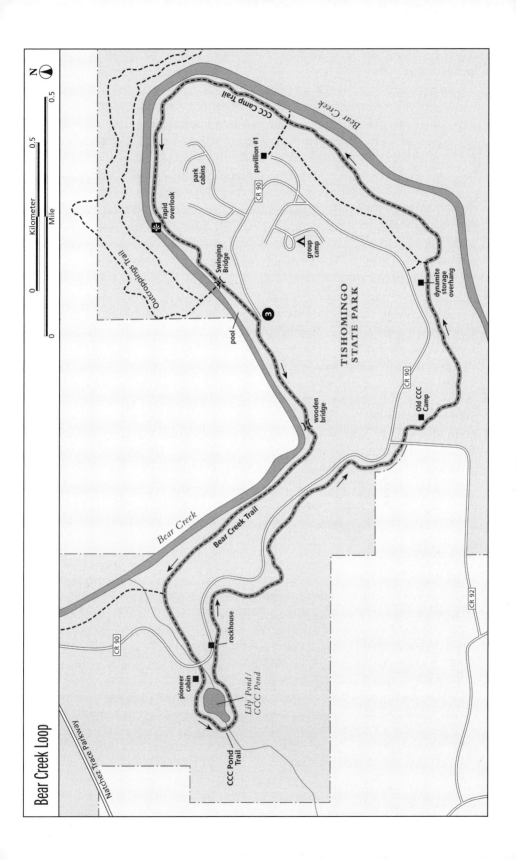

TISHOMINGO STATE PARK

CCC Camp Trail

Bear Creek

park cabins

pavillion #1

rapid overlook

CR 90

Swinging Bridge

pool

Outcroppings Trail

group camp

dynamite storage overhang

Old CCC Camp

CR 90

wooden bridge

CR 90

Bear Creek

Bear Creek Trail

rockhouse

pioneer cabin

Lily Pond / CCC Pond

CCC Pond Trail

Natchez Trace Parkway

CR 92

N

Kilometer

0   0.5   0.5

Mile

0

foot trail bordered by many sandstone outcrops and cabin-size boulders. Cross the stream that feeds the pond, looking just downstream for a large rock outcrop beside the watercourse. Other rock outcrops beg a scramble.

Reach a full-blown rockhouse beyond the pond, about 10 by 20 feet with a level floor; many fallen former overhangs are near this rockhouse. The trail is fainter beyond the rockhouse, winding along hillsides covered in thick forest and broken with innumerable rock outcrops, which are the upper border of Bear Creek Canyon.

▶ **Woodall Mountain, at 906 feet, is the highest point in Mississippi. It is in Tishomingo County, just a few miles north of Tishomingo State Park.**

The main park road isn't far away, but don't let that distract you from this unique Magnolia State hike. Expect the going to be slow with all the rocks on the trail, while twisting through boulder gardens.

The CCC camp through which you next pass housed the young men who developed the state park back in the 1930s. About fifteen concrete foundations remain scattered in the woods, one of which you pass. The trail drops through a cliffline to reenter the Bear Creek Canyon upstream of where you were, since the stream makes a ninety-degree curve in the park. The stony and cumbersome track weaves through more gorgeous rock gardens on a south-facing slope.

The outcrops and overhangs become too numerous to mention; however, look to the left for an overhang that has some stone bricked into its lower portion—it was the dynamite storage spot during park development. Watch for stone steps going left to the bluff top and right downhill. If you walk up the steps and turn right, you can stay on top of the bluff on an alternate trail. However, the best route is to take the stone steps steeply downhill through a boulder garden never imagined in Mississippi. Bear Creek is now to your right. The Bear Creek Loop picks up an old roadbed and the walking becomes easier, passing shoals beneath a high sandbar before returning to the developed area of the park.

Miles and Directions

0.0 Start at the end of the road beyond the swimming pool, walk west through picnic area and along holes of a disc golf course on Bear Creek Trail.

0.3 Cross a wooden bridge over a tributary of Bear Creek.

0.8 Stay left at trail junction on a connector trail, as the Bear Creek Trail leaves right toward Natchez Trace and Tishomingo State Park campground.

0.9 Cross the main park road and reach 1840s pioneer cabin and CCC Pond, also known as Lily Pond. Circle pond on CCC Pond Trail.

1.2 Pass overhanging rockhouse after circling CCC Pond, now on CCC Camp Trail. Stone steps lead left down from the rockhouse to a parking area where visitors can access the CCC Pond. Stay right now on a much fainter trail.

1.6 Briefly dip into bottomland as a tributary stream breaks through the Bear Creek Canyon. Resume traveling along upper canyon wall.

2.2 After passing through a grassy spot with a power line overhead, the trail then enters a dense pine-holly forest, to cross Tishomingo County Road 92. Stay on the trail, returning to woods.

2.4 Pass through Fatman's Squeeze, splitting tight boulders, and continue along a cliffline.

2.6 Pass an overhang with bricks added onto it. This was the dynamite storage area during the park's construction.

2.7 Stone steps lead left to bluff top and a trail leading atop bluff, or right, down to continue loop. Stay right, down stone steps.

3.2 Reach four-way trail junction. To your right it is but a short distance to rocky Bear Creek and the remains of an old suspension bridge washed away by flood in 1974. To your left a trail leads uphill to Pavilion #1, with a fountain, after passing underneath a massive rockhouse with a small spring in it. The rockhouse is worth a look. This loop continues forward.

3.8 Reach a gravel road and follow it to the Swinging Bridge over Bear Creek.

4.1 Arrive back at trailhead after passing swimming pool.

More Information

Local Information
Tishomingo County Tourism Council, 1001 Battleground Drive, Luka, MS 38852; (662) 423-9933; www.tishomingo.org.

Local Events/Attractions
Tishomingo County Archives & History Museum, 203 East Quitman Street, Luka, MS 38852, (662) 423-3500. Set in the 1870 courthouse for Tishomingo County, it offers two stories of photographs and history, with rotating exhibits.

4 Outcroppings Trail

Take a rugged hike at Tishomingo State Park. Here, the Appalachian foothills have stuck their toe into Mississippi and Bear Creek has cut a rocky gorge through sandstone, making for a park unlike any other in this book. The Outcroppings Trail travels high and low through the Bear Creek Canyon, revealing a rocky stream and stone features such as rockhouses, overhangs, and clifflines.

Start: Swinging Bridge
Distance: 2.0-mile loop
Approximate hiking time: 1.5 to 2.5 hours
Difficulty: Moderate, relatively short hike
Trail surface: Rock and dirt in woods
Seasons: Early fall through late spring
Other trail users: Rock climbers
Canine compatibility: Leashed dogs permitted
Land status: State park

Nearest town: Tishomingo
Fees and permits: Park entry fee required
Schedule: Open year-round
Maps: Tishomingo State Park trails; USGS maps: Belmont
Trail contacts: Tishomingo State Park, P.O. Box 880, Tishomingo, MS 38873; (662) 438-6914; http://home.mdwfp.com/parks.aspx

Finding the trailhead: From Tupelo, take the Natchez Parkway northeast to milepost 304 and an intersection. Turn left at the intersection and follow the paved road 0.5 mile, then turn right to reach the state park entrance station. Continue on the main park road and after 2.9 miles stay forward at an intersection, following signs for the Swinging Bridge and swimming pool. Follow the road to the Swinging Bridge, which will be on your right. *DeLorme: Mississippi Atlas & Gazetteer:* Page 21 F10. GPS trailhead coordinates: N34 36' 9.98" / W88 11' 0.79".

Rock overhangs such as this one are a surprise for Mississippi hikers

The Hike

The Swinging Bridge, built in 1939 by the Civilian Conservation Corps (CCC), is approximately 6 feet wide and spans Bear Creek between rustic stone abutments. The bridge, in many ways the enduring symbol of this park, is just one example of the handiwork of the CCC boys that has resulted in the entire state park being put on the National Register of Historic Places. The level track, marked with red paint blazes, meanders through creekside woodland dominated by white oaks and pines. Ground cover is dense with lush ferns that reflect the physiographic region that is an extension of the Appalachian foothills. Intermittent feeder streams trickle across the trail from a hillside to your left where the first rock outcrops are revealed. These outcrops throughout the state park are popular with climbers. Approximately 1,500 to 2,000 climbing permits are issued per year. The stone features will be more visible when the leaves are off the trees. Bear Creek, 30 to 40 feet wide, flows to your right in noisy shoals. It is a popular canoeing stream. The park rents canoes and offers a shuttle for a fee.

Musclewood and cypress trees grow on the water's edge, while just a short ways inland sycamore, tulip, and beech—along with the ever-present sweetgum—shade the path before it turns away from Bear Creek. Wander among colossal boulders, some partly clothed with vegetation, others rising forth naked from the forest floor. This Highland Church Sandstone from the Paleozoic era has eroded slower than the other rock, leaving these bluffs, boulders, and other formations. The rock coloration ranges from white to gray to rust, depending upon the exposure to sunlight and moisture. Notice another Appalachian relic, mountain laurel, growing below the outcrops. The trail is quite steep here and meets a loop shortcut. Keep alongside the bluff, reaching two huge rock shelters up the hill that people can't resist visiting. You can actually walk between the twin overhangs and climb to the top of them, standing out on their lips, which extend over the shelters themselves.

The gravel track continues winding below the outcrops. Shortly cross a small branch. Don't pass up the spur trail leading right to a waterfall. There, a small stream drops 15 feet over a stone lip and to a dark, mossy cathedral. On a hot day the water and air will be cool in the small, mossy cave-like setting. The splashing cataract promotes the growth of moss and forms a microclimate here.

The main Outcroppings Trail passes more impressive sandstone features including a rockhouse with a collapsed roof just beyond the junction with the Waterfall Trail. Ahead, reach a large formation, Jean's Overhang, which is popular with rock climbers. After circling a feeder branch, the trail offers a different perspective: From atop the bluffline, you now look down into the wooded Bear Creek Canyon. This bluff-top forest is more xeric—heavy with oaks, hickories, sparkleberry, and sweetgum, which contrasts with the moister valley below. Watch for fallen boulders that have tumbled from the bluff upon which you travel. At 1.7 miles, drop off the bluffline and reach a second waterfall, descending about 12 feet into a semicircular amphitheater. This intermittent cascade can nearly run dry in the late summer and fall.

Outcroppings Trail

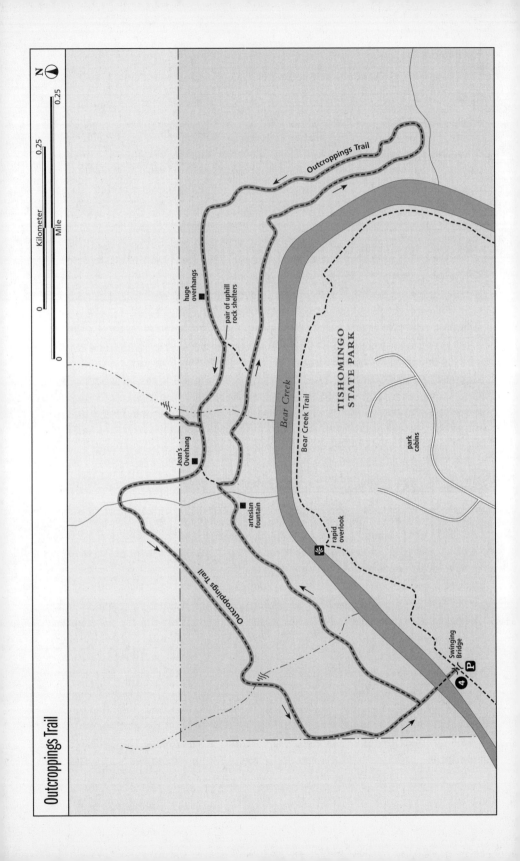

N

0   0.25   Kilometer

0   0.25   Mile

Outcroppings Trail

huge
overhangs

pair of uphill
rock shelters

Jean's
Overhang

Bear Creek

Bear Creek Trail

artesian
fountain

TISHOMINGO
STATE PARK

park
cabins

rapid
overlook

Outcroppings Trail

Swinging
Bridge

4

P

Wooden steps take you down away from the bluffs through pines, then back to the suspension bridge over Bear Creek. Return to bottomland before reaching the suspension bridge with the twin stone arches.

Miles and Directions

0.0 Start at the Swinging Bridge. Cross bridge then turn right, upstream along Bear Creek at a trail junction immediately following bridge crossing. The path going straight is your return route. Spur trails split off the main track up Bear Creek.

0.3 Pass an artesian spring around which the Civilian Conservation Corps built a rock fountain. The path then crosses a perennial stream. Just beyond the stream a trail splits left, short-cutting the loop.

0.8 Turn away from Bear Creek, briefly following a tributary, passing rock outcrops before climbing away from the tributary and now turning back downstream in the Bear Creek Valley. Impressive sandstone bluffs rise uphill to your right.

1.0 Cross the rocky streambed, then climb alongside a small overhang. The Outcroppings Trail continues along the base of an impressive cliffline.

1.1 Come to the first of the huge rockhouses.

1.2 Reach a pair of large rockhouses uphill from trail after passing loop shortcut. Look under them, then scramble atop them.

1.3 Cross a small branch then reach a trail junction. Follow the trail uphill to your right to reach a low-flow waterfall dropping 15 feet over the lip of a rock overhang.

1.4 Reach Jean's Overhang. Spur trail leads left, shortcutting the loop to end near artesian fountain. Main loop keeps forward, passing under the huge outcrop, then circles around a small tributary of Bear Creek.

1.7 Drop off the bluffline, then pass small waterfall and semicircular amphitheater. Continue descending on wooden steps.

2.0 Cross suspension bridge a second time and arrive back at trailhead.

More Information

Local Information

Tishomingo County Tourism Council, 1001 Battleground Drive, Luka, MS 38852; (662) 423-9933; www.tishomingo.org.

Local Events/Attractions

Tishomingo County Archives & History Museum, 203 East Quitman Street, Luka, MS 38852, (662) 423-3500. Set in the 1870 courthouse of Tishomingo County, it offers two stories of photographs and history, with rotating exhibits.

5 Nature Trail at Wall Doxey State Park

Want to visit a crystalline spring-fed lake? Then come here to Wall Doxey State Park, where you'll find some of the most appealing water in Mississippi. The hike leaves developed park facilities and works its way among undulating shoreline past some of the 200 springs that flow into the lake, including Spring Creek.

Start: Park picnic area
Distance: 2.0-mile loop
Approximate hiking time: 1.5 to 2 hours
Difficulty: Easy
Trail surface: Gravel, dirt, leaves, roots
Seasons: Year-round
Other trail users: Hikers only
Canine compatibility: Leashed dogs permitted
Land status: State park

Nearest town: Holly Springs
Fees and permits: Park entrance fee required
Schedule: Open year-round
Maps: Wall Doxey State Park; USGS maps: Waterford
Trail contacts: Wall Doxey State Park, 3946 Highway 7 South, Holly Springs, MS 38635; (662) 252-4231; http://home.mdwfp.com/parks.aspx

Finding the trailhead: From the junction of Highway 30 and Highway 7 near Oxford, head north on Highway 7 for 21 miles. From Holly Springs, head south for 6 miles on Highway 7 to reach the park entrance, on the west side of Highway 7. Keep going beyond the entrance station, then continue beyond the stone park lodge/office building. Turn right into the day use picnic area and park closest to the lake. *DeLorme: Mississippi Atlas & Gazetteer:* Page 19 E7. GPS trailhead coordinates: N34 39' 41.39" / W89 27' 56.11".

The Hike

Restrooms, a playground, and shaded picnic pavilions are at the trailhead. The trail is not immediately evident from the parking area. Walk toward Spring Lake. You'll have covered picnic pavilions to your left and the old bathhouse to your right. The trail begins just beyond Picnic Shelter #3. This is a gorgeous picnic area. Sycamores, cedars, and oaks shade the tables and pavilions that overlook Spring Lake. Begin walking a gravel track along the lake with the park fishing pier to your right. Woods and kudzu are off to your left.

The loud noise of falling water drifts into your ears. That is the lake spillway that continues as Spring Creek. The Nature Trail passes a second spillway—the crystal clear water disappears into a thick cypress slough. The path stays level as you cross the earthen dam holding back the waters of Spring Creek. Turtles will slip into the water and splash off logs in the lake. After leaving the dam area, a tree canopy shades the trail. Here, cypress trees grow in the lake away from shore and are quite picturesque.

▶ Spring Lake recharges itself every fifty-one hours from the abundant springs feeding it.

Overlooking spring-fed Wall Doxey Lake

Beyond the dam, the trail passes by a clear spring, the first of innumerable feeder branches you will see. Stop and feel the water—it is quite chilly. The trail splits—stay right with the footpath traveling along the lake. The trail leading left follows an old roadbed farther above the lake and reconnects with the Nature Trail later. The Nature Trail narrows and travels under a heavy canopy of hardwoods. Look closely along the shoreline—you'll see more springs feeding the lake. The lakeside terrain steepens, and the trail becomes correspondingly more uneven. Scattered contemplation benches offer varied watery perspectives. The path uses wooden steps to ascend a steep hill. At times, the hillside is so vertical railings have been installed to aid your passage and prevent a fall. Other places have boardwalks where the trail crosses more spring seeps. These wetlands are sensitive areas and are part of what makes Wall Doxey State Park special. The spring seeps become so continual as to create a permanent wetland between the trail and Spring Lake below you.

Who was Wall Doxey? He holds the honor of being the only United States senator to also serve as Senate sergeant-at-arms. Raised in nearby Holly Springs, he went to Ole Miss, getting an undergraduate and law degree before running for the U.S. House and winning. In 1941, he ran to fill the unexpired term of Senator Pat Harrison, who died in office. Doxey only served one-and-a-half years in "the world's greatest deliberative body," then lost his reelection campaign. But he made friends during his short stint in the Senate, which led to his serving as sergeant-at-arms from 1943 to 1947. Doxey passed away in 1962.

In leafless winter, lake views will not stop. But during summer, the lake becomes obscured by thick vegetation, though you can gain glimpses. You'll undoubtedly notice the amazing clarity of the water, especially looking down from this steep bluff. The Upper Trail comes in from your left and the main track widens, then becomes less hilly. Upper Spring Creek, bordered with alder bushes growing so dense as to prevent passage by man or beast, rushes beneath the narrow boardwalk, which you cross. Watch the underwater vegetation sway in the swift flow. The path begins making its big turn to circle around the north side of Spring Lake in a deep hardwood forest. More spring seeps feed the still water.

Lose sight of the lake but enjoy the depths of the forest before the woods give way and you reach the park cabins on your left. Don't miss a short little deck extending into the water where picturesque cypress trees grow beyond the shore of this quiet lake. Only trolling motors are allowed here, making it a quiet venue for paddlers, boaters, anglers, and hikers.

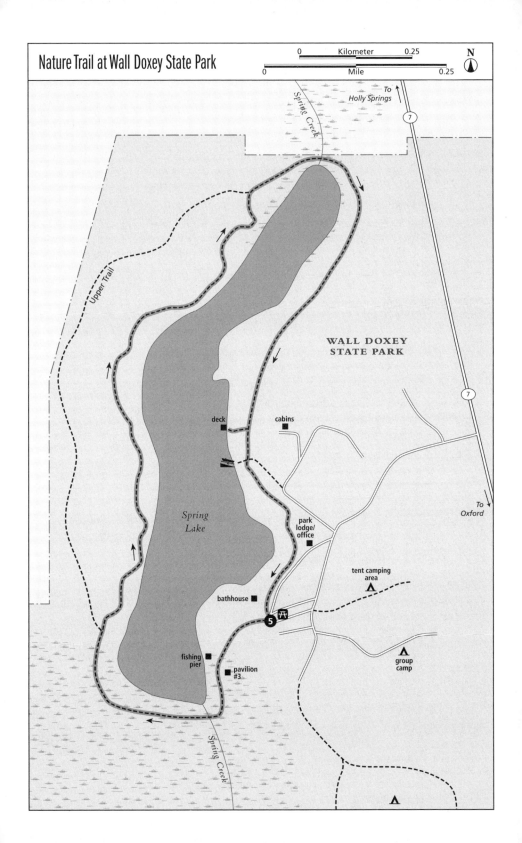

The trail then follows a paved road a short distance, then veers off to the right, just after passing a spur road to the park cabins. Cruise behind the park lodge, staying on the hill above the lake. While you are here, appreciate the stonework of the Civilian Conservation Corps boys, who first put this park together. Of course they had the wonderful springs and scenic hills with which to work. Circle behind the old bathhouse and diving platform. Swimming is no longer allowed, since the lawyers in Jackson got involved. What a shame. The hike ends back at the picnic area.

While you are here, consider enjoying more of the park than the Nature Trail. The old stone facilities add a quaint touch to the natural setting. Camping is a good option, as Wall Doxey offers a full-facility campground. Each site has a picnic table, grill, fire ring, water, and electricity, as well as a bathhouse, under the shade of thick widespread oaks. It also has a primitive tent camping area stretched along a gravel road in a mix of woods and small clearings. These sites have picnic tables, fire rings, and upright grills. Enjoy the disc golf course or go fishing in Spring Lake.

Miles and Directions

0.0 Start by Spring Lake near the picnic area.

0.4 Trail reaches the first cool, clear spring. Alternate path leaves left and uphill.

0.7 Trail uses wooden steps to ascend especially steep portion of lakeside terrain.

1.2 Alternate path descends to meet Nature Trail.

1.3 The path reaches and spans boardwalk over upper Spring Creek.

1.7 Leave thick woods and open onto park cabins to your left. A small deck leads to lake's edge and view.

2.0 Pass behind old bathhouse, reach picnic area, and arrive back at the trailhead.

More Information

Local Information
Holly Springs Chamber of Commerce, 148 E. College Avenue, Holly Springs, MS 38635; (662) 252-2943; www.hollyspringsmschamberofcommerce.org.

Local Events/Attractions
Kudzu Festival, www.visithollysprings.org. Held on the square in fall, it offers a carnival, a gospel jamboree, a political rally, arts and crafts, a rodeo, and a barbecue cook-off.

Holly Springs Pilgrimage, www.visithollysprings.org. Tour all the historic antebellum homes of the city; a place spared the destruction of the Civil War.

6 Puskus Lake Interpretive Trail

This hike takes place at one of the finer recreation areas of the Holly Springs National Forest, Puskus Lake. Leave the lake boat ramp and follow the interpretive trail as it wanders through the lakeside woodland and ends up making a double loop. During this hike you can enjoy views of the lake as well as learn a thing or two about the environment with the interpretive information scattered about the trail.

Start: Near lakeside boat ramp
Distance: 1.7-mile double loop
Approximate hiking time: 1 to 1.5 hours
Difficulty: Easy
Trail surface: Grass, pine needles under trees
Seasons: Year-round
Other trail users: Hikers only
Canine compatibility: Leashed dogs permitted
Land status: National forest
Nearest town: Oxford

Fees and permits: Recreation area entry fee required
Schedule: Open year-round
Maps: Holly Springs National Forest; USGS maps: Puskus Lake
Trail contacts: Holly Springs National Forest, 1000 Front Street, Oxford, MS 38655; (662) 236-6550; www.fs.fed.us/r8/mississippi/hollysprings

Finding the trailhead: From the intersection of Highway 7 and Highway 30 just north of Oxford, take Highway 30 east for 9.1 miles to Forest Road 838/Lafayette County Road 2090. Turn left and follow it for 2.5 miles to enter the recreation area, then stay left with Forest Road 838B and follow it for 0.2 mile to the trailhead on your left near the boat ramp. *DeLorme: Mississippi Atlas & Gazetteer:* Page 19 H8. GPS trailhead coordinates: N34 26' 10.97" / W89 21' 6.92".

The Hike

The Puskus Lake Interpretive Trail is but one part of the Puskus Lake Recreation Area experience. The recreation area also offers water, restrooms, and nineteen lakefront campsites. To reach the alluring hardwood-shaded campsites, you can park your car and walk down beyond a split rail fence. Most have stellar lake views. Each site offers a picnic table, lantern post, fire ring, and tent pad. Some of them also have either a land peninsula extending into the water or a small dock to better fish and enjoy the water from your camp. You can vie for largemouth bass, catfish, bluegill, and crappie. Boatless anglers can use the fishing pier, conveniently located near the trailhead and boat ramp. The lake offers paddling opportunities for canoes and kayaks, but be apprised that small motors are allowed. The restrooms are on the old side, and that is the only shortcoming of this recreation area. The day use area is closer to the dam and offers picnic tables, a restroom, and fishing docks.

Puskus Lake stretches resplendently in a frame of trees

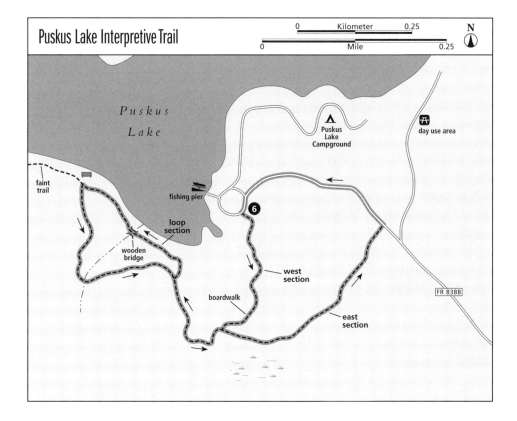

Puskus Lake Interpretive Trail

0   Kilometer   0.25

0   Mile   0.25

N

Puskus Lake

Puskus
Lake
Campground

day use area

faint
trail

fishing pier

6

loop
section

wooden
bridge

west
section

boardwalk

east
section

FR 838B

White paint blazes and metal hiker symbols nailed to trees mark the Puskus Lake Interpretive Trail. Widespread mature pines greet hikers as they follow the wide track over a hill and down to a boardwalk in moist terrain. Occasional contemplation benches are scattered along the way.

You will see the first of the interpretive signs placed here to aid your understanding of the flora and fauna of the national forest. The west section drops to cross

Dogwoods are plentiful in Mississippi. The short tree with scaly brown bark and widespread crown is easy to identify. It is widely regarded as one of the most beautiful trees in the East and ranges from east Texas north to Michigan, east to Massachusetts, and south to Florida. It grows in both moist and dry soils throughout Mississippi. In the spring dogwoods offer showy white blooms that can be pinkish as well. After greening up in the warm season, dogwoods produce a shiny red fruit in fall. These small berry-like fruits are bitter to humans but are an important food for birds. Dogwood is extremely hard and is used to make mallet heads, jewelers' blocks, and spools.

another boardwalk over a second streamlet to meet the loop section of the Puskus Lake Interpretive Trail.

The path remains in lush bottomland and shortly spans a stream via wooden bridge. In fall this stream will be completely dry, simply a bed of sand and leaves. More boardwalks cross streamlets coming from the hills that encircle Puskus Lake. The actual loop begins at 0.4 mile in full-fledged bottomland. The footing is irregular here, a result of the hardwood forest being periodically inundated. The trail stays within sight of Puskus Lake. During summer the water is barely visible due to the lush vegetation thriving at the lake's edge. Bridge an intermittent streambed as the trail nears the lake now and offers some improved views.

The path reaches a contemplation bench where you can overlook Puskus. A faint trail continues beyond the bench, and if you follow it you will see an old bridge over a wash. This part of the trail is no longer maintained but could be a way for adventurous trekkers to get in additional mileage. The loop portion of the trail turns away from the water at the bench. Complete the lake loop, wandering through hillier terrain, enjoying more interpretive information, then backtrack.

The east section slowly makes its way out of the bottom into pines, still accompanied by numerous interpretive signs explaining the forest. Top out and reach FR 838B. Turn left to trace the road back to the trailhead.

Miles and Directions

0.0 Start at the parking area near the boat ramp. Enter widespread shortleaf pines on the west section of the Puskus Lake Trail. The wide track climbs over a little hill, then drops to span a wetland on a boardwalk.

0.2 Meet loop section of trail. Stay right here.

0.4 Stay right with the actual loop portion of the hike.

0.7 The trail saddles alongside Puskus Lake and turns away from it near a contemplation bench. A faint trail continues along the lake.

1.1 After completing loop and backtracking, join east section of trail on hillier terrain.

1.4 Meet FR 838B after climbing the east section. Turn left and follow the forest road.

1.7 Arrive back at the trailhead.

More Information

Local Information
Oxford-Lafayette County Chamber of Commerce, 299 W. Jackson Avenue, Oxford, MS 38655; (662) 234-4651; www.oxfordms.com.

Local Events/Attractions
University of Mississippi football games, www.olemiss.edu. See the Rebels tackle foes on the gridiron.

Oxford Film Festival, P.O. Box 727, Oxford, MS 38655, www.oxfordfilmfest.com. It's held each February.

7 North Cypress Nonmotorized Trail

This hike, located in the Holly Springs National Forest, loops around North Cypress Lake, an impoundment within the preserve. The Forest Service put the word "non-motorized" in the trail name to emphasize that the path is only for hikers, bikers, and equestrians. It offers undulating terrain as it rolls through piney woods divided by moist bottomland. Along the way the well-maintained trail crosses the dam of North Cypress Lake and offers watery views.

Start: Trailhead off Forest Road 862
Distance: 3.3-mile loop
Approximate hiking time: 1.5 to 2 hours
Difficulty: Moderate
Trail surface: Gravel, leaves
Seasons: Year-round
Other trail users: Hikers, mountain bicyclists, equestrians
Canine compatibility: Leashed dogs permitted
Land status: National forest

Nearest town: Oxford
Fees and permits: No fees or permits required
Schedule: Open year-round
Maps: Holly Springs National Forest; USGS maps: Puskus Lake
Trail contacts: Holly Springs National Forest, 1000 Front Street, Oxford, MS 38655; (662) 236-6550; www.fs.fed.us/r8/mississippi/hollysprings

Finding the trailhead: From the intersection of Highway 7 and Highway 30 just north of Oxford, take Highway 30 east for 10.1 miles to Forest Road 862 and a sign for the North Cypress Nonmotorized Trail. Turn right on FR 862 and follow it for 0.5 mile to reach the trailhead. *DeLorme: Mississippi Atlas & Gazetteer:* Page 19 H8. GPS trailhead coordinates: N34 24' 32.1" / W89 19' 56.3".

The Hike

This trail is a response to the increased demand for recreational opportunities in the Holly Springs National Forest. You will find the going easy here and the track simple to follow. This wide trail is shared with horses and bikers. The Forest Service has laid

Sassafras trees are easy to identify. Their leaves have three basic shapes: oval, three-lobed, and mitten-shaped. Mature sassafras trees have a reddish-brown, deeply furrowed bark. Sassafras trees are known for their aromatic scent. Scratch the bark away from a twig and the sweet smell is unmistakable. American natives used sassafras for medicinal purposes. Pioneers made tea from boiling sassafras roots, and some modern Mississippians do this, too. It was one of the first exports from America to Europe during colonial days. Birds eat the berries. The wood of sassafras shrinks when dried and is used for fence posts and hand tools.

Author treks downhill near North Cypress Lake

gravel throughout the path. Pines and white oaks grow tall overhead. Sassafras is a major understory tree. The open areas may be brushy later in summer.

The terrain is surprisingly hilly as it drops off to your right steeply toward the wetlands surrounding North Cypress Lake. The trail follows suit, descending to cross a branch on a wooden bridge, then continues in the flat. Look for ferns growing along the creekbeds during the warm season. Enter a younger section of pine trees, some of which appear to be planted in rows.

The North Cypress Nonmotorized Trail travels the margin between the hardwood bottomland to your right and the pines to your left, crossing intermittent feeder branches as it wanders southeasterly. Leave the tree canopy and join an old forest road. The sun is open overhead and the walking is easy as you cruise past young pines and sweetgum that will shade the trail in the future.

Reach the dam for North Cypress Lake. It was drained and the levee repaired in 2007. As you cross the dam, look for signs of beavers along the water's edge and on the downstream side of the dam. Leave the open dam area and reenter shady woodland. The pines here are much more mature than those on the other side of the lake.

Mississippi beavers are so prolific as to be a nuisance. A poor fur market and a lack of predators have allowed the beaver to expand throughout the state. Their dams are estimated to cost up to $5 million a year in damage, from flooding timber and agricultural fields to undermining roadways and other man-made structures. Property owners need no permit or license to control beavers on their land. However, a professional trapper is recommended for beaver removal.

The North Cypress Nonmotorized Trail opens onto a grassy wildlife clearing. The track splits left just after entering the clearing to descend off the hill and cross a small branch on a wooden bridge. Interestingly, this stream flows directly into West Cypress Creek and not into the lake that the trail encircles. Your climb away from North Cypress Creek subtly brought you into another watershed.

The trail rolls along a ridgeline, then turns right to reach and follow Forest Road 837G, before leaving the developed road and turning back north toward the trailhead at the path's high point. The trail here is partly canopied. Sumac grows in sunnier margins. It's mostly downhill from this point, dropping over 100 feet. Some sections of the path may be muddy despite the erosion control work the Forest Service has done on this path.

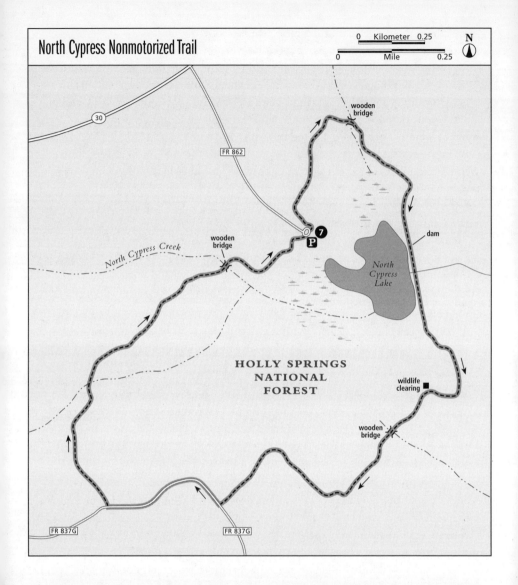

North Cypress Nonmotorized Trail

0   Kilometer   0.25

0   Mile   0.25

N

30

FR 862

wooden
bridge

wooden
bridge

7
P

dam

North Cypress Creek

*North
Cypress
Lake*

HOLLY SPRINGS
NATIONAL
FOREST

wildlife
clearing

wooden
bridge

FR 837G

FR 837G

Originally created in the 1930s, the Holly Springs National Forest primarily consisted of relatively small parcels of agriculturally depleted, abandoned, and eroded hilly lands in the Little Tallahatchie River basin whose owners were eager to sell. After the national forest first came to be, the Civilian Conservation Corps originally replanted the eroded farmlands with loblolly pines. The loblollies could grow in the diminished soil and their heavy needles stabilized the ground, helping to prevent further erosion.

Reach bottomland in thick, vine-draped woods. The lushness of the locale is subject to change as the Forest Service uses prescribed fire that thins the underbrush. Leave the bottom and climb into the open woods, losing your canopy overhead. A steep downhill leads you ever closer to the trailhead. A wooden bridge takes you over the primary tributary, North Cypress Creek, which feeds North Cypress Lake. Enjoy a bottomland hardwood cruise before opening onto the lower gravel parking area. The main trailhead is within sight uphill.

If you are interested in camping, the turn to Puskus Lake Recreation Area is 1 mile west on Highway 30. The Puskus Lake Interpretive Trail begins from this area.

Miles and Directions

0.0 Start near the shaded picnic tables and a restroom. As you face the restroom, take the trail to your left, heading east. Follow the gravel track away from parking area to shortly pass a bench. You are roughly paralleling the forest road entered.

0.4 Descend from hills to cross a wooden bridge over feeder of North Cypress Lake. Trail continues in flats near stream.

0.7 Join the dam that holds back the waters of North Cypress Lake. Cruise southerly atop the dam, enjoying views of the impound.

1.2 Enter a wildlife clearing. The trail veers left just as it enters the clearing. Most hikers keep walking through the clearing as it is the most open area. Continue rolling through mixed pine-oak timber.

1.9 Continue through tall woods to reach FR 837G. Turn right here on the gravel road.

2.2 Leave right from the forest road. This is the high point of the entire hike, over 500 feet, lofty ground for the Holly Springs National Forest.

2.6 Reach bottomland in lush woods, make one last climb, and lose the overhead canopy.

3.0 Cross North Cypress Creek on a wooden bridge. Walk beneath tall bottomland forest.

3.3 Open onto lower parking area and arrive back at the trailhead.

More Information

Local Information
Oxford–Lafayette County Chamber of Commerce, 299 W. Jackson Avenue, Oxford, MS 38655; (662) 234-4651; www.oxfordms.com.

Local Events/Attractions
University of Mississippi football games, www.olemiss.edu. See the Rebels take on SEC rivals, among other foes.

Oxford Film Festival, P.O. Box 727, Oxford, MS 38655, www.oxfordfilmfest.com. It is held annually in February. Consider submitting your own film.

8 Clear Creek Loop at Sardis Lake

The following loop is within a trail system primarily used by mountain bikers. Starting near the Clear Creek Recreation Area, the hike curves through hills and hollows along the shore of Sardis Lake, where a watery vista awaits. The mostly singletrack path nearly curves back upon itself numerous times, attempting to get the most mileage in a small area before returning to the trailhead.

Start: Clear Creek Recreation Area
Distance: 3.6-mile loop
Approximate hiking time: 1.5 to 2.5 hours
Difficulty: Moderate
Trail surface: Leaves and needles under forest cover
Seasons: Fall through spring
Other trail users: Mountain bicyclists
Canine compatibility: Leashed dogs permitted
Land status: Army Corps of Engineers property

Nearest town: Oxford
Fees and permits: No fees or permits required
Schedule: Open year-round
Maps: Sardis Lake Mountain Bike Trail; USGS maps: Coles Point
Trail contacts: U.S. Army Corps of Engineers, 29049 Highway 315, Sardis, MS 38666-0186; (662) 563-4531; www.mvk.usace.army.mil/Lakes/mssardis

Finding the trailhead: From exit 243A on Interstate 55, Batesville/Oxford, take U.S. Highway 278/Highway 6 east 21 miles to Oxford and West Jackson Avenue. Veer left on West Jackson Avenue and follow it for 2.3 miles. Turn left on College Hill Road, Highway 314 West, which is just across from the University of Mississippi. After 5.6 miles it becomes Lafayette County Road 100; keep going straight. After 12 miles, enter Clear Creek Recreation Area. Continue 0.7 mile farther, then turn left for primitive camping and bicycle trails. The trailhead will be on your left. Water, restrooms, and tent pads for camping are provided at the trailhead. *DeLorme: Mississippi Atlas & Gazetteer:* Page 18 H15. GPS trailhead coordinates: N34 25' 31.92" / W89 41' 36.49".

The Hike

This trail system, shared by hikers and mountain bikers, was designed by mountain bikers from the nearby University of Mississippi, the Oxford Bike Club, and the Army Corps of Engineers. Despite the name—Sardis Lake Mountain Bike Trail—hikers are welcome on the trail that weaves through the undulating landscape, not going anywhere in particular, just covering scenic terrain. I suggest hikers do the same, but keep an ear open, listening for fast pedalers.

The singletrack path descends from the trailhead into attractive hickory-oak woodland through the hills and hollows surrounding the Clear Creek drainage, which flows into the south side of Sardis Lake. Sweetgum and cedar trees dominate the forest. Carsonite posts mark the trail in half-mile increments. The narrow dirt track makes for an intimate experience in deep woodland.

The trail is going more west than anything, heading toward Sardis Lake, and frequently undulates, providing exercise value as it joins an old roadbed bordered with tall oaks and a few pines. At this point you drop on and off an old roadbed, heading ever so gently toward Sardis Lake. Enter a water-bordered peninsula, though you might not even know it as the leafed-out forest blocks the aquatic views. Shortly open onto a riparian area. You are on the edge of the Clear Creek embayment. Sardis Lake is clearly visible here. After the summer lake drawdown, you must walk down to the lake. When the water is up it will be trailside. Enjoy this scenic vantage.

The singletrack path now turns away from the lake and begins heading up the right-hand side of an embayment, partially obscured by vegetation. You are now in mixed woodland and gaining a little elevation before drifting into creek bottoms, staying in the margin between the bottom and the steep hillside above it. Picturesque bluffs border the trail. Gain occasional close-ups of the creeks that created the bottoms. After rains, some of these streams will have little waterfalls, but this occurs infrequently. Consider yourself lucky—or wet—if you're here when this happens.

Ferns grace the hillsides in this dark, moist hardwood hollow, which resembles the Southern Appalachian Mountains to the east. The trail begins curving in and out of tributary hollows that feed Clear Creek. Watch for rock outcrops, unusual for this area. You'll also notice the characteristics often exhibited with mountain bike trails—

Views of Sardis Lake open 1.7 miles into the hike

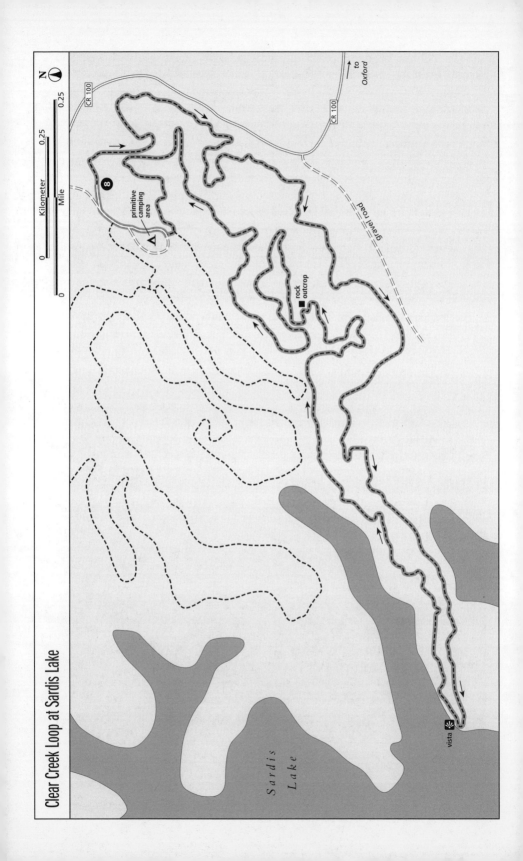

Clear Creek Loop at Sardis Lake

N

Kilometer
0   0.25   0.25

Mile
0   0.25

CR 100

to
Oxford

CR 100

gravel road

primitive
camping
area

8

rock
outcrop

vista

S a r d i s
L a k e

turns so tight and trails so close to one another you can see where you will be in a little while. In this instance the path heads along a ridgeline, then curves directly back down it before dipping into a hollow once again.

▶ Clear Creek Recreation Area offers thirty-two water and electric campsites, hot showers, a swim beach, a boat ramp, and a fishing area. The trailhead camps with tent pads, water, and portable restrooms are free.

Enjoy the creekside cruise amid white oaks, sweetgum, and tulip trees. Cane also grows here. Ferns are rife and guard the trail in spots. Enjoy this lush greenery and even a few more scattered rock outcrops. Pass the 3.5-mile marker as you leave the bottomland. The trail is still making some solid ups and downs but is more up than down before reaching an auto-accessible campsite near the trailhead. Leave the path and join the gravel campground road, shortly returning to the trailhead.

Miles and Directions

0.0 Start at Clear Creek primitive camping and mountain bike trailhead. Enter the woods at kiosk near the road you came in.

0.2 Come near Lafayette County Road 100. Continue roughly paralleling the road, aiming southwesterly.

0.7 Turn away from Lafayette CR 100 and roughly parallel a ridgeline.

1.5 Enter a dense stand of young sweetgum. The tall, spindly trees crowd the trail and contrast with other forested areas along the trail.

1.7 Open onto a riparian area at the low point of your hike. Views open of Sardis Lake. Trail turns away from the lake, heading northeasterly.

2.6 Watch for rock outcrops beside the trail as it winds through hollows.

3.6 Come alongside primitive camping area near trailhead. When you come directly beside a tent pad, leave right away from the trail and walk on the gravel road back to trailhead.

More Information

Local Information
Oxford–Lafayette County Chamber of Commerce, 299 W. Jackson Avenue, Oxford, MS 38655; (662) 234-4651; www.oxfordms.com.

Local Events/Attractions
University of Mississippi football games, www.olemiss.edu. Watch the Rebels on the gridiron, tackling SEC opponents among others.

Oxford Film Festival, P.O. Box 727, Oxford, MS 38655, www.oxfordfilmfest.com. It is held each February. Consider submitting your own film.

$\mathbb{9}$ Thacker Mountain Trail at Oxford

The Thacker Mountain Trail is a trunk path following an old railroad grade, with numerous singletrack paths splintering from it. Located in Oxford, the rail trail is popular with walkers, hikers, and runners, while the dirt trails that spur off it are mainly traveled by the mountain bike set.

Start: Trailhead near the Whirlpool plant
Distance: 6.0 miles out-and-back
Approximate hiking time: 2.5 to 3.0 hours
Difficulty: Rail trail is easy; spur trails more difficult with hills
Trail surface: Gravel, cinder on old railroad grade
Seasons: Fall through spring
Other trail users: Walkers, mountain bicyclists, University of Mississippi cross-country team

Canine compatibility: Leashed dogs permitted
Land status: City of Oxford property
Nearest town: Oxford
Fees and permits: No fees or permits required
Schedule: Open year-round
Maps: USGS maps: Oxford South
Trail contacts: Oxford Pathways Commission, 107 Courthouse Square, Oxford, MS 38655; (662) 236-1310; www.oxfordms.net

Finding the trailhead: From U.S. Highway 278/Highway 6 freeway on the south side of Oxford, take the Coliseum Drive exit southbound. At 0.2 mile you will see the guard shack for the Whirlpool plant. The Thacker Mountain Trail starts on your right before the guard shack. Park on the right-hand side of the road, near the trailhead gate, but do not block the gate, which is normally closed. *DeLorme: Mississippi Atlas & Gazetteer:* Page 25 B6. GPS trailhead coordinates: N34 21' 13.1" / W89 32' 36.2".

The Hike

The wide former railbed is the main route into a trail system with numerous spur paths splitting off. These are mainly mountain bike trails and hiking trails that twist and turn back on themselves. These unorganized trails were developed by users and change over time. Therefore, if you want to enjoy them, I recommend repeatedly visiting this spot and learning and developing your own routes, using this rail trail as the trunk of your hiking experience here.

First, pass around a trailhead pole gate, which is normally closed, and join a level grade that once was part of the Mississippi Central Railroad line, laid in the 1850s. At this point, the grade is elevated and the forested woodland below you drops off sharply. This rail trail is closed to all vehicles, except University of Mississippi trucks. The gravel and cinder track continues its level course through the surrounding hilly landscape. The old railroad grade had to keep a level track, since trains were not able to go up and down sharp hills.

Pass the paved Oxford Mixed Use Pathway, which is part of a growing trail system extending through Oxford and Lafayette County. By this point, other singletrack

This old railroad grade was originally laid out in the 1850s

trails have already split away from the main railbed, as this is a major destination for mountain bikers, who primarily use the spur trails. The trunk path is at times wide open and at other times hemmed in. It's a strange thing, a result of the railbed being cut into forested hillside, which then rises on both sides of you. Yet at other times you will be looking down upon the woodland as the hills fall away. The woods grow thick here, with dense thickets of young pine—along with ranks of oak, sweetgum, dogwood, cedar, and pine. In still other places, kudzu has overgrown the trees and everything between them. The forest canopy gives way in these kudzu zones, splashing sunlight onto the path. In the gravel below your feet, watch for old bolts, coal, crushed glass, and pieces of railroad tie, from the days when this track was active.

▶ **The Mississippi Central passed through Oxford for thirteen decades, ending service for good in 1982. Passenger service through Oxford stopped in the 1940s.**

The northern section of the railbed has been turned into a mixed-use trail known as the Oxford Depot Trail, and is named for the restored rail depot that is the pride of Oxford residents.

An occasional house stands near the trail. The railbed is a right-of-way; therefore some private land extends to it. Nevertheless, the scenery remains wooded and/or natural nearly the whole time. The trailside landscape resumes its pattern, as the former track cuts between hills, then keeps its level course as the hills fall away to offer views of the valleys below. The track has been traveling generally southwest, but as it gets near Thacker Mountain, it begins to turn more southerly in a gentle fashion. Just as a railroad cannot handle steep irregular grades, it cannot make sharp turns. The path remains partly canopied. Pines cloak adjacent hills.

The current trail ends at a farm gate and Thacker Mountain Road. You can see the railbed continuing beyond the gate. This is your turnaround point.

Miles and Directions

0.0   Start at the Whirlpool trailhead. Pass around a metal gate and join a former railbed of cinder and gravel.

0.2   Paved greenway leads left under a power line.

0.7   A road leads right, uphill. The rail trail continues forward around metal barriers.

0.9   The trail crosses a culvert. Here, the modern trail dips, whereas in the railroad days this culvert was spanned by a bridge.

1.3   Private gravel road crosses old railbed.

2.9   Pass under a transmission line.

3.0   The trail reaches gravel Thacker Mountain Road. The abandoned railroad right-of-way is blocked by a gate. Old Taylor Road is visible to the left. Turnaround point.

6.0   Arrive back at the trailhead.

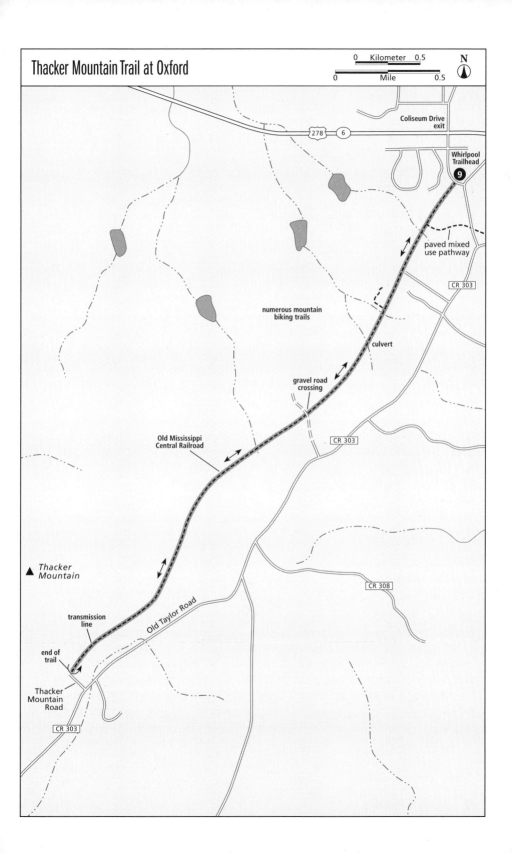

Thacker Mountain Trail at Oxford

0   Kilometer   0.5
0   Mile   0.5

N

Coliseum Drive
exit

278   6

Whirlpool
Trailhead
9

paved mixed
use pathway

CR 303

numerous mountain
biking trails

culvert

gravel road
crossing

CR 303

Old Mississippi
Central Railroad

CR 308

▲ Thacker
Mountain

Old Taylor Road

transmission
line

end of
trail

Thacker
Mountain
Road

CR 303

More Information

Local Information
Oxford–Lafayette County Chamber of Commerce, 299 W. Jackson Avenue, Oxford, MS 38655; (662) 234-4651; www.oxfordms.com.

Local Events/Attractions
University of Mississippi football games, www.olemiss.edu. Watch the Rebels on the gridiron, tackling SEC opponents among others.

Oxford Film Festival, P.O. Box 727, Oxford, MS 38655, www.oxfordfilmfest.com. It is held each February. Consider submitting your own film.

10 Natchez Trace at Tupelo

This there-and-back hike leaves the Natchez Trace Parkway Tupelo Visitor Center and roughly parallels the Parkway amid the rolling woods and fields of suburban Tupelo. Along the way it passes the Old Town Overlook, then ends at the site of a former Chickasaw Indian village, where a short nature trail starts that identifies important plants used by the Chickasaw. This village can also serve as an alternate trailhead if you want to do the hike one way.

Start: Parking area across from the Tupelo Visitor Center
Distance: 9.4 miles out-and-back
Approximate hiking time: 4.0 to 5.5 hours
Difficulty: Difficult due to length
Trail surface: Pea gravel, dirt, rock, grass, boardwalks
Seasons: Early fall through late spring
Other trail users: Hikers, joggers, local cross-country teams

Canine compatibility: Leashed dogs permitted
Land status: National park
Nearest town: Tupelo
Fees and permits: No fees or permits required
Schedule: Open year-round
Maps: Natchez Trace National Scenic Trail; USGS maps: Tupelo
Trail contacts: Natchez Trace Parkway, 2680 Natchez Trace Parkway, Tupelo, MS 38804; (800) 305-7417; www.nps.gov/natr

Finding the trailhead: From Tupelo, take the Natchez Trace Parkway northeast to milepost 260 and the Tupelo Visitor Center. The trailhead is across the road from the visitor center. Leave the visitor center and follow the road crossing the south side of the Parkway. Follow it a short distance as it veers left to reach the trailhead. The alternate south trailhead can be reached by taking the Natchez Trace Parkway south from the Tupelo Visitor Center to milepost 261.8. Turn into the road leading to a parking area at the Chickasaw Village site. *DeLorme: Mississippi Atlas & Gazetteer:* Page 26 B4. GPS trailhead coordinates: N34 19' 47.4" / W88 42' 47.4".

The Hike

The Natchez Trace National Scenic Trail extends for 62 miles in four sections along the Natchez Trace Parkway. This is one of three open sections in Mississippi. The national scenic trail was to have paralleled the entire Natchez Trace Parkway. Though completion of the entire trail is a long way off, plans are for the trail to be expanded. This particular section extends 7 miles one way, and this hike covers 4.7 miles of that in suburban Tupelo where civilization is never far away.

A widespread mature oak tree at the trailhead offers a shady picnic place. Immediately enter oak-pine woods on a gravel track. Trailside vegetation can be very brushy as the pea gravel track crosses Old Highway 45. Most lands along the Trace were inhabited before the parkway was begun in 1937 and brought into the national park system in 1938. The Parkway was finally completed in 2005. The trailway passes an old storm shelter as evidence of such past use before dropping off a hill into bottomland, where river birches proliferate. Ramble through oak woods, with the Parkway off to your left. The Natchez Trace foot trail continues to go up and down. Cedar, persimmon, and sweetgum now cover land formerly tilled for cotton. Enter bottomland in forest that will be inundated during wetter periods. Notice how the bases of the trees are slightly more buttressed at the bottom due to this part-time flooding of the woodland floor.

Interpretive signs mark a Chickasaw Village

The scenic trail opens onto a meadow to your left and modern cropland to your right. The parkway is visible to your left. This will give you a close-up view of Mississippi agriculture.

▶ Cotton, soybeans, and rice, in that order, are the most valuable crops grown in Mississippi.

At 1.7 miles, use the Parkway road bridge to cross Town Creek. Return to the foot trail by dropping right, continuing southbound. Curve away from the Parkway heading toward Old Town Overlook. Span an intermittent stream by bridge and then rise to reach Old Town Overlook. Gain a view of the area just passed.

The Trace is using all the tricks in the book to navigate through the outskirts of Tupelo as it spans U.S. Highway 78. Reenter cedar woods beyond the crossing. Viney thick woods screen civilization. However, in winter it will be more open. Ahead, the path crosses Lakeshire Drive and a road connecting the Parkway to Highway 178, then uses the parkway to span Highway 178. The Trace then makes its way to the Chickasaw Indian village site after passing one end of a nature trail. Interpretive signs explain the site.

The Chickasaw Nation stretched through northeast Mississippi into west Tennessee. Along the Trace interpretive information shows the building placements of the village known as Ackia. In the spring of 1736, the Chickasaws, known for their ferocity, and proud of it, defeated the French and Choctaw near this site. The Choctaw roamed farther south in present-day Mississippi. In less than one hundred years, the Chickasaws would be removed to Oklahoma under the Treaty of Pontotoc. The Natchez Trace harbors a largely untapped resource of historical and archaeological resources associated with the Chickasaw nation. Long-term park plans include developing and displaying these resources at a Chickasaw cultural interpretive center. For now, an interpretive walk shows the locations and functions of various structures that were there during the time the village was occupied.

Miles and Directions

0.0 Start at the trailhead across from Tupelo Visitor Center. Follow pea gravel track into pine-oak woods.

0.2 Reach and cross Old Highway 45. Reenter thick woods and rolling terrain.

0.5 A wooden footbridge spans intermittent tributary of Town Creek. The trail keeps southwest.

0.9 Travel extensive boardwalk through a low forest. Emerge onto field beyond the boardwalk.

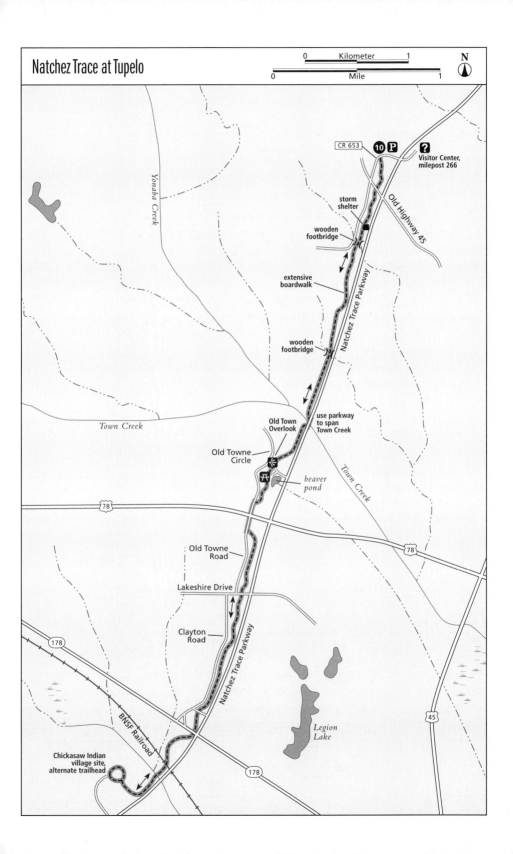

Natchez Trace at Tupelo

N

0 — Kilometer — 1

0 — Mile — 1

CR 653

10 **P** **?**

Visitor Center,
milepost 266

Old Highway 45

Yonaha Creek

storm
shelter

wooden
footbridge

Natchez Trace Parkway

extensive
boardwalk

wooden
footbridge

Town Creek

use parkway
to span
Town Creek

Old Town
Overlook

Town Creek

Old Towne
Circle

*beaver
pond*

78

78

Old Towne
Road

Lakeshire Drive

Clayton
Road

45

Natchez Trace Parkway

178

BNSF Railroad

*Legion
Lake*

Chickasaw Indian
village site,
alternate trailhead

178

1.2 Cross a channeled stream by wooden footbridge. The trail may seem confusing here but keep heading southbound in the grassy margin between the Parkway to your left and field to your right. Span another wooden bridge over small ditch.

2.1 Reach Old Town Overlook in woods after climbing over a small ditch. Views open to the northeast from where you just came, Town Creek, and the adjacent floodplain.

2.2 Trail continues through piney woods beyond overlook, then opens onto a picnic area and beaver pond. The trail resumes at the end of picnic area.

2.3 Reach another road, Old Towne Circle, and join it left, spanning US 78. After crossing US 78, veer left into woodland, bordered by the Parkway to your left and Old Towne Circle to your right.

2.9 Cross Lakeshire Drive. The Trace stays in thick woods on a wide dirt and gravel track.

3.7 Cross road connecting Natchez Trace Parkway to Highway 178. Immediately reenter woods.

3.8 Use the Parkway to span Highway 178. Descend right from the Parkway to reach picnic table under shade tree.

4.2 Carefully cross the Burlington Northern and Santa Fe railroad tracks and reenter woods rife with hackberry. Span wooded wetland on a pair of long boardwalks.

4.6 Reach one end of interpretive nature trail. To the right the nature trail curves into woods with interpretive signage displaying use of plants by Chickasaw Indians. The Trace continues forward.

4.7 Open onto parking area and village site. Retrace steps back to trailhead, or use this alternate trailhead for one-way hike.

9.4 Arrive back at the trailhead if you are completing the out-and-back hike.

More Information

Local Information
Tupelo Convention & Visitors Bureau, P.O. Drawer 47, Tupelo, MS 38802-0047; (800) 533-0611.

Local Events/Attractions
Elvis Presley Birthplace Museum, 306 Elvis Presley Drive, Tupelo, MS 38801, (662) 841-1245, www.elvispresleybirthplace.com. Tour the place where it all started.

11 Rocky Ridge Trail at Enid Lake

This trail has seen better days in the past, and hopefully will see improved days in the future. It cruises hills above the shoreline of Enid Lake, offering watery vistas as it makes a loop. The path, open to horses and hikers, unfortunately has been overrun by ATVs. Having said that, the trek still has scenic value, is adequately marked, and in passable shape.

Start: Plum Point Recreation Area
Distance: 4.2-mile lollipop
Approximate hiking time: 2.5 to 3.5 hours
Difficulty: Moderate, some ups and downs
Trail surface: Gravel, dirt, leaves in lakeside woods
Seasons: Early fall through late spring
Other trail users: Horses, illegal ATVs
Canine compatibility: Leashed dogs permitted
Land status: Army Corps of Engineers property

Nearest town: Batesville
Fees and permits: No fees or permits required for hiking, fee required for use of swim beach. Both share the same parking area.
Schedule: Open year-round
Maps: Enid Lake; USGS maps: Shuford
Trail contacts: Enid Lake Field Office, P.O. Box 10, Enid, MS 38927-0010; (662) 563-4571; www.mvk.usace.army.mil/Lakes/msenid

Finding the trailhead: From exit 233 on Interstate 55, take Yalobusha County Road 36 east for 0.8 mile to Enid Dam Road. Turn left on Enid Dam Road and follow it for 2.3 miles to Chapel Hill Road. Turn right on Chapel Hill Road and follow it 1.3 miles to Pope–Water Valley Road. Turn right and go for 4.0 miles on Pope–Water Valley Road to Plum Point Road. Turn right on Plum Point Road. Go for 2.3 miles and then veer right, following the signs for the campground and swim beach, then bear left for the swim beach and horse trail. *DeLorme: Mississippi Atlas & Gazetteer:* Page 24 D3. GPS trailhead coordinates: N34 36' 12.57" / W88 10' 50.00".

The Hike

The Rocky Ridge Trail is signed with Carsonite posts with arrows indicating the proper direction for the trail. The green arrow means you are heading away from Plum Point and the red arrow means you are returning toward Plum Point. Though the trail is closed to motor vehicles, four-wheelers are blatantly violating this regulation. Leave the trailhead, heading steeply downhill toward Enid Lake. Once down the hill, you can gain a good water vantage from the lakeshore. The swim beach is just off to your right. Cut acutely left back into the woods. Climb into pines then reach a backyard at the edge of Army Corps of Engineers property. Turn acutely right back into dense woods.

The track is about 4 or 5 feet wide. The surrounding woodland is quite scenic with its steep terrain forested with oaks, dogwood, and hickory. Lake views continue as you descend to an intersection in a fast reforesting clearing where the trail splits. One trail heads toward the lake, while the main track heads left.

The main track then drops off the hill and bridges bottomland on a wide elevated dike with a large concrete culvert underneath it. Level out and reach the Army Corps of Engineers property boundary. These are the yellow-banded trees you see adjacent to the trail in places. The path continues winding northeasterly in high pines. ATV trails spur off the main path but the Army Corps of Engineers has done a good job marking the confusing areas with the Carsonite posts. Too bad they can't do as good a job enforcing the "no motorized vehicles" regulation. The trail continues rolling, dropping into a bottom where sycamores and other moisture-loving trees survive and ascending into oak-pine areas at the higher points.

▶ **Plum Point Recreation Area has several tent-friendly campsites, each with a picnic table, fire ring, lantern post, and tent pad. Water, flush toilets, and upright grills complement the camping and picnic area here. A boat ramp allows easy water access and the swim beach is next to the trailhead.**

Just before reaching Midway Road, turn right at a junction, almost due south, and begin heading toward Enid Lake and the undeveloped Midway Recreation Area, joining Midway Road. This is part of a spur loop. Walking down to the lake, you can see a large channel marker beside the point. The swim area at Plum Point can be seen, as well as Enid Lake Dam.

Enid Lake is ringed in sylvan forestland

Rocky Ridge Trail at Enid Lake

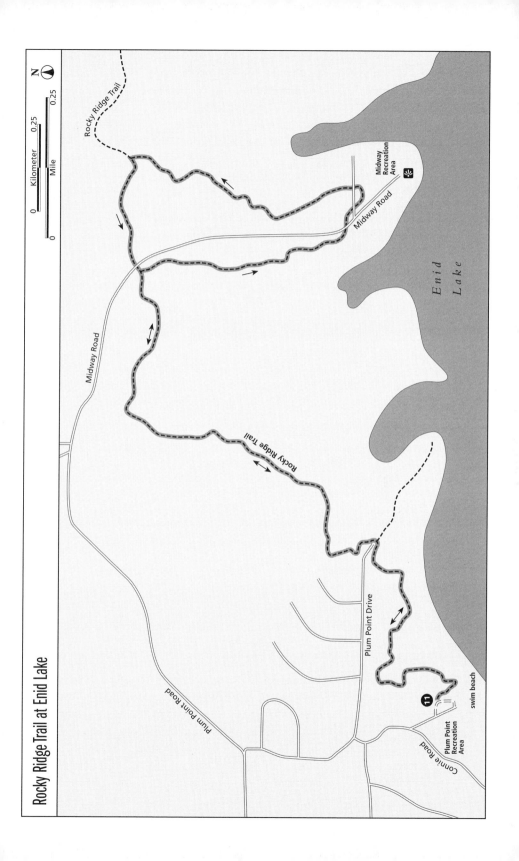

Head away from Midway in pine-oak woods. The trail continues undulating in and out of small bottoms, keeping your heart moving. Soon you will reach the main Rocky Ridge Horse Trail and begin heading back toward Plum Point; you'll cross Midway Road a second time, now backtracking to the trailhead.

In the winter when the lake is down, you could theoretically return along the exposed lakeshore from Midway, but don't try it when it's been raining recently. You will get yourself in a muddy mess.

Miles and Directions

0.0 Start at the swim beach and horse trail parking area at Plum Point. Descend steeply from trailhead toward lake before turning acutely left and uphill.

0.2 Turn right after approaching corps property boundary.

0.8 Cross bottomland and a stream on an elevated track via culvert.

1.5 Reach a trail junction; this loop turns right and main trail continues forward to shortly meet Midway Road. The portion of trail heading toward Midway Road is your return route.

1.9 Meet Midway Road. Turn right heading down the gravel road to gain good views from this undeveloped recreation area. The trail follows the road toward the lake briefly before turning left and climbing away from the lake.

2.5 Reach a heavily used dirt road, which at this point is the main Rocky Ridge Horse Trail. If you go right with the green arrows, you will bridge a perennial stream flowing beneath a culvert. Beyond this stream a small farm field opens up. This loop turns left, however, now going with the red arrows back toward Plum Point, uphill and away from the small field.

2.7 Reach and cross Midway Road a second time. To your right at the road is a gate and private property. Keep going straight across the road, descending to a trail junction. You've been here before. Backtrack 1.5 miles to the trailhead.

4.2 Arrive back at the trailhead.

More Information

Local Information

Batesville, Mississippi Chamber of Commerce, 107 Public Square, Batesville, MS 38606; (662) 563-3126; www.cityofbatesvillems.com.

Local Events/Attractions

Watermelon Carnival, 206 Main Street, P.O. Box 726, Water Valley, MS 38965; (662) 473-1122; www.watervalleychamber.com. The annual festival, held each August, is centered on the popular crop in Yalobusha County, in which lies most of Enid Lake.

12 Sandbar Trail at Great River Road State Park

This is one of the most unusual hikes in the state. A trail leaves the shoreline of the Mississippi River and heads out to a waterside sandbar. A trip here will help you gain an understanding of the massive size of Old Man River. Be apprised that when the river is up, the trail will be inundated. Fall is the best time to enjoy this trek, as it exposes the most sandbar.

Start: Trailhead near the park visitor center
Distance: 2.0 miles out-and-back
Approximate hiking time: 1 to 1.5 hours
Difficulty: Tougher than you might think, due to loose sand
Trail surface: Mostly sand
Seasons: Year-round
Other trail users: Hikers only
Canine compatibility: Leashed dogs permitted
Land status: State park

Nearest town: Rosedale
Fees and permits: Park entrance fee required
Schedule: Open year-round
Maps: Great River Road State Park; USGS maps: Rosedale
Trail contacts: Great River Road State Park, P.O. Box 292, Rosedale MS 38769; (662) 759-6762; http://home.mdwfp.com/parks.aspx

Finding the trailhead: From Cleveland, take Highway 8 west 18 miles to its end in Rosedale and Highway 1. Turn left on Highway 1 south and go just a few feet, then turn right on State Park Road. Continue for 1.2 miles and turn right toward the visitor center. The Sandbar Trail starts at the picnic area near the visitor center, toward the river. *DeLorme: Mississippi Atlas & Gazetteer:* Page 22 H1. GPS trailhead coordinates: N33 50' 51.7" / W91 3' 6.4".

The Hike

The Sandbar Trail leaves the picnic area to cross a wooden bridge over a wetland. The bridge was an Eagle Scout project by Rob Crump. The river is already visible in the distance, even at low water, which is when you should be doing this hike. If the water is high, there will be no sandbar exposed and the flowing waters will be relatively close. Begin heading toward the Mississippi before curving right, running parallel and upstream with the river. The trailbed is sandy, with some grass in spots. This sand walking will train you for the sandbar crossing. It isn't long before the trail reaches a dike, then turns westerly along the dike, aiming for Big Muddy.

A line of willows divides the riverbank and the sandbar. The path cuts through this line and opens into a sand desert—in late summer and fall of normal precipitation years. In winter and spring you will be reaching water. Before undertaking this hike, call the state park office to see if the river is up or down, if you are unsure. Potholes and old river channels may be partly filled with water. To your left as you face out to the river, there is generally a water-filled slough.

A very few young cottonwood trees survive out here. Most vegetation can't endure the intermittent flooding. Driftwood large and small is scattered about. The river is due west and Arkansas lies beyond it. The sandbar rises. But it isn't all sand. Depending upon the river flows, gravel, mud, and other particles will come together, each in their own places. Just think about what you're walking on: soils that have come from as far as Montana, Minnesota, and New York, all melding here on Mississippi shoreline.

This gigantic sandbar is an indicator of what an enormous watercourse is the Mississippi River. Consider the area that it drains: Starting in the West it is fed by streams coursing off the Rocky Mountains from Montana to New Mexico. Now add the entire Midwest to northern Minnesota and the Mississippi's official headwaters at Lake Itasca. Then look east, its drainages ranging from New York to the Southern Appalachian Mountains and down Dixie way. All told the Mississippi drains all or parts of thirty-one states and two Canadian provinces—1.5 million square miles. This aggregate river flow averages 600,000 cubic feet per second in New Orleans, moving 436,000 tons of soil per day. Only two rivers on the planet have larger drainage basins—the Amazon and the Congo.

View of Big Muddy from the park observation tower

Sandbar Trail at Great River Road State Park

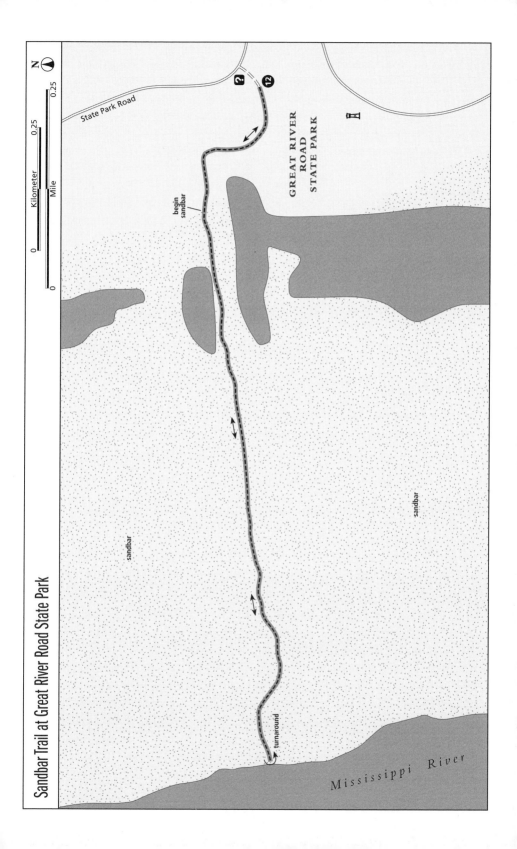

State Park Road

N

Kilometer
0   0.25

Mile
0   0.25

begin
sandbar

GREAT RIVER
ROAD
STATE PARK

sandbar

sandbar

turnaround

Mississippi River

Then there are the man-made aspects of the Mississippi River. The Arkansas shoreline is riprap, rock piles spread along the shoreline to prevent erosion. If you look way up or downstream, you will see wing dams. These are stone walls extending from the bank into the river to concentrate and accelerate the river current. It is likely that during your trek out here you will see a tugboat rolling by. Nearing the river, you will see more potholes and semi–dried-up channels that may be muddy. Be prepared to work around them. And then you reach the Father of Waters. It is amazing to think about where the water flowing before you came from. The Mississippi River is truly the aquatic pulse of our country.

▶ Over 60 percent of American grain exports travel down this river. Gravel, sand, and assorted liquids are also pushed along by pilots and crews who have their own subculture, living on the tugs for weeks on end.

You may want to ramble around and explore the sandbar. Look for animal tracks such as beaver and coyote. When you return from the river, note the park observation tower and stay left of it, and when you get a little closer use the visitor center as your guide. By the way, climbing the observation tower is mandatory if you come here. The view is well worth the climb. The park also has a fine campground that is worth a night of your life.

Miles and Directions

0.0 Start at the parking/picnic area toward the river.

0.3 Drop off the bank, passing through willows to reach the sandbar.

1.0 Reach the river at low water. Arkansas stands before you. Explore then backtrack.

2.0 Arrive back at trailhead.

More Information

Local Information
Cleveland Tourist Council, 600 3rd Street, Cleveland, MS 37832; (800) 295-7473; www.visitclevelandms.com.

Local Events/Attractions
Crossroads Blues Festival, www.crossroadsbluessocietyrosedalems.com. This music festival takes place on the second Saturday of May in Rosedale, which is adjacent to Great River Road State Park. The festival features local blues musicians.

13 Lost Bluff Trail at Grenada Lake

This is one of the best hikes in the entire state. Enjoy a well-marked and maintained trail through some of the steepest terrain around. In addition to experiencing some vertical variation, you'll also explore a Civil War fort site, all within the realm of Grenada Lake.

Start: Lost Bluff trailhead near Grenada Lake Dam
Distance: 2.1-mile loop
Approximate hiking time: 1 to 2 hours
Difficulty: Difficult for a short hike due to steep climbs
Trail surface: Sand, dirt, wooden steps
Seasons: Year-round
Other trail users: Hikers only
Canine compatibility: Leashed dogs permitted

Land status: Army Corps of Engineers property
Nearest town: Grenada
Fees and permits: No fees or permits required
Schedule: Open year-round
Maps: Lost Bluff Trail, Grenada Lake; USGS maps: Grenada
Trail contacts: Grenada Lake Field Office, P.O. Box 903, Grenada, MS 38902-0903; (662) 226-5911; www.mvk.usace.army.mil/Lakes/msgrenada

Finding the trailhead: From exit 207 on Interstate 55, Highway 7/Highway 8, Grenada/Greenwood, take Highway 8 east for 4.7 miles and turn left on Scenic Loop Highway 333. Follow Highway 333 for 0.4 mile and veer left, staying with the Scenic Loop Road to enter the greater Grenada Lake area after 0.4 mile. Continue for 1.0 mile farther, a total of 1.4 miles, then turn left into the signed parking area for the Lost Bluff Trail. *DeLorme: Mississippi Atlas & Gazetteer:* Page 30 A5. GPS trailhead coordinates: N33 47' 53.70" / W89 46' 5.60".

The Hike

This well-maintained path is part of a nice recreation area run by the Army Corps of Engineers. Unlike some trails, this trailhead parking area is in great shape and is indicative of the shape of the trail itself. Leave the signboard and kiosk to enter a mixed woodland of pine, oak, and hickory. The singletrack sand and dirt corridor curves along the edge of some ultra-steep dropoffs. Notice the trailside rock outcrops. The path winds among oaks, dogwood, hickory, and regal white oaks. Beech trees grow in the cooler margins. In places, the dropoff to your right is nearly vertical—true bluffs. Cane grows, not only in the bottoms, but also on the hills you are walking.

The course drops off the bluff amid thick woods. The downgrade becomes such that the Army Corps of Engineers has installed handrails along the trail and even steps that lead off the hillside into the bottoms. You will be amazed at the bluffs now above you. Beech trees tower over ferns deep in this hollow. A footbridge straddles a

Steps ease the climb and cut down on erosion

sand-bed stream, cutting this hollow ever deeper. Reach a second set of steps beyond a second bridging of the creek.

The steepness of the steps matches the steepness of the bluff that they surmount. The eighty stairs lead you most of the way up the bluff and replace a rougher gravel track that had a metal cable with which to haul yourself up. Beyond the stairs, climb a little bit more, this time on regular dirt, to a junction. Turn right here to head to an overlook of the Old Yalobusha River Channel and the main emergency spillway for the dam. Beyond the spillway, you can see Grenada Lake shimmering in the distance. A contemplation bench begs a seat.

Backtrack to the main trail and continue along the ridgeline bordered by sparkle-berry and yaupon, passing a loop shortcut. Intrepid hikers carry on and dive into another steep hollow, this time with fewer steps. This descent is mostly over dirt and roots, using only thirty-seven steps to hit the base of the bluff. The trail then crosses a couple of hollows on footbridges. Return to a regular foot trail atop a slender ridgeline with precipitous deeply wooded bluffs plunging to bottomland. The passageway briefly tops out in pines before descending to perhaps the steepest bluff of them all, the one bordering the old river channel, the former channel of the Yalobusha River.

Another beech-shaded contemplation bench is stationed where you can overlook the river. Head upstream along a tiny creek that must have taken a long time to cut so deep a hollow. Of course, most bluff cutting happens during floods. Besides, Mother Nature is much more patient than modern man. Bridge the stream to leave the hollow. Another solid climb leads to a ridgeline and easy level hiking, where you can catch your breath.

This old roadbed seems wide, level, and easy compared to the other trail sections you've been tracking. Pass the other end of the loop shortcut while looking for exposed rock. This old road has been in use a long time and is eroded, even though it has reverted to footpath. Pass back under the power line, then come to the old Confederate fort. Steps and scattered rocks lead uphill left to the fort remnants. During the Civil War, trees around the edges were cut to allow viewing. The Confederate soldiers dug "moats" to make it difficult for Union troops to scale the perimeter. Other earthworks and foundations are within the fort perimeter. This fort never saw action. A short walk leads to the trailhead.

FYI: This is one of eight earthen forts built in a semicircle around Grenada. The fort, constructed in 1862, overlooked the Yalobusha River. Cannons were placed here to prevent the Yankees from crossing the river. This fort has deteriorated somewhat, but is being left in its natural condition to contrast with the restored fort you pass on the drive to the trailhead.

Miles and Directions

0.0 Start at the Lost Bluff trailhead near the information kiosk, heading forward on a wooded singletrack path.

Lost Bluff Trail at Grenada Lake

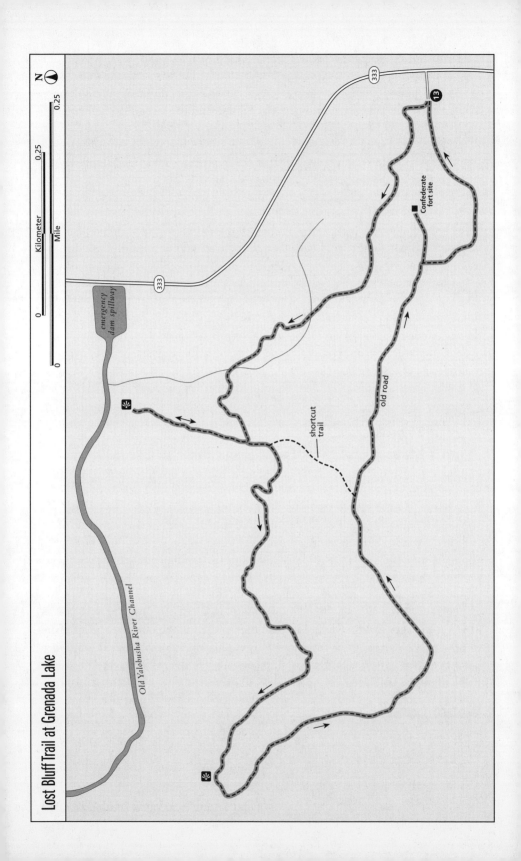

N

0   0.25   Kilometer

0   0.25   Mile

Old Yalobusha River Channel

emergency dam spillway

333

333

Confederate fort site

old road

shortcut trail

13

0.2 The trail passes under a descending power line.

0.5 Reach a junction. Spur trail leaves right to overlook of Old Yalobusha River channel. Soon pass a loop shortcut.

1.2 Drop sharply to reach overlook of Old Yalobusha River Channel. A very steep bluff drops from this overlook.

1.5 Join an old ridgetop roadbed after climbing away from old river channel. Turn left upon reaching the roadbed.

1.7 Pass the other end of the loop shortcut. Keep forward on old roadbed.

1.9 Pass spur trail leading left to old Confederate fort.

2.1 Arrive back at the trailhead, completing loop.

More Information

Local Information
Grenada Tourism Commission, 95 SW Frontage Road, Grenada, MS 38901; (800) 373-2571; www.grenadamississippi.com.

Local Events/Attractions
Grenada Crappie Classic, www.grenadacrappieclassic.ms. This is a spring fishing tournament that draws in anglers from near and far to Grenada Lake.

Grenada Downtown Jubilee, www.grenadamississippi.com. Arts and crafts, music, and entertainment takes place on the square in Grenada, held annually in September.

14 Leflore Trail at Malmaison WMA

This trail system, which combines human and natural history on the edge of the Delta, has had a recent facelift. Hike through the Loess Hills to a historic cemetery and the homesite of an early Mississippi settler, Jackson Leflore. Pass through a pecan grove to finish your loop.

Start: Leflore trailhead near Malmaison WMA Headquarters
Distance: 2.5-mile loop
Approximate hiking time: 1.0 to 1.5 hours
Difficulty: Moderate due to some hills
Trail surface: Dirt and grass along wooded hills
Seasons: Year-round
Other trail users: Hikers only
Canine compatibility: Leashed dogs permitted
Land status: State wildlife management area

Nearest town: Holcomb
Fees and permits: No fee, but you must register at trailhead
Schedule: Open year-round
Maps: USGS maps: Louisville North
Trail contacts: Malmaison Wildlife Management Area, 628 Malmaison Headquarters Road, Holcomb, MS 38490; (662) 453-5409; http://home.mdwfp.com/parks.aspx

Finding the trailhead: From exit 206 on Interstate 55, Grenada/Greenwood, take Highway 7 south/Highway 8 west. Drive through Holcomb, then keep going on Highway 7 south. Go for a total of 15.5 miles from I-55 and turn left on Malmaison Headquarters Road, ignoring the previous right turn on Malmaison Road. Follow the wide gravel road for 0.6 mile as it curves to the wildlife management headquarters. Drive past the large metal building and park across from the trailhead kiosk. *DeLorme: Mississippi Atlas & Gazetteer:* Page 30 B2. GPS trailhead coordinates: N33 40' 59.2" / W90 3' 3.6".

Sign marks spot where Jackson Leflore lived in the 1840s and early 1850s

The Hike

This set of hiking trails was originally developed in 1980 by the Greenwood Garden Club, in cooperation with the Mississippi Department of Wildlife Conservation. Over the years, the paths became overgrown and somewhat neglected. However, recent infusions of money and interest have combined to restore this trail system. This transformation was ongoing while this book was being written, and hopefully you will find the trail system improved.

First, make sure and fill out a user permit at the trailhead before you hit the Long Trail. Lush woods, including ash, magnolia, and cypress, veil the hills and the adjoining clear creek. Its waters, shaded by sycamore, flow over a sand bed into Beauty Bayou, which forms in the Delta beyond these hills. Travel betwixt steep bluffs to your left and the meandering watercourse to your right. By now you may have noticed the old interpretive signs that have been placed along the trail. Perhaps they will be replaced or refurbished in the future. Occasional wooden benches stand trailside for your resting and contemplation.

After passing the bridge to the Footbridge/Wilderness Trail, the Long Trail keeps going north on a doubletrack to reach another junction, where the Short Trail bears left and uphill. The Long Trail is still straddling the margin between the alluvial bottom and the bluffs to your left in tall, viney woods. The trail then turns left and begins to climb, splitting again as the Cemetery/Homesite Trail leaves right and avails the most interesting option.

On the Cemetery/Homesite Trail you will soon see the Leflore Cemetery, with its graves mostly untended, left to time and the elements, now shaded by trees that have sprung up over the past few decades, giving it a haunting look. Area residents were interred here from the latter 1800s to as recently as 1959. Heavy iron fences circle some of the graves.

The wide, shady track curves to pass the other end of the Footbridge/Wilderness Trail, leaving the lush dark hollow to tackle a hilltop, reaching the Jackson Leflore homesite. Not much is left here. At first glance, the only evidence is the cleared area and the sign. Note the huge cedar trees and privet, a common ground cover found at homesites.

After rejoining the Long Trail, the hike reaches its highest point, then begins working back downhill toward the WMA Headquarters. Enjoy the woodland walk on an extended downgrade over a grassy track, eventually to meet the Short Trail again. The Long Trail curves right through a large pecan grove and rejoins a wide path, which soon leads down to Malmaison Headquarters Road. The trailhead is to your left.

Miles and Directions

0.0 Start at the covered information kiosk and head away from the headquarters up the green mown Long Trail, which is quite wide at this point.

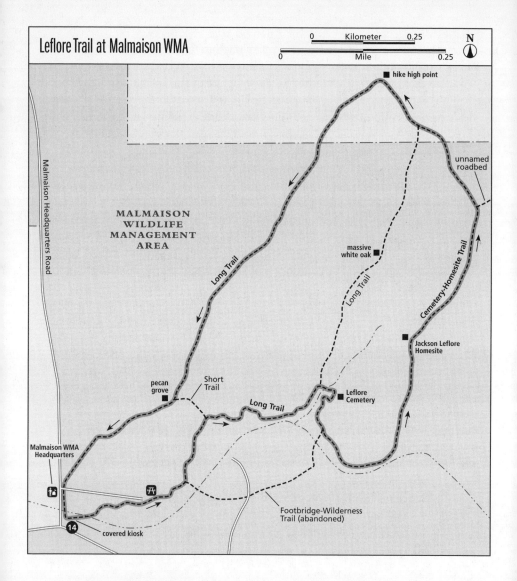

Leflore Trail at Malmaison WMA

0   Kilometer   0.25

0   Mile   0.25

N

■ hike high point

unnamed roadbed

MALMAISON
WILDLIFE
MANAGEMENT
AREA

Long Trail

massive
white oak ■

Long Trail

Cemetery-Homesite Trail

Malmaison Headquarters Road

Jackson Leflore
Homesite ■

pecan
grove ■

Short
Trail

Long Trail

■ Leflore
Cemetery

Malmaison WMA
Headquarters

🏕

Footbridge-Wilderness
Trail (abandoned)

14

covered kiosk

0.2   Reach the shaded picnic area.

0.3   Come to an enormous beech tree, just before reaching the bridge leading right to the Footbridge/Wilderness Trail. Unfortunately this trail has been overtaken by kudzu. Hopefully it will be restored in the future.

0.4   Reach an intersection. Here, the wide Short Trail leads left uphill and cuts over to the pecan orchard. Stay right with the Long Trail, immediately crossing a streamlet via culvert.

0.6   The right turn to the Cemetery/Homesite Trail is easy to miss. Watch for old steps with a handrail leading right and downhill just after you start climbing. Follow these steps down and circle around the ravine ahead of you to join a wide roadbed at the Leflore Cemetery. (Side trip: Continue forward on the Long Trail to see massive white oak to left of the path.)

0.7 The Leflore Cemetery is to the left of the trail amid the trees. Gravesites rise up the hill. The hike continues to pass the other end of the abandoned Footbridge/Wilderness Trail.

1.0 Reach the Jackson Leflore homesite, after leaving the hollow and climbing a hill. (FYI: Leflore, who lived here in the 1840s and early 1850s, put his homesite up here to minimize insect troubles and enjoy summer breezes.)

1.2 Stay left as a roadbed veers acutely right, northeast. Resume climbing.

1.4 Meet the Long Trail as it comes in from your left. Keep going in a northwesterly direction, climbing a bit more.

1.5 Small spur trail leads right to open field at the high point of the hike. Stay left and begin downhill ridgeline walk.

2.1 Reach a trail junction. The Short Trail leads left. This hike turns right and passes through the center of the pecan grove. Join roadbed heading downhill at the far end of the pecan grove.

2.4 Emerge onto Malmaison Headquarters Road. Turn left and follow the road toward the trailhead.

2.5 Arrive back at the trailhead.

More Information

Local Information

Grenada Tourism Commission, 95 SW Frontage Road, Grenada, MS 38901; (800) 373-2571; www.grenadamississippi.com.

Local Events/Attractions

Cottonlandia Museum, 1608 Highway 82 West, Greenwood, MS 38930, (662) 453-0925, www.cottonlandia.org. This attraction offers not only a glimpse at the agricultural past, but reflections on all aspects of area history from the Choctaw to the Confederates.

Heart of
Mississippi

15 Double Loop at Plymouth Bluff

British civil engineer Bernard Romans described Plymouth Bluff in 1771: "We saw a very remarkable bluff on the west side, rising about 50 feet out of the present level of the water . . . it looks as if made by art, and placed near any town of note, I do not doubt would be much used as a walk . . . it's being in the form of a crescent, makes it have a very romantic appearance." And now, over 200 years later, his vision has come true and you can walk this double loop along the old Tombigbee River and Plymouth Bluff.

Start: Plymouth Bluff Center
Distance: 3.9-mile double loop
Approximate hiking time: 2 to 2.5 hours
Difficulty: Moderate with hills and steps
Trail surface: Pavement, boardwalk, steps, natural surfaces
Seasons: Year-round
Other trail users: Hikers only
Canine compatibility: Leashed dogs permitted
Land status: Army Corps of Engineers,

Mississippi University for Women
Nearest town: Columbus
Fees and permits: No fees or permits required
Schedule: Open year-round
Maps: Plymouth Bluff Environmental Center Site; USGS maps: Columbus North, Waverly
Trail contacts: Plymouth Bluff Center, Mississippi University for Women, 2200 Old West Point Road, Columbus, MS 39701; (662) 241-6214; www.plymouthbluff.com

Finding the trailhead: From Columbus, take U.S. Highway 82 west over the Tennessee-Tombigbee Waterway, then take the first exit west of the waterway, U.S. Highway 45 south, Macon/Meridian. Head right toward the Stennis Lock and Dam to reach a T intersection and Old West Point Road. Turn left on Old West Point Road, following it for 0.6 mile to turn right into Plymouth Bluff Environmental Center. *DeLorme: Mississippi Atlas & Gazetteer:* Page 33 E8. GPS trailhead coordinates: N33 30' 52.49" / W88 29' 46.53".

The Hike

Plymouth Bluff Center is located adjacent to the old Tombigbee River and offers facilities for groups from workshops to educational programs to family reunions. The 190-acre area is mostly wooded, has a quality trail system, and is managed for wildlife as well. Start your hike on the Lake Trail, following the asphalt pavement through the woods, and then begin circling left around the lake. Osage orange and cedar trees are prevalent.

Join a fence line marking the border of Army Corps of Engineers property. Yaupon bushes crowd the trail as you encounter tall pines and hardwoods. The wide-limbed oaks have resurrection ferns atop them. Stay left joining the Bluff Trail as it traverses varied environments, including dense cedar thickets, to bridge a few ravines. This is now Mississippi University for Women property. Fields are visible beyond the

The Osage orange is also known as a hedge-apple. The heavy yellow-green ball that falls from the tree in autumn best identifies it. Inside the ball are light brown nutlets. This fruit is eaten by livestock, which has given rise to the name "horse-apple." The native range of this tree is uncertain, as it has been naturalized and planted in many states east of its primary Oklahoma-Texas range. Out there, the spiny tree served as fence lines before barbed wire.

trees. The trail emerges at the bluff and you can see the old Tombigbee River channel below through the trees. The bluff below you is much more vegetated than it used to be before the Tennessee-Tombigbee Waterway was opened in 1985. No longer does the Tombigbee River scour the shore.

▶ After the 1830 Treaty of Dancing Rabbit Creek opened the area to white settlement, one Clark Howell prepared for the influx of white settlers by surveying land around his house just north of this bluff, naming the town Plymouth. The town didn't last long but the name stuck to the bluff.

White-trunked sycamores rise at the water's edge. Pass a contemplation bench and bluff overlook. Occasional fencing borders the steep parts of the bluff. The views just keep on coming. The old channel is now a backwater, since the Waterway was dug. Leave the bluff and travel through woods before returning to the Lake Trail. Return to the conference center.

The second loop leads you down to the banks of the Tombigbee River. Note the saw palmetto as you come alongside the old river channel. Vine-draped moisture-loving species such as ironwood and buckeye shade the track. Pass the first of many grassy food plots, designed to attract wildlife. Keep your eye peeled as the old river channel merges with the Waterway downstream. This confluence is visible from the trail, despite the thick growth, as cane has become more prevalent.

The loop turns back north on the Buckeye Trail. It follows a rudimentary transportation track now reverted to hiking trail. A haunting cypress/tupelo swamp lies to the left of the trail. The path leaves the lower river area, then works its way back up Plymouth Bluff, passing over a couple shallow drainages underneath cedars and chestnut oaks, a rare tree in Mississippi. Backtrack to the conference center.

Miles and Directions

0.0 Start at the Harry Logan Sherman Conference Center. As you face the conference building, the hike starts to your left on the paved Lake Trail. Stay left following the asphalt bordered with lanterns. (FYI: The university property upon which this hike travels was originally purchased by The Nature Conservancy in 1965.)

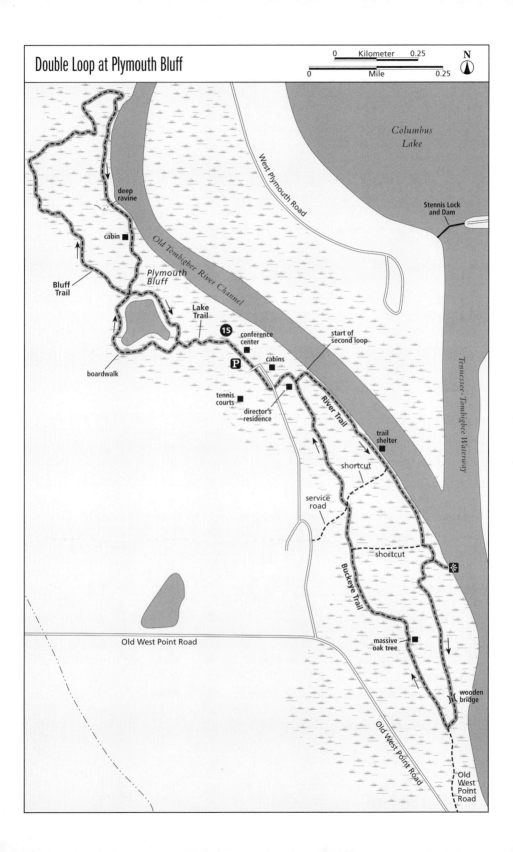

Double Loop at Plymouth Bluff

Columbus Lake

West Plymouth Road

Old Tombigbee River Channel

Tennessee-Tombigbee Waterway

Stennis Lock and Dam

deep ravine

cabin

Bluff Trail

Plymouth Bluff

Lake Trail

boardwalk

15

conference center

cabins

start of second loop

River Trail

trail shelter

tennis courts

director's residence

shortcut

service road

shortcut

Buckeye Trail

massive oak tree

wooden bridge

Old West Point Road

Old West Point Road

N

Kilometer   0.25
Mile   0.25

0.1 Shortly reach the split of the Lake Trail. To your right a path leads down to a small lake. This is your return route. Stay left for now under tall cedar trees and the lake will be on your right. Traverse a boardwalk near the lake. Note the Osage orange trees.

0.4 Watch for a break in the fence line to the left and a pair of trails leading away. Pass through the fence line break and stay left, now on the Bluff Trail. The path is now on a completely natural surface in tall woodland of pine, cedar, and oak.

0.5 The trail crosses a gravel road. Veer slightly right after the crossing. The track is quite wide for a short distance, then veers left to cross a little boardwalk in a dense cedar thicket.

1.1 Reach Plymouth Bluff. Trails go both left and right, but the official trail heads right. Pass an old Army Corps of Engineers survey marker from 1978.

1.5 Descend off the bluff, then reach a trail junction. To the left a bridge crosses an incredibly steep ravine, then leads down steps to reach a gravel bluff just above the river channel. To the right, the main trail bridges the ravine, then climbs a series of steps to rejoin Plymouth Bluff near a cabin. Join the gravel cabin access road.

1.6 Veer left away from the gravel cabin access road.

1.7 Complete the Bluff Trail. Turn left and rejoin the paved Lake Trail, crossing the lake dam and passing the outdoor amphitheater.

1.8 Stay left at the trail junction and return to the conference center, completing the first loop.

2.1 Begin the second loop, following an asphalt path across from the tennis courts. Pass behind the director's residence, then reach a set of steps leading down to the lower river.

2.4 Pass a trail shelter adjacent to the river, then pass a food plot and wide track leading right to shortcut the loop.

2.6 Come out under a power line and reach a junction. A spur trail leads right and shortcuts the loop. However, turn left here toward the river in a grassy mown area adjacent to the waterway. Ahead, the main path enters the woods to parallel the waterway and travels briefly to reach another junction. Here you can continue hiking just a short distance to gain a view of the waterway and maybe even see a tugboat and barge. Main loop turns right, away from the river.

2.9 Traverse a wooden bridge over a ravine.

3.0 Intersect Old West Point Road. This should be called Older West Point Road, since you drove in on Old West Point Road. This loop turns back acutely right, northbound, joining the Buckeye Trail.

3.2 Pass a massive, lightning-struck oak tree to the right of the trail.

3.4 Pass back under the power line. Keep forward on the Buckeye Trail.

3.5 Open onto another grassy food plot. Pay attention here. A gravel road leads left to Old West Point Road. Keep forward along the edge of the food plot, just past the gravel road, then look for the trail leading into the woods away from the food plot. If you continue forward, a roadbed will lead you back to the River Trail. This left turn just beyond the gravel road is hard to find and easy to miss.

3.8 Complete the lower loop behind the director's house after climbing up Plymouth Bluff. Begin backtracking.

3.9 Arrive back at the conference center.

More Information

Local Information
Columbus Convention & Visitors Bureau, P.O. Box 789, Columbus, MS 39703; (800) 327-2686; www.columbus-ms.org.

Local Events/Attractions
Tennessee Williams Home/Columbus Welcome Center, 300 Main Street, Columbus, MS 39701-4532; (662) 328-0222. Tour the home of the famous Southern playwright and learn about other tourism opportunities in the great Columbus area.

16 Lake Lowndes Horse and Bike Trail

This trail is actually a series of loops that range through hills and streams on the east side of Lake Lowndes at Lake Lowndes State Park. Though it is officially called a horse and bike trail, truth is it is only lightly used by both groups, with the lightest use by equestrians. Hikers often travel these loops and also use the Opossum Nature Trail as part of the greater state park trail network. Another benefit of these multiple loops is being able to alter the distance you want to hike on the fly.

Start: Trailhead near park entrance station
Distance: 6.2 miles (all loops)
Approximate hiking time: 3 to 4 hours
Difficulty: Somewhat difficult due to elevation changes and numerous trail junctions
Trail surface: Dirt and leaf roadbeds, also singletrack natural surface trails
Seasons: Fall through spring
Other trail users: Equestrians, mountain bicyclists
Canine compatibility: Leashed dogs permitted

Land status: State park
Nearest town: Columbus
Fees and permits: Park entry fee required
Schedule: Open year-round
Maps: Opossum Nature Trail; USGS maps: New Hope
Trail contacts: Lake Lowndes State Park, 3319 Lake Lowndes Road, Columbus, MS 39702; (662) 328-2110; http://home.mdwfp.com/parks.aspx

Finding the trailhead: From the intersection of Highway 182 and Highway 69 on the east side of Columbus, take Highway 69 south for 4.9 miles, then veer left on Lake Lowndes Road. Follow it for 3.3 miles to enter the state park. Pass the entrance station, then immediately turn left onto the signed gravel road shortly leading to a large parking area. *DeLorme: Mississippi Atlas & Gazetteer:* Page 33 F9. GPS trailhead coordinates: N33 26' 24.0" / W88 18' 12.7".

The Hike

Don't expect this to be a muddy track where you are dodging horse poop every other step. This trail is underutilized by all groups who use it—equestrians, mountain bikers, and hikers. You may find some trail intersections confusing, so on your first trip here, don't be surprised if you get lost. However, the worst-case scenario is getting a little extra mileage in while getting out.

The trail is blazed in orange. At first you will follow a closed roadbed, passing over Ellis Creek, which feeds Lake Lowndes. A tall forest with a healthy dose of dogwoods keeps things well shaded. The trail rolls between hill and bottom as it skirts the edge of the park. It is making the most of the park property and therefore comes near civilization.

Hiker-eye view while descending to Ellis Creek

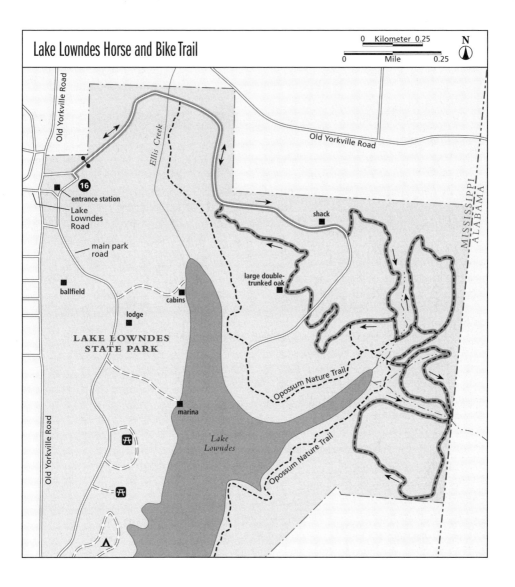

Lake Lowndes Horse and Bike Trail

0   Kilometer   0.25

0   Mile   0.25

N

Old Yorkville Road

Ellis Creek

Old Yorkville Road

MISSISSIPPI

ALABAMA

16

entrance station

Lake
Lowndes
Road

main park
road

shack

large double-
trunked oak

ballfield

cabins

lodge

LAKE LOWNDES
STATE PARK

Opossum Nature Trail

marina

Lake
Lowndes

Opossum Nature Trail

Old Yorkville Road

The trail dips into a valley with a streambed off to your left as you drop to a major intersection by a stream. Here is where a GPS will come in handy. If you mark the intersections, you will find yourself returning to them later, and watching your progress adds to the fun. After leaving the main roadbed at 1.1 miles, you will have to pay closer attention to the trail. It is blazed in orange and will have small metal signs with a horse stamped onto it at the key junctions. Here is another tip: If in doubt, stay left at just about every trail junction on the Horse and Bike Trail and you will do the complete set of loops. The few exceptions are when it reaches connector trails to the Opossum Nature Trail.

The path returns to the streams flowing off the Alabama hills to feed Lake Lowndes before beginning the second loop, which turns away from the streams and lake to climb a wooded hilltop, then descend to another watercourse. The third and final loop begins on the far side of the bridged watercourse. The vegetation is much more open and brushy here. Shade is next to nil. Avoid this loop on a hot day. The loop tops an open hill and nears a timbered area. As you curve around, Lake Lowndes becomes visible to your left.

After the third loop is complete, you are officially on the return journey to the trailhead, which will entail a mix of new trail and backtracking. Hopefully the intersections won't all look the same. Your wanderings are heading generally northwest. Don't miss the large double-trunked oak to the left of the trail at 5.0 miles. It would take three people interlinked to stretch their arms around the forest giant. It divides about 7 feet above ground level and this imperfection may have spared it the logger's ax. The numerous dogwoods will brighten the woods in spring with their blossoms and color the woods in burgundy during autumn. Shortly pop out on the roadbed that took you in here, then backtrack to the trailhead.

Miles and Directions

0.0   Start at the parking area near the park entrance station. Join a roadbed leading away from the entrance, passing around a pole gate. The roadbed winds through piney hills, crossing a bottomland stream, Ellis Creek, after climbing the second hill.

0.5   Reach a trail junction. Here, the Opossum Trail leads right. The Horse and Bike Trail continues on the roadbed.

0.7   A singletrack trail comes in on your right just as you begin to climb out of a bottom. This is your return route. Continue forward on the wide roadbed.

1.0   Reach a hilltop. A shack lies off to the left. Keep straight going downhill.

1.1   The Horse and Bike Trail leads acutely left away from the roadbed you've been following, now on a narrower track.

1.6   Junction. A trail leads uphill and to your right. Continue straight and downhill.

1.7   Reach another trail junction. Here, a short trail leads right connecting to the Opossum Trail. Turn left here, immediately crossing a stream, then continue up the valley you were just heading down.

2.2   Complete the first loop. Keep forward here to reach the other two loops.

2.4   Reach important intersection. Here, a short trail heads straight to intersect the Opossum Trail. The Horse and Bike Trail curves left and immediately crosses a wooden bridge over a stream.

2.5   Stay left at the intersection to begin second loop.

2.8   Reach a junction after dropping off a hill. A trail leads acutely right. Keep going straight to immediately bridge a small stream, then reach the third loop.

3.4   Reach a trail junction in a brushy area. A short path leads left to the Opossum Trail.

3.7   After completing the third loop, bridge the small stream again and stay left at the next junction.

3.9 Complete the second loop and stay left.

4.0 To get the maximum trail mileage, turn right at the next junction.

4.2 Reach first loop and turn left here.

4.3 Turn left at the intersection.

4.4 Turn left on narrow trail after crossing a stream then turning back up along it.

4.5 Cross a roadbed and keep forward on the narrow trail.

4.8 Cross main park service road.

5.0 Note large double-trunk oak to the left of the trail.

5.1 The trail takes an abrupt left atop a hill, now heading down after left turn.

5.5 After a final steep drop, return to the roadbed that brought you in. Turn left here, now backtracking to the trailhead.

6.2 Arrive back at the trailhead.

More Information

Local Information

Columbus Convention & Visitors Bureau, P.O. Box 789, Columbus, MS 39703; (800) 327-2686; www.columbus-ms.org.

Local Events/Attractions

Tennessee Williams Home/Columbus Welcome Center, 300 Main Street, Columbus, MS 39701-4532, (662) 328-0222. Tour the home of the famous Southern playwright and learn about other tourism opportunities in the great Columbus area.

17 Opossum Nature Trail at Lake Lowndes State Park

This track makes a loop around 150-acre Lake Lowndes. It starts off as a narrow footpath and winds along the east shore of the impoundment through hill country, crossing small streams. It eventually joins a closed road and works its way back to the main area of the park, where you trace the main park road to complete the loop.

Start: Lake Lowndes Dam
Distance: 4.8-mile loop
Approximate hiking time: 2.5 to 3 hours
Difficulty: Moderate with some hills, many level sections too
Trail surface: Grass, natural surface under forest, dirt, pavement
Seasons: Fall through spring
Other trail users: Hikers only
Canine compatibility: Leashed dogs permitted

Land status: State park
Nearest town: Columbus
Fees and permits: Park entry fee required
Schedule: Open year-round
Maps: Opossum Nature Trail map; USGS maps: New Hope
Trail contacts: Lake Lowndes State Park, 3319 Lake Lowndes Road, Columbus, MS 39702; (662) 328-2110; http://home.mdwfp.com/parks.aspx

Finding the trailhead: From the intersection of Highway 182 and Highway 69 on the east side of Columbus, take Highway 69 south for 4.9 miles, then veer left on Lake Lowndes Road. Follow it for 3.3 miles to enter the state park. Pass the entrance station and take the main park road all the way down to the end of the lake. You'll find a parking area under some pines across from the assistant manager's residence. *DeLorme: Mississippi Atlas & Gazetteer:* Page 33 F9. GPS trailhead coordinates: N33 25' 25.6" / W88 18' 15.0".

The Hike

Lake Lowndes is the centerpiece of this state park located south of Columbus. First dug half a century ago, it was originally a county lake open to the public. Later, the lake and adjacent 600 acres were deeded to the state, and Lake Lowndes State Park came to be. Your path, the Opossum Nature Trail, was built by the Youth Conservation Corps in 1980.

The Opossum Trail begins by crossing the Lake Lowndes dam. Along the way it offers good views north of the impoundment and where you will be going. The trail is identified with yellow blazes and circular metal tags with a hiker symbol. Trailside posts mark distance in half-mile increments. Bottomland hardwoods stretch out on the lower side of the dam. The setting becomes most enjoyable once the trail starts meandering through hills on the east side of Lake Lowndes. Pines shade the track as it travels

The Opossum Trail overlooks Lake Lowndes

along the steep shoreline. Wooden steps have been placed in the most declivitous areas. Begin circling around a cove, descending to nearly lake level before rising again.

Occasional short wooden bridges span intermittent drainages. Beech trees can be found in the bottoms near these bridges. Note how the beeches are well carved by passersby, especially the bigger ones.

Beech trees range over most of Mississippi, generally in moist hollows. They sometimes occur in nearly pure stands. It is thought they might produce a chemical that discourages other growth. The beech faces a new threat, not from the knives of passersby but from an exotic bug known as the beech scale insect. First found in Nova Scotia in the late 1800s, it has been working its way south ever since. Less than half of the mature beech trees are left in New England, where the beech scale insect has been since the turn of the century. The closest place the beech scale insect is to Mississippi is east Tennessee in the Smokies. The trees of the Magnolia State will probably decline over a long time. As of today, there is no way to stop the bug, but some trees in the North are resisting this European invader, offering hope for the future.

Holly trees add year-round greenery. Curve around the largest embayment of the lake, where the tree canopy gives way. Come within 1,000 feet of the Alabama state line as you bridge an unnamed Lake Lowndes tributary. Keep circling around the embayment in rich bottomland woods, passing trails connecting to the Lake Lowndes Horse and Bike Trail. In case you get confused, stay with the yellow blazes. Roll over hills to join the uppermost reaches of the lake. The open water gives way to a large wetland and the Ellis Creek drainage.

After joining a closed road, the path winds back toward the park entrance station and the developed facilities. The return part of the loop now follows the main park road. You will pass a ball field and tennis courts. Join in on a game if the hike hasn't worn you out enough. Ahead, you will see the park campgrounds. They have a primitive camp and a more developed overnight area. I have enjoyed a night here before. It is a great base camp in which to enjoy yourself at this state park on the outskirts of Columbus.

Miles and Directions

0.0 Start at the parking area across from the assistant manager's residence near the lake dam. A concrete channel lies between the parking area and the beginning of the trail. You can cross it on the road that continues beyond the assistant manager's residence, or find the low concrete plank crossing the channel. Either way, look for the Opossum Trail sign

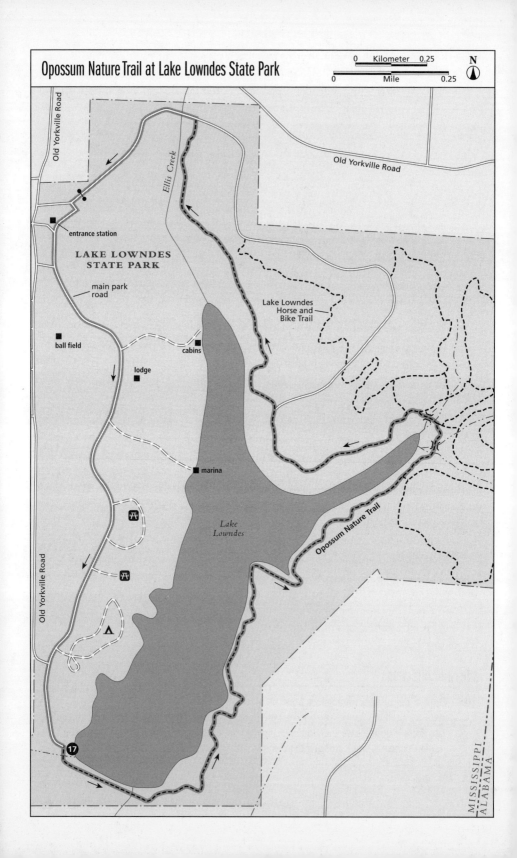

Opossum Nature Trail at Lake Lowndes State Park

0 Kilometer 0.25
0 Mile 0.25

N

Old Yorkville Road

Ellis Creek

Old Yorkville Road

entrance station

LAKE LOWNDES
STATE PARK

main park
road

Lake Lowndes
Horse and
Bike Trail

ball field

cabins

lodge

marina

Opossum Nature Trail

Lake
Lowndes

Old Yorkville Road

17

MISSISSIPPI
ALABAMA

at the beginning of the Lake Lowndes dam. Immediately join the dam, an arrow-straight earthen structure covered in grass.

0.2 Leave the dam to enter woods on an old roadbed, which climbs a hill and leads to a clearing encircled by pines. Look for the trail sign leading left, still on a roadbed. Soon leave the roadbed at the edge of the woods, picking up a narrow singletrack foot-only trail.

0.8 The trail comes directly alongside Lake Lowndes.

1.5 Short path in brushy area leads right to Lake Lowndes Horse and Bike Trail.

1.6 Bridge a stream feeding an embayment of Lake Lowndes.

1.7 Reach a trail junction in thick woods. Here, a short trail leads right connecting to the Lake Lowndes Horse and Bike Trail. The Opossum Trail continues forward, immediately crossing a wooden bridge.

1.8 Cross another wooden bridge. A trail comes in on the right just beyond the last bridge. Stay left traveling between young dense pines. Stay left at next junction. Continue in woods toward the main body of Lake Lowndes.

2.3 Leave abruptly left from old roadbed you have joined after climbing a hill away from Lake Lowndes.

3.0 The foot trail reaches a closed roadbed under a big pine. Turn left here, crossing Ellis Creek on a culvert, then climb a hill. The wide dirt track is mostly shaded, and you can hear the sounds of civilization not too far in the distance.

3.5 Reach the park entrance station and join the main park road heading back toward the trailhead. Pass numerous park facilities.

4.8 Arrive back at the trailhead.

More Information

Local Information
Columbus Convention & Visitors Bureau, P.O. Box 789, Columbus, MS 39703; (800) 327-2686; www.columbus-ms.org.

Local Events/Attractions
Tennessee Williams Home/Columbus Welcome Center, 300 Main Street, Columbus, MS 39701-4532, (662) 328-0222. Tour the home of the famous Southern playwright and learn about other tourism opportunities in the greater Columbus area.

18 Little Mountain

This trail travels an outlier of the Appalachian Mountains along the Natchez Trace. The trek starts unconventionally at the top of the mountain, offering far-reaching views of the Magnolia State, goes past springs, then makes a loop before reaching its low point at Jeff Busby Campground, all a part of the Natchez Trace Parkway. Therefore, you can combine hiking, picnicking, camping, and scenic driving all in one segment of beautiful Choctaw County.

Start: Summit of Little Mountain at Jeff Busby Recreation Area
Distance: 2.0 miles out-and-back
Approximate hiking time: 1 to 1.5 hours
Difficulty: Moderate
Trail surface: Pea gravel, leaves, dirt, pine needles
Seasons: Fall through spring
Other trail users: Hikers only

Canine compatibility: Leashed dogs permitted
Land status: National park
Nearest town: Ackerman
Fees and permits: No fees or permits required
Schedule: Open year-round
Maps: USGS maps: Tomnolen
Trail contacts: Natchez Trace Parkway, 2680 Natchez Trace Parkway, Tupelo, MS 38804; (800) 305-7417; www.nps.gov/natr

Finding the trailhead: Jeff Busby Recreation Area is located at milepost 193.1 of the Natchez Trace Parkway, near the town of Ackerman. *DeLorme: Mississippi Atlas & Gazetteer:* Page 31 F10. GPS trailhead coordinates: N33 24' 49.74" / W89 15' 39.42".

The Hike

Mountain hikes usually start at the bottom and climb to a view, but this one goes in reverse—it is still rewarding nonetheless. Though Little Mountain, at 590 feet, is a good 200 feet lower than Mississippi's highest point—Woodall Mountain—this peak still sports quite a view. At the trailhead you will find a picnic area, restrooms, and informative displays. The mountaintop has cleared overlooks both to the east and west. You may want to time your visit to enjoy sunrise and sunset from the peak. Leave the parking area descending on a gravel footpath. Interpretive information about fossilized trees and other items are posted trailside. The hillsides are draped in a hickory-oak hardwood forest with a few scattered pines. The trail makes a pair of switchbacks, working down the east

▶ The Jeff Busby Recreation Area is named in honor of the Mississippi congressman Thomas Jefferson Busby. He got the Natchez Trace Parkway on its feet, spearheading a survey of the Natchez Trace in 1934 that led the historic road to become a part of the national park system. Approximately 310 miles of the Parkway travel through Mississippi and provide scenic and recreational venues, such as this one, for state residents.

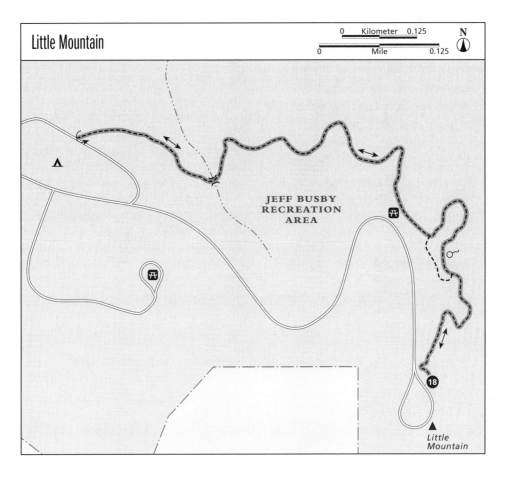

0   Kilometer   0.125

0   Mile   0.125

N

JEFF BUSBY
RECREATION
AREA

18

Little
Mountain

slope of Little Mountain. Continue descending into a hollow to meet a springhead. Here, the trail splits and you begin a short loop. A boardwalk crosses the seep of the spring branch. A contemplation bench begs a rest. Shortly pass a second springhead where a second boardwalk crosses the outflow. In the summer the air will be cooler around the springs than in the surrounding woods.

The Little Mountain Trail travels over extremely sloped ground, but the trail itself has been leveled. Curve around a rib ridge of Little Mountain. Reach another junction, keeping right toward the campground. The sloped woodland you are traveling is truly reminiscent of the Southern Appalachian Mountains. Though Little Mountain is appropriately named in comparison to its larger sister peaks to the east, the wooded hillsides add a special physiological component to the Mississippi landscape.

Come very near the Little Mountain access road before turning away on another rib ridge. Continue winding through some of the most beautiful woodland in the state, heading ever downward. Soon skirt the campground, straddling the margin

► Back in the early 1800s, during the heyday of traveling the Trace from Natchez, Mississippi, to Nashville, an arduous trip was virtually assured. Flooded rivers, robbers, bad weather, hostile Indians, and the rigors of day-after-day, self-propelled travel made the journey challenging. The perils that befell Natchez Trace travelers were said to be the work of the devil, and the name "Devils Backbone" sprang up as a moniker for the Trace.

between a bottomland and the hillside to your left. From here, the path cruises below the camping area before it rises, making the north side of the campground loop.

If you're thirsty, grab some water at the campground, which also has restrooms. Your return trip will be more challenging as you have a 200-foot climb ahead of you. On your return trek, don't forget to do the upper part of the loop, which offers a top-down perspective of the mountainside springs.

Miles and Directions

0.0 Start at the summit of Little Mountain at Jeff Busby Recreation Area on the Natchez Trace Parkway.

0.2 Reach a hillside springhead. Here the trail splits. Take the right-hand part of the loop to pass a second spring.

0.3 Reach the other side of the loop. Stay right here heading toward the recreation area campground.

0.4 Pass a small picnic area beside Little Mountain access road.

0.7 Bridge an intermittent streambed.

1.0 Reach the recreation area campground. Water and restrooms are available. This is where you turn around and begin the climb up Little Mountain.

2.0 Arrive back at the top of Little Mountain.

More Information

Local Information

Choctaw County, 115 E. Quinn, P.O. Box 737, Ackerman, MS 39735; (662) 285-3778; www.choctawcountyms.com.

Local Events/Attractions

Pioneer Day, www.frenchcamp.org/NatchezTrace_site/. Old-time lifeway demonstrations such as basket weaving, cooking, weaponry, music, and crafts can be found 12 miles south of Jeff Busby at mile 180.7 of the Natchez Trace Parkway. It is held annually in early May. Sorghum molasses is made on weekends in October.

19 Headwaters Trail at Choctaw Lake

This trail winds through the hills and hollows above Choctaw Lake Recreation Area. Carved out of an abandoned nature trail, it offers a multitude of environments—lush rich hollows, pine-oak ridgetops, and a wooded marsh, plus occasional man-made wildlife clearings.

Start: Chata trailhead on the southwest side of Choctaw Lake
Distance: 3.7-mile double loop
Approximate hiking time: 2 to 2.5 hours
Difficulty: Moderate with hills
Trail surface: Dirt, leaves, gravel
Seasons: Fall through spring
Other trail users: Hikers only
Canine compatibility: Leashed dogs permitted
Land status: National forest

Nearest town: Ackerman
Fees and permits: Recreation area user fee
Schedule: Open year-round, Choctaw Lake campground closed in winter
Maps: Choctaw Lake Wildflower Viewing Trails; USGS maps: Ackerman
Trail contacts: Tombigbee National Forest, P.O. Box 1912, Highway 15 South, Ackerman, MS 39735; (662) 285-3264; www.fs.fed.us/r8/ mississippi/tombigbee

Finding the trailhead: From the intersection of Highway 12 and Highway 15 in Ackerman, take Highway 15 south and go for 4.2 miles, then turn left on Choctaw Lake Road. Go for 1.2 miles and turn left into Choctaw Lake Recreation Area. Ahead, veer left toward the campground, passing the swim area on your right, then look left for the Chata trailhead. Note that the trail cannot be directly accessed when Choctaw Lake Recreation Area is closed. If Choctaw Lake Recreation Area is closed, veer right, away from the campground and swim area, to reach the Noxubee Hills trailhead on the far side of Choctaw Lake dam. Take the Lakeside Trail for 1 mile to meet the Headwaters Trail. *DeLorme: Mississippi Atlas & Gazetteer:* Page 20 H1. GPS trailhead coordinates: N33 16' 23.6" / W89 8' 43.3".

The Hike

Choctaw Lake Recreation Area, one of the finest national forest facilities in Mississippi, offers a campground open during the warm season, fishing, and swimming, in addition to hiking. The Chata Trail heads away from Choctaw Lake, tracing an old roadbed through stone gates that once led to cabins, built when the Civilian Conservation Corps (CCC) originally developed the recreation area in the 1930s. Though the cabins are now gone, much of the CCC handiwork is visible elsewhere in the recreation area. The blazed path climbs away from the water. Keep forward as a road leads left uphill. A lush hardwood forest grows overhead, with oaks the dominant tree. Ferns line the hollows below gray beech trees. Choctaw Lake is visible beyond the forest.

After passing the Cabin Lake Trail, stay left and join the Headwaters Trail as it works up a hollow, soon bridging a tributary of the main stream you are following.

The Headwaters Trail was resurrected in 2007, roughly following an abandoned trail. You can still see the white paint blazes of the abandoned trail here and there. The revitalized trail system is now marked with plastic blazes nailed to trees. Continue up the hollow, dipping when crossing side tributaries. Tulip trees are abundant in this hollow. Watch for shagbark hickories, too. The hollows get smaller, the hills higher, and the pines more frequent the farther you get from Choctaw Lake. The Headwaters Trail meanders over rib ridges between hollows, most without benefit of footbridge. You begin to get a sense of how many streams do come together to form a creek and why this is called the Headwaters Trail. Some of the watercourses are flowing year-round, such as the one you bridge at 1.4 miles. In its quest to never remain level, this trail climbs away from the clear stream to bisect a linear wildlife clearing atop a hill in a thick forest, dipping over a couple more hollow/hill combinations, with short bridges at the low point of the hollows. Watch for a wildlife clearing to the right of the trail at 2.0 miles. These wildlife clearings are just one example of how the land-scape is managed for game within the Choctaw Lake Wildlife Management Area.

The trail leaves the headwaters area, descending to come alongside a big, brushy wetland and the main tributary of Choctaw Lake. This open, flat bottomland contrasts with the hilly terrain you've been traveling. Cane covers the bottoms beneath rich woods. Reach the edge of the wetland, then intersect the Lakeside Trail. The board-walk extending to your left offers a good vantage for observing the wetland. This loop

Trailside wetland along Choctaw Lake

0   Kilometer   0.25

0   Mile   0.25

N

TOMBIGBEE
NATIONAL
FOREST

wildlife
clearing

wetland

Lakeside
Trail

Choctaw
Lake

Chata Trail

Lakeside Trail

briefly join
closed forest road

Choctaw Lake
Campground

Cabin Lake
Trail

gazebo

Choctaw Lake Road

Headwaters Trail

Cabin Lake

19

Cabin Lake Trail

Chata Trail

stays right on the gravel track to bridge a creek, and the lake comes into view near a restroom. A walkway leads left to an island in Choctaw Lake.

This loop turns right here and heads up the Chata Trail, thickly flanked with cane, as it ascends away from Choctaw Lake, up yet another headwater hollow. Surmount a ridge then dip to Cabin Lake. The first junction with the Cabin Lake Trail leads left to the campground, but you keep going straight, crossing a long boardwalk to a second junction with the Cabin Lake Trail. Stay left and cruise the south side of Cabin Lake on an easy track. The campground is across the water. Hickory and beech trees grow thick here. Nesting boxes are scattered about Cabin Lake, another effort of wildlife managers to enhance species. Note that Cabin Lake is separated from Choctaw Lake by a small dam. The gravel track meanders along the shoreline, where man-made peninsulas jut into the water and are primarily used by anglers. Reach the campground access road. To your left the pavement leads to the campground. The Chata trailhead is a short distance down the road to your right.

Miles and Directions

0.0 Start at the Chata trailhead. Follow an old roadbed through stone gates.

0.3 Bridge a rocky streambed before rising into hills.

0.5 Intersect the Cabin Lake Trail. Turn left, joining a gravel track. Walk just a short distance then intersect the Headwaters Trail, and stay left again.

1.0 Drop to span another creekbed on a wooden bridge.

1.4 Bridge a perennial stream after sharp drop.

1.5 Reach a linear wildlife clearing atop a hill. Turn right to join a closed forest road. Leave left from the closed forest road after 70 yards.

2.0 Pass a wildlife clearing to the right of the trail. Ahead, climb a high piney hill.

2.2 Trail turns abruptly southeast, descending with a wetland to left of the trail.

2.7 Intersect the Lakeside Trail. Stay right to complete loop.

2.8 Briefly travel a gravel path, bridge a stream, then reach another junction near restroom. Leave the Lakeside Trail and turn right, ascending Chata Trail.

3.4 After surmounting a hill, pass Cabin Lake Trail leading sharply left to Choctaw Lake Campground. Keep straight, crossing a long boardwalk to complete loop portion of hike. Stay left again at second Cabin Lake Trail junction along south side of Cabin Lake.

3.7 After reaching campground road, follow pavement right to arrive back at Chata trailhead.

More Information

Local Information
Choctaw County, 115 E. Quinn, P.O. Box 737, Ackerman, MS 39735; (662) 285-3778; www.choctawcountyms.com.

Local Events/Attractions
Pioneer Day, www.frenchcamp.org/NatchezTrace_site/. Old-time lifeway demonstrations such as basket weaving, cooking, weaponry, and music and crafts, all near the Natchez Trace Parkway. It is held annually in early May. Sorghum molasses is made on weekends in October.

20 Lakeside Trail at Choctaw Lake

This all-accessible trail loops around charming Choctaw Lake, and makes for one pretty stroll that complements other paths in the area. Contemplation benches, fishing piers, boardwalks, and other amenities enhance the natural setting.

Start: Boat ramp near dam on the southeast side of Choctaw Lake
Distance: 2.5-mile loop
Approximate hiking time: 1 to 1.5 hours
Difficulty: Easy due to flat trail
Trail surface: Gravel
Seasons: Year-round
Other trail users: Hikers only
Canine compatibility: Leashed dogs permitted
Land status: National forest

Nearest town: Ackerman
Fees and permits: Recreation area user fee
Schedule: Open year-round, Choctaw Lake campground closed in winter
Maps: Choctaw Lake Wildflower Viewing Trails; USGS maps: Ackerman
Trail contacts: Tombigbee National Forest, P.O. Box 1912, Highway 15 South, Ackerman, MS 39735; (662) 285-3264; www.fs.fed.us/ r8/mississippi/tombigbee

Finding the trailhead: From the intersection of Highway 12 and Highway 15 in Ackerman, take Highway 15 south, go for 4.2 miles, then turn left on Choctaw Lake Road. Go for 1.2 miles and turn left into Choctaw Lake Recreation Area. Ahead, veer right, away from the campground and swim area, to reach the Noxubee Hills trailhead on the far side of Choctaw Lake dam. *DeLorme: Mississippi Atlas & Gazetteer:* Page 20 H1. GPS trailhead coordinates: N33 16' 29.5" / W89 8' 16.7".

The Hike

As you face the dam, head right, away from it. The pea gravel Lakeside Trail, about 4 feet wide, offers a foot-friendly environment open to everyone. Contemplation benches have been placed here for your pleasure. The trailside environment is partly landscaped, complemented with neatly mown grass, and makes the setting quite attractive. The lake will be off to your left the entire trip. Pines and oaks shade parts of the path. Shortly cross your first boardwalk, the first of many. The second boardwalk crosses an embayment. A big peninsula juts into Choctaw Lake and was built for bank fishermen. Bird boxes have been placed to aid wildlife. You may see herons perched on the old pilings of former docks in the lake. Ahead, a fishing pier is another angling venue. Bass, bream, crappie, and catfish inhabit the lake.

The trail curves away from the main body of the lake. Pass an old structure before entering a long boardwalk, crossing an extensive wetland thick with brushy alders. The path briefly curves away from the lake and climbs. Since this is an all-accessible trail, the slope of the climb is within the Americans with Disabilities Act guidelines. The path ends up a good 30 feet above the river on a bluff, and offers an elevated vantage. The trail returns to the lowlands, crossing a pair of boardwalks over alder-rich wetland to make a junction. Here the Headwaters Trail leads right. The Lakeside Trail continues on the pea gravel track, crossing a bridge, then comes to another trail junction. Here, the Chata Trail leads right. A restroom is here for your convenience. For fishing and lake viewing, take the arched bridge reaching out to an island in Choctaw Lake.

Hills rise higher from this side of the lake. Look for trailside red maples growing here. Interestingly, for nearly the entire hike you can see both where you have been and where you are going. After the path curves into the main lake, reach another boat ramp and fishing pier just below the campground. Choctaw Lake offers twenty-one campsites with water, electricity, and hot showers, and is a good recreation destination and hiker base camp. The Choctaw Lake trails and the Noxubee Hills trail system are in the immediate vicinity. The path curves around an arm of the lake to reach a wooden gazebo over the water. It beckons you to leave the trail and walk out to it. When the recreation area was first built, a dance floor over the lake was a popular drawing card. The gazebo does much the same. The trail makes a slight uptick as it passes through the day use area dotted with cedars.

Here, you have a high road and a low road. The high road curves back and forth, keeping its grade moderate. The low road curves by the sand beach of the swim area.

Nearly continuous views accompany the Lakeside Trail

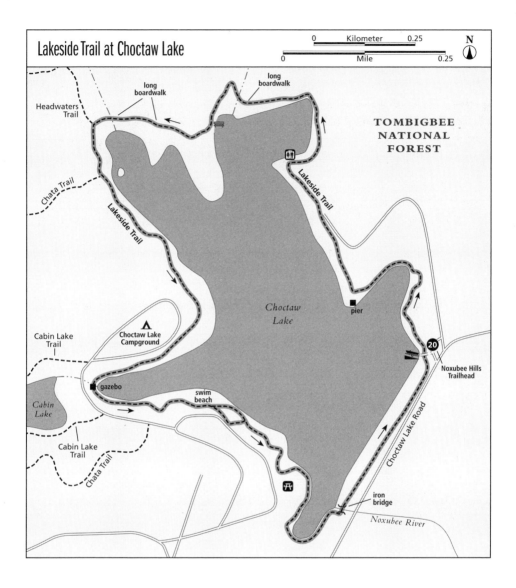

Lakeside Trail at Choctaw Lake

Kilometer 0 0.25

Mile 0 0.25

N

long boardwalk

long boardwalk

Headwaters Trail

TOMBIGBEE NATIONAL FOREST

Chata Trail

Lakeside Trail

Lakeside Trail

Choctaw Lake

pier

Cabin Lake Trail

Choctaw Lake Campground

gazebo

Cabin Lake

Cabin Lake Trail

Chata Trail

swim beach

20

Noxubee Hills Trailhead

Choctaw Lake Road

iron bridge

Noxubee River

The two paths come together before reaching the picnic area. You'll note that the grounds are very attractive, with regal trees shading the scattered picnic tables overlooking Choctaw Lake.

Beyond the picnic area, the path curves around one last embayment before reaching an iron bridge spanning the lake spillway, which is now the Noxubee River. A very long boardwalk takes you over the dam, offering great views of Choctaw Lake, and keeps you off the road crossing the dam. You can see the trailhead, and you'll soon arrive there to complete the hike.

Miles and Directions

0.0 Start at the Noxubee Hills trailhead. Follow pea gravel track away from Choctaw Lake dam.

0.2 Pass a fishing pier extending into the lake.

0.5 Pass a restroom and contemplation bench before curving back into thicker woods.

0.9 Reach contemplation bench and view atop a bluff after crossing a long boardwalk across a brushy wetland.

1.0 Intersect Headwaters Trail after passing a pair of lengthy boardwalks over wetlands. Continue on the Lakeside Trail.

1.1 Intersect the Chata Trail near a restroom. An arched bridge leads to a small island. The Lakeside Trail stays on the pea gravel track.

1.5 After curving back into the main body of Choctaw Lake, reach a boat ramp and fishing pier just below the recreation area campground.

1.8 Pass the swim beach amid cedars. Trail briefly splits into the high road and low road before coming together again.

2.0 Pass beneath well-groomed picnic area.

2.3 Use an iron bridge to cross the Choctaw Lake spillway. Hike a boardwalk the length of Choctaw Lake dam.

2.5 Arrive back at the trailhead, completing loop hike.

More Information

Local Information
Choctaw County, 115 E. Quinn, P.O. Box 737, Ackerman, MS 39735; (662) 285-3778; www.choctawcountyms.com.

Local Events/Attractions
Pioneer Day, www.frenchcamp.org/NatchezTrace_site/. Old-time lifeway demonstrations such as basket weaving, cooking, weaponry, and music and crafts, all near the Natchez Trace Parkway. It is held annually in early May. Sorghum molasses is made on weekends in October.

21 North Noxubee Hills Loop

This is a challenging hike utilizing a mix of paths in the Noxubee Hills trail system. It explores bottomland terrain as well as hilly country while circling the greater Noxubee River Valley, which is a good wildflower destination. Several shortcut trails allows you to shorten the loop if it becomes tiring. The paths are well marked and maintained, and some intersections even have trail maps encased in plastic.

Start: Boat ramp near dam on the southeast side of Choctaw Lake
Distance: 11.4-mile lollipop
Approximate hiking time: 5 to 6.5 hours
Difficulty: Difficult due to length and hills
Trail surface: Dirt, leaves, roots, gravel
Seasons: Fall through spring
Other trail users: Mountain bicyclists
Canine compatibility: Leashed dogs permitted
Land status: National forest

Nearest town: Ackerman
Fees and permits: Recreation area user fee
Schedule: Open year-round, Choctaw Lake campground closed in winter
Maps: Noxubee Hills Trails; USGS maps: Ackerman, Sturgis, Highpoint, Louisville North
Trail contacts: Tombigbee National Forest, P.O. Box 1912, Highway 15 South, Ackerman, MS 39735; (662) 285-3264; www.fs.fed.us/r8/mississippi/tombigbee

Finding the trailhead: From the intersection of Highway 12 and Highway 15 in Ackerman, take Highway 15 south and go for 4.2 miles, then turn left on Choctaw Lake Road. Go for 1.2 miles and turn left into Choctaw Lake Recreation Area. Ahead, veer right, away from the campground and swim area, to reach the Noxubee Hills trailhead on the far side of Choctaw Lake dam. *DeLorme: Mississippi Atlas & Gazetteer:* Page 20 H1. GPS trailhead coordinates: N33 16' 29.5" / W89 8' 16.7".

The Hike

The Noxubee trail system was the hard work of volunteers in cooperation with national forest personnel. Join the singletrack Beaver Lodge Trail as it courses through a fire-managed pine forest, shortly crossing an intermittent streambed. Note how the forest is thicker around the moist ravine. The level trekking is a breeze as you enjoy the pines mixed with sweetgum and a few oaks. The lower areas will have more hardwoods. Bridge a second streambed, continuing southeasterly, now nearing the lush Noxubee River bottoms. Swamps, beaver dams, and beaver lodges are visible to your right. The trail soon rises to a little bluff above the bottom before passing a very large beech tree directly beside the trail.

The trail joins Walker Wood Road, then twice-gated Lost Cemetery Road on a grassy doubletrack. Young pines border the now-level trail. The trail remains level here, then dips into bottomland just before bridging the Noxubee River, which is but 20 to 30 feet wide. It will be quite sluggish in the late summer and fall. Intersect the North Trail just beyond the bridge. Stay right, now in full-fledged river bottom.

Signs warn that the trail can be submerged. A large wildlife clearing is the only inter-ruption in the lush woods. Come alongside canalized Noxubee Creek. Vine-draped hardwoods, dominated by musclewood trees, canopy the track. After a while you can see private land across Noxubee Creek.

Singletrack trails predominate in the North Noxubee Hills

The path angles left away from the bottom to enter hills, just after passing the first potential shortcut trail. A steep climb leads you into pine, hickory, oak, and sweetgum woods. Dogwoods and redbud form an understory. Keep ascending to intersect the second connector trail. Steep hollows begin to drop off to your left. Pass the third connector trail on a descent. If this loop is getting a little long for you, these connector trails can shortcut your hike. Soon reach a major intersection with gated Rock Crusher Road. Stay left here, ascending toward Pigeon Roost Road, then begin a prolonged downgrade to pass the final connector trail, and your final chance to shortcut the loop.

Continue moderate ridge running to reach Pigeon Roost Road. This is a more developed gravel road, and will contrast mightily with the North Trail that you are fixing to join. Many consider the North Trail to be the most scenic of them all, as it travels into rich hollows divided by low ridges. The forest immediately changes to hardwoods, including tall tulip trees among others. Being on the north slope of the ridge leaves this area richly vegetated.

The North Trail works west, occasionally dipping into drainages flowing toward the Noxubee River. You are now following yellow blazes, since you are heading toward Choctaw Lake. The path is fun to follow as it twists all over the place. You will once again meet the connector trails, this time in reverse order, starting with D. Continue bisecting rich drainages filled with ferns. Crest out, intersecting Connector Trail C at the top of the ridge. The North Trail stays on a northbound oak ridge. At times young trees crowd the path. The challenging path includes up and down stretches before intersecting Connector Trail B. Stay along the ridgeline before drifting into the greater Noxubee River bottom, before you intersect Connector Trail A. Continue in beautiful rich woods, bridging a tributary. Soon come alongside the Noxubee River. Complete the loop portion of your hike upon reaching the bridge over the Noxubee River. While backtracking to Choctaw Lake, look for wildflowers in spring and fall.

Miles and Directions

0.0   Start at the Noxubee Hills trailhead. Cross the gravel road heading away from Choctaw Lake to join the singletrack Beaver Lodge Trail.

0.7   Briefly follow then bridge a streambed.

1.7   The Beaver Lodge Trail emerges onto closed Walker Wood Road. Turn left here, passing around a Forest Service gate.

1.8   Reach a four-way junction and turn right, passing around a Forest Service pole gate to join Lost Cemetery Road.

2.0   A grassy road leads left; however, you continue forward, still on Lost Cemetery Road.

2.6   Intersect North Trail just after bridging Noxubee River. Stay right with the Lost Cemetery Road.

3.4   After curving away from Noxubee Creek, Lost Cemetery Road intersects 0.5-mile long Connector Trail A. Stay with Lost Cemetery Road and enter hills.

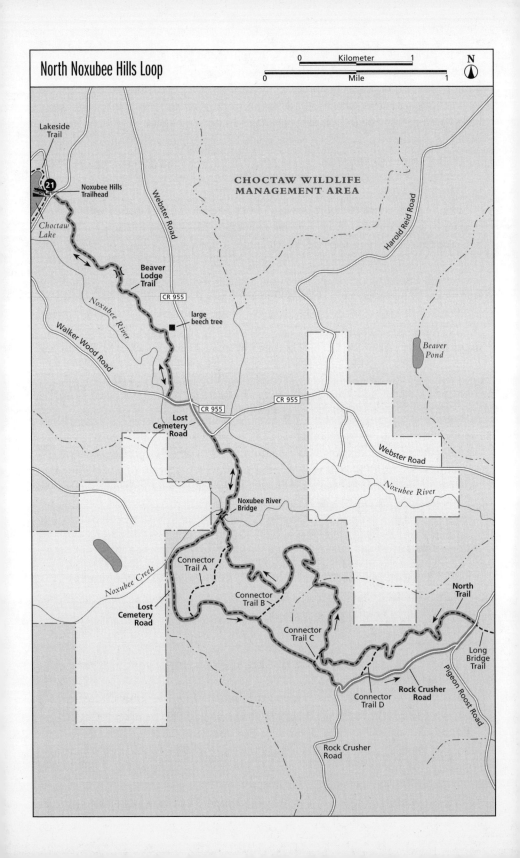

0   Kilometer   1

0   Mile   1

N

Lakeside
Trail

21

Noxubee Hills
Trailhead

*Choctaw
Lake*

Webster Road

**CHOCTAW WILDLIFE
MANAGEMENT AREA**

Harold Reid Road

**Beaver
Lodge
Trail**

CR 955

large
beech tree

Noxubee River

Walker Wood Road

*Beaver
Pond*

CR 955

CR 955

**Lost
Cemetery
Road**

Webster Road

Noxubee River

Noxubee River
Bridge

Noxubee Creek

**Connector
Trail A**

**Lost
Cemetery
Road**

**Connector
Trail B**

**Connector
Trail C**

**North
Trail**

**Connector
Trail D**

**Rock Crusher
Road**

**Long
Bridge
Trail**

Pigeon Roost Road

Rock Crusher
Road

3.9 Connector Trail B, 0.3 mile in length, leaves left.

4.3 Connector Trail C, 0.1 mile in length, leaves left.

4.5 Intersect Rock Crusher Road. Stay left, ascending.

4.7 Connector Trail D, 0.2 mile in length, leaves left.

4.8 Pass under the major power line.

5.3 Reach Pigeon Roost Road after passing around a pole gate. Stay left on developed gravel road open to vehicles.

5.5 At a four-way junction, leave left on scenic singletrack North Trail, which constantly curves.

6.3 Pass under the first of a few power lines, then intersect Connector Trail D.

6.9 Intersect Connector Trail C after a steep climb. Trail keeps north.

7.4 Cross a wash and a low point after a long descent. Resume climbing.

8.0 Intersect Connector Trail B.

8.6 Intersect Connector Trail A after descending into bottomland.

8.8 End North Trail and complete loop portion of your hike. Bridge the Noxubee River and begin backtrack.

11.4 Arrive back at the trailhead.

More Information

Local Information
Choctaw County, 115 E. Quinn, P.O. Box 737, Ackerman, MS 39735; (662) 285-3778; www.choctawcountyms.com.

Local Events/Attractions
Pioneer Day, www.frenchcamp.org/NatchezTrace_site/. Old-time lifeway demonstrations such as basket weaving, cooking, weaponry, music, and crafts, all near the Natchez Trace Parkway. It is held annually in early May. Sorghum molasses is made on weekends in October.

22 Sheepranch Loop

This challenging, but well-marked and well-signed loop in the Noxubee Hills offers not only vertical variation but also a forest mosaic to please the eye. The path is almost all singletrack, and the rugged terrain makes the footing tough. The interconnected trails of this area create a worthy backpacking destination, too. You will be sharing this loop with mountain bikers.

Start: Noxubee Hill Cemetery trailhead
Distance: 11.1-mile loop
Approximate hiking time: 4.5 to 6 hours
Difficulty: Difficult due to length and hills
Trail surface: Dirt, leaves, roots, gravel
Seasons: Year-round
Other trail users: Mountain bicyclists
Canine compatibility: Leashed dogs permitted
Land status: National forest

Nearest town: Louisville
Fees and permits: No fees or permits required
Schedule: Open year-round
Maps: Noxubee Hills Trail; USGS maps: Louisville North
Trail contacts: Tombigbee National Forest, P.O. Box 1912, Highway 15 South, Ackerman, MS 39735; (662) 285-3264; www.fs.fed.us/ r8/mississippi/tombigbee

Finding the trailhead: From the intersection of Highway 25 and Highway 15, just north of Louisville, take Highway 25 north for 2.2 miles, then turn left on Poplar Flat Road. Go for 2.5 miles and turn left on Sheepranch Road. Drive for 1 mile and the trailhead is on your left. The Charlotte's Web Trail starts on the right-hand side of Sheepranch Road. *DeLorme: Mississippi Atlas & Gazetteer:* Page 38 A2. GPS trailhead coordinates: N33 12' 26.7" / W89 4' 27.5".

The Hike

The loop starts with the Charlotte's Web Trail, a singletrack path blazed with yellow plastic diamonds, roughly paralleling Noxubee Hill Road to your left. The northbound trail slopes and is rarely level as it works along a steep hillside, ultimately switchbacking downward into a cane-filled hollow only to climb out again, still along a hillside with a sharp drop to your right. The trail returns within sight of Noxubee Hills Road. The dropoffs here are very steep, and the trail stays within the margin of the hillside with the road to the left and desiccated hollows to the right.

▶ This area once was cut over and farmed, resulting in horrific erosion, which rendered the land worthless. This was why the land was bought by the U.S. Forest Service. They planted trees, which, coupled with the passage of time, have allowed the land to recover to become a gem of the state rather than an eyesore.

The Charlotte's Web Trail sometimes dips into ferny hollows, where redbuds, tulip trees, water oaks, beech trees, and vines tangle tightly along the often sloped and irregular trailbed, which goes where you think it won't or shouldn't go. It is obvious that scenery and challenging terrain were taken into account constructing this trail, which was created with the intent of being a scenic trail, rather than following old logging or settlement roads, like national forest trails often do.

The Charlotte's Web Trail travels the border between the lush riparian forest to your left and open piney woods to your right, eventually heading west into gently undulating mixed woods. The hiking is easy and the trees are relatively widely spaced from one another. The sparse understory allows long looks through the woods here.

You will see milepost markers on the path. They indicate the distance from Choctaw Lake and the Noxubee Hill trailhead. While walking through this area, look for the undulations of the old row crops. Noxubee Hill Road is off to your right now, and occasionally comes into view. This is a rich wildflower habitat. Climb by switchbacks into high pines to reach a trail junction. Note the bricks and old stone fireplace foundation at the junction. This may have been a homesite.

► Distinguishing between sugar maples and red maples is easy. Look at the leaf of a sugar maple. The curves between lobes of the sugar maple are U-shaped, whereas the curves between lobes of the red maple are at right angles.

Turn left here on a closed forest road, joining the Log Jump Trail, now tracing blue blazes. Follow the closed forest road briefly, then split right. The closed forest road heads down to a field below. This trail comes alongside that field before reaching a junction. The Log Jump Trail leads left and avails your first shortcut opportunity, but why miss the fun? Instead, continue forward on Connector Trail E, toward Pigeon Roost Road. This is an interesting area as the scenes change quickly—first pass a large trailside beech tree, then climb to a sheer bluff overlooking a tributary below. The path then meets planted pines before reaching Pigeon Roost Road, which offers another chance to shortcut this loop.

The singletrack Three Bridges Trail rolls through the high country of Noxubee Hill in planted pines before dipping into hardwood bottoms and passing the first two bridges of the Three Bridges Trail. Enter a tight young forest with closely spaced trees, replacing open lands. Note in the past few miles that the forest has changed dramatically and often. It reveals how site, situation, and forest management practices affect what grows. To confirm this fact, the Three Bridges Trail drifts in and out of dense woods, now paralleling a small creek to your right with lots of paw paw, holly, and maple in this valley. Sugar maple even grows here.

Beyond the last of the three bridges, the trail rises dramatically into hilltop pines and meets Rock Crusher Road, a mostly shaded doubletrack. The Sheepranch Trail is your grand finale and travels the steepest terrain, doing much as the Charlotte's Web Trail does, traveling the margin between a nearby road and sheer bluffs. It comes within sight of the Sheepranch Road several times. Note the occasional rock outcrops.

The trail doesn't always skirt the edge of the dropoffs, rather descending into shallow hollows or otherwise running along the main ridgeline when Sheepranch Road is off the crest. It also occasionally joins a doubletrack covered in pine needles. After briefly joining Sheepranch Road, the trail travels along some extremely sheer bluffs as they break off the hillside.

Hickory, pine, and sparkleberry grow in the more level areas, such as when the trail passes under power lines before making Pigeon Roost Road. After passing through a flat, return to wandering along sharp dropoffs and on and off old logging roads. This is complemented by a constantly changing forest as well. One minute it will be young sweetgums and pines and the next you will be in shady hardwoods. This area offers the highest elevations of the entire loop.

Beyond the intersection with the Log Jump Trail, the Sheepranch Trail follows a narrow singletrack on a slope in full-blown woods that form an overhead cathedral, especially impressive compared to the younger forest you just passed through. Now you are below the bluffline, working your way along moist slopes, among dogwoods, sourwoods, sweetgums, and tulip trees, and cutting across shallow drainages. It soon joins the younger ridgetop forest, where sumac borders the path, which has been jumping on and off old roadbeds. Pass one last section of incredibly vertical terrain before passing just below Noxubee Hill Cemetery and the end of the hike.

Miles and Directions

0.0 Start at the Noxubee Hills Cemetery trailhead on the singletrack Charlotte's Web Trail, across Sheepranch Road from the trailhead parking area.

0.9 Come within sight of Noxubee Hill Road after climbing out of a cane-filled hollow.

1.9 The Charlotte's Web Trail dives off the ridge into the Noxubee River bottom.

2.5 After coursing through bottoms, join Noxubee Hill Road and turn right, bridging two tributaries of the Noxubee River.

2.8 Leave left away from Noxubee Hill Road, back on singletrack trail.

4.1 Reach a trail junction near Noxubee Hill Road. Long Bridge Trail leads right across road. This loop heads left on Log Jump Trail, briefly following closed forest road, then angling right and downhill.

4.4 The Log Jump Trail intersects Connector Trail E. Continue straight on Connector Trail E, while the Log Jump Trail heads left.

4.8 After climbing through planted pines, reach and cross Pigeon Roost Road, now joining the Three Bridges Trail.

5.4 After crossing two bridges, intersect the 0.7-mile Powerline Trail. It offers a steep shortcut to this loop. Three Bridges Trail passes under a power line.

5.8 Span the third bridge over a deep ravine, then make a heart-pounding ascent.

6.2 Turn left onto Rock Crusher Road.

6.4 Leave Rock Crusher Road and turn left onto Sheepranch Trail.

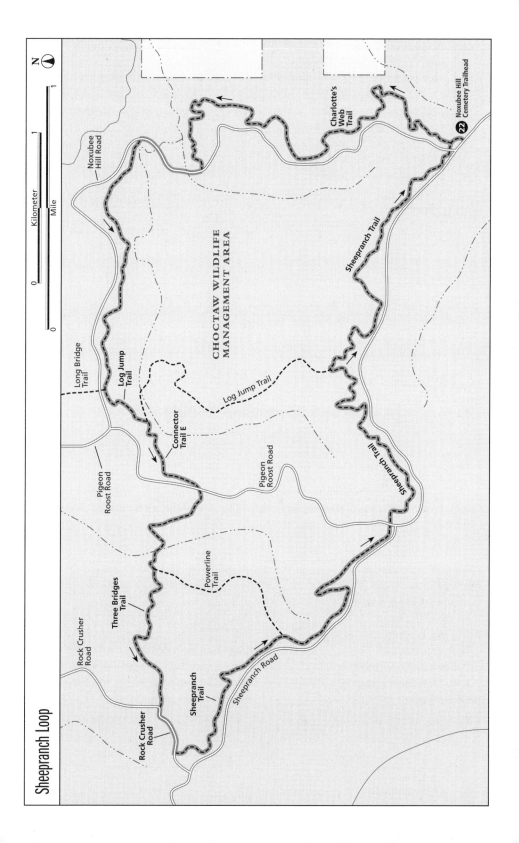

Sheepranch Loop

N

Kilometer

0   1

Mile

0   1

Rock Crusher Road

Rock Crusher Road

Three Bridges Trail

Sheepranch Trail

Sheepranch Road

Powerline Trail

Pigeon Roost Road

Connector Trail E

Pigeon Roost Road

Long Bridge Trail

Log Jump Trail

Log Jump Trail

Noxubee Hill Road

Sheepranch Trail

Sheepranch Trail

CHOCTAW WILDLIFE MANAGEMENT AREA

Charlotte's Web Trail

22 Noxubee Hill Cemetery Trailhead

7.3 Reach the other end of the Powerline Trail. The Sheepranch Trail soon joins Sheepranch Road for a short distance.

8.4 Meet and cross Pigeon Roost Road, still on the Sheepranch Trail.

9.6 Pass the south junction with the Log Jump Trail. Sheepranch Trail continues southeasterly, alternating between singletrack path and doubletrack roadbed, as well as alternating between ridgetop and hillside.

11.0 After traveling just below Noxubee Hill Cemetery, cross Noxubee Hill Road. Intersect the Charlotte's Web Trail and turn right.

11.1 Arrive back at the trailhead.

More Information

Local Information
Winston County Economic Development Partnership, P.O. Box 551, 311 W. Park Street, Louisville, MS 39339; (662) 773-8719; www.winstoncounty.com.

Local Events/Attractions
Red Hills Festival, www.winstoncounty.com. This great family event offers an art show, a car show, music, speakers, food, sidewalk sales, and games. It is the primary event in the Noxubee Hills of Winston County and is held each May.

23 Scattertown Trail at Noxubee Wildlife Refuge

This is a beautiful hiker-only trail that loops through the Red Hills in the Little Yellow Creek watershed. If the distance seems a little short, visit some of the other nearby trails in the refuge. A picturesque visitor center set on the shores of Bluff Lake offers interpretive displays and other trail information. It also has a picnic area overlooking Bluff Lake.

Start: Bevil Hill Road trailhead
Distance: 1.6-mile loop
Approximate hiking time: 1 to 1.5 hours
Difficulty: Moderate with hills
Trail surface: Leaves, needles, forest duff
Seasons: Year-round
Other trail users: Hunters in season
Canine compatibility: Leashed dogs permitted
Land status: National wildlife refuge

Nearest town: Starkville
Fees and permits: No fees or permits required
Schedule: Open year-round
Maps: Noxubee National Wildlife Refuge Hunting Regulations map; USGS maps: Betheden
Trail contacts: Noxubee National Wildlife Refuge, 2970 Bluff Lake Road, Brooksville, MS 39739; (662) 323-5548; www.fws.gov/noxubee

Finding the trailhead: From Highway 12 in Starkville, within sight of the MSU Stadium, head south on Spring Street. After 0.9 mile, you reach a roundabout. Continue in a southerly direction on the other side of the roundabout, now on Oktoc Road. Stay forward on Oktoc Road. Go for 11.3 miles, then reach a T intersection. Turn right here on Skinner Road and enter the refuge after 0.8 mile. Stay with the main refuge road to reach the refuge headquarters in the visitor center after 3.4 miles. Continue beyond the refuge, now on Bluff Lake Road, for 9 miles and turn left at Bevil Hill Road. This is also the location of Bevil Hill Church. Bevil Hill Road immediately turns into gravel. Follow the road just a short distance beyond the church and look for the trailhead on your left. There is parking for one or two cars here. *DeLorme: Mississippi Atlas & Gazetteer:* Page 38 A3. GPS trailhead coordinates: N33 13' 44.8" / W88 54' 46.9".

The Hike

This hike, the Scattertown Trail, travels through numerous hardwoods in the Red Hills, which makes this loop trail a good fall color destination. However, the refuge is a popular hunting locale, so check ahead of time for hunting dates and also be prepared to wear orange during such times if you choose to hike.

Noxubee National Wildlife Refuge was established at the same time as the nearby Tombigbee National Forest, in the 1930s. Both now-public lands had been farmed using poor practices and overgrazed by cattle. The 48,000 acres of the refuge were restored with an eye toward enhancing flora and fauna habitats, from alligators to woodpeckers, and from bottomland cypresses to upland oaks. Migratory birds gather on the refuge waterways. You can enjoy the varied habitats on the hiking trails offered here.

Follow the metal arrows nailed to trees. They help indicate the way, which passes underneath a tall forest. Sparkleberry is a prominent understory tree. Pass a small wooden footbridge, then roll over more hills to reach a second bridge spanning Little Yellow Creek. The narrow footpath continues winding through heavily wooded oak-covered hills mixed with cedar. You are heading downstream in the Little Yellow Creek drainage. Dip to Little Yellow Creek again and make the first of several wooden footbridges crisscrossing the now-larger stream in narrow bottomland bordered with high hills. Note how the stream has cut small vertical bluffs into the hills as it curves through the narrow hollow. Ferns spread their greenery along the waterway.

The path then leaves the Little Yellow Creek hollow, regaining the upland hills. The trail winds the mid-slope area between the lowlands to your right and the hill crest to your left. Drift in and out of shallow drainages that rarely flow except during rains, before returning to the trailhead.

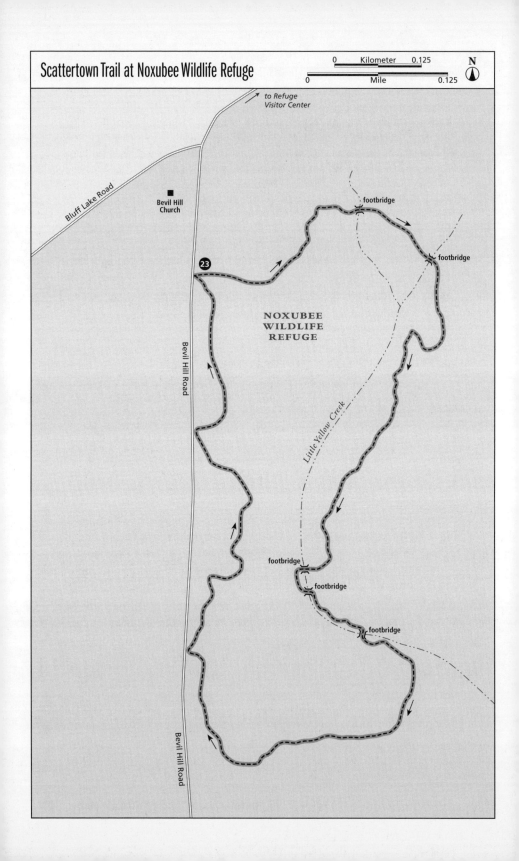

Scattertown Trail at Noxubee Wildlife Refuge

0　　　Kilometer　　0.125

0　　　Mile　　　0.125

N

to Refuge
Visitor Center

Bluff Lake Road

Bevil Hill
Church

23

Bevil Hill Road

NOXUBEE
WILDLIFE
REFUGE

footbridge

footbridge

footbridge

Little Yellow Creek

footbridge

footbridge

footbridge

Bevil Hill Road

Though none of the hiking trails at the refuge are long, there are many of them. The Bluff Lake Boardwalk makes a short meander through cypress woods along Bluff Lake. The Trail of the Big Trees was once 4 miles long and traveled through the Noxubee River bottomlands, but many of the big trees fell during Hurricane Katrina. It is currently 0.75 mile one way. The 4-mile Wilderness Trail is closed, but watch for it to reopen. The Beaver Dam Trail is another bottomland hardwood trek that is 2 miles long. The refuge has still other nature paths, and when you add up the mileage there is plenty to hike. Call ahead at the visitor center for the latest trail updates.

Miles and Directions

0.0 Start at the Bevil Hill trailhead. Leave the trailhead and immediately enter a tall mixed pine forest on a leafy track. It is but a short distance before you cross the first drainage.

0.2 Cross a streambed on a wooden footbridge.

0.7 Make the first of numerous bridge crossings of Little Yellow Creek.

1.6 Arrive back at the trailhead after circling around upper Little Yellow Creek drainage.

More Information

Local Information

Greater Starkville Development Partnership, 200 East Main Street, Starkville, MS 39759; (662) 323-3322; www.starkville.org.

Local Events/Attractions

Mississippi Horse Park and Agri-Center, 716 E. Poorhouse Road, Starkville, MS 39759; (662) 325-9350; www.msucares.com/centers/agricenter/. This one hundred-acre park, developed by the Mississippi State University and the town of Starkville, hosts events and exhibits including racing.

24 Legion State Park Loop

This relatively short hike takes a watery trip at historic Legion State Park. The trail travels not only along the lake, but also through wetlands and hills. Though the trail is short, it packs a lot of climbing and descending into the trek. Occasional interpretive signs are scattered along the path.

Start: Legion Lake trailhead
Distance: 1.5-mile loop
Approximate hiking time: 1 to 1.5 hours
Difficulty: Easy, but has some short steep sections
Trail surface: Dirt, grass, gravel, leaves
Seasons: Year-round
Other trail users: Hikers only
Canine compatibility: Leashed dogs permitted

Land status: State park
Nearest town: Louisville
Fees and permits: Park entrance fee required
Schedule: Open year-round
Maps: USGS maps: Louisville North
Trail contacts: Legion State Park, 635 Legion State Park Road, Louisville, MS 39339; (662) 773-8323; http://home.mdwfp.com/parks.aspx

Finding the trailhead: From the intersection of Highway 15 and Highway 14 west of Louisville, take Highway 14 east for 1.9 miles and reach the town square. Turn left on Columbus Street at the Confederate soldier monument and follow Columbus Street for 1.7 miles to Legion State Park. Turn left on Legion State Park Road and continue beyond the entrance station and the campground toward the park lodge. At 0.9 mile, reach a circular driveway and the park lodge. Bear left here on a gravel road to reach the trailhead overlooking Legion Lake. Alternate directions from Starkville: Take Highway 25 south to the signs for Legion State Park. Turn left on Columbus Avenue and follow it 3.5 miles to the state park, which will be on your right. Once inside the park, follow above directions. *DeLorme: Mississippi Atlas & Gazetteer:* Page 38 B2. GPS trailhead coordinates: N33 9' 20.74" / W89 2' 44.35".

The Hike

This hike takes place at one of the four Mississippi state parks developed by the Civilian Conservation Corps. Many other impressive works still remain from the CCC days, including the park lodge, which is in sight of the trailhead. Today, the lodge is used for business meetings, church functions, and family gatherings.

Walk downhill from the parking area into pines. Legion Lake lies before you. Immediately traverse a pair of bridges, which use the original footings from the CCC trail built here many decades distant. The trail you are following has been refurbished since then. Pass the remains of the old CCC-built bathhouse before crossing the dam. The grassy earthen barrier was also constructed by the young men in the 1930s. Atop the dam you can look south into the lake.

The gravel track enters pine, oak, maple, and sweetgum woods. Sourwoods and cedars also find their place. Occasional swing benches are placed along the trail, and make for great relaxing spots. The trail curves away from the water, climbing sharp terrain. After all, this is the part of the state known as the Red Hills. You can see a lakeside wetland below, before dropping precipitously to cross the upper part of this marshy drainage on a footbridge. Turn up the moist hollow, where beech trees thrive, before climbing then curving to a jutting promontory, where you can gain views through the trees here.

Not surprisingly, the trail drops yet again to bridge an abrupt ravine. It looks as if you are leaving the lake—and you are—to explore its headwaters. Cross another footbridge, then go up yet again. Open onto a clearing, where young pines are sprouting up everywhere. And—as you might guess—the trail tumbles, leaving the sunny clearing for thick bottomland hardwoods and a stream spanned by a bridge. This

Even turtles love Legion State Park

watercourse is the main tributary of Legion Lake. Here the trail diverges. A wide track heads straight ahead while the narrow foot trail splits left. Stay left, following the stream you just crossed toward the lake. Work your way down the hollow, filled with Christmas ferns, passing a spur trail to a CCC park cabin. After nearing the lake, the course turns away and climbs steps to reach a cluster of cabins.

The path drops toward Legion Lake. Along the water's edge, fallen timber provides sunning spots for turtles that will dive into the water as you pass. The trailside gazebo provides a shady spot to overlook the lake. Take note of the persimmon trees growing just beyond the gazebo near the shore. They will be laden with fruit in early autumn.

Persimmon trees grow throughout Mississippi, and range in the southeastern United States from east Texas to eastern Pennsylvania and down through Florida. Look for furrowed bark broken in squares. In the fall you will see sweet, orange persimmon fruit among the leaves and overhead, still on the tree even after its leaves have fallen. This fruit recalls the flavor of dates. Hard, unripe fruits are unpalatable. Make sure to get a softer, riper fruit. American Indians made persimmon bread and also stored the dried fruit like prunes. Many old-timers believe persimmons shouldn't be eaten until after the first frost. Possums, raccoons, skunks, deer, and birds also enjoy the fruit, which contains a few seeds.

The narrow path now squeezes between the water and a very steep hillside. Bridge a streambed, taking note of the old foundations built by the CCC. Curve around to the trailhead, completing the loop.

Miles and Directions

0.0 Start at the Legion Lake trailhead near the park lodge. Follow the loop counterclockwise.

0.4 Span a wetland via footbridge after sharp drop.

0.6 Bridge a steep ravine.

0.9 After passing through a clearing with young pines, the Lake Trail dips to bottomland and crosses the bridge spanning the primary feeder stream of Legion Lake. Just beyond the bridge, a wide track keeps going straight, whereas the Lake Trail turns left down the hollow, northbound back toward Legion Lake.

1.1 Climb a hill to reach a cluster of CCC cabins. The Lake Trail crosses the road, angling slightly right, then drops away from the cabin access road, toward Legion Lake.

1.3 Reach the gazebo overlooking Legion Lake. Continue along the shoreline.

1.5 Arrive back at the trailhead, completing the loop.

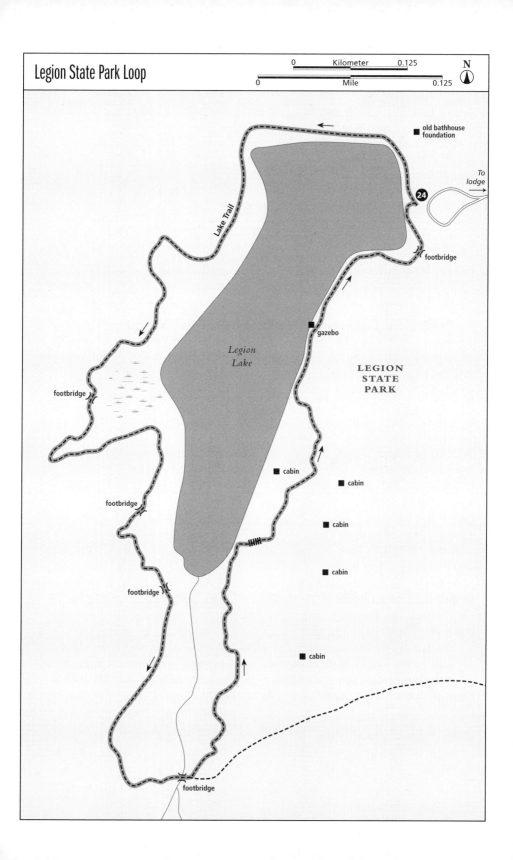

More Information

Local Information
Winston County Economic Development Partnership, P.O. Box 551, 311 W. Park Street, Louisville, MS 39339; (662) 773-8719; www.winstoncounty.com.

Local Events/Attractions
Red Hills Festival, www.winstoncounty.com. This great family event offers an art show, a car show, music, speakers, food, sidewalk sales, and games. It is the primary event in the Noxubee Hills of Winston County and is held each May.

25 Double Loop at Leroy Percy State Park

This trek offers two loop hikes from one trailhead at one state park. First, cruise around the shores of Alligator Lake, a cypress-bordered natural body of water, with boardwalks that get you up close to the scene. Pass the Alligator Pond, where you can see some reptiles. The second loop explores deep bottomland hardwoods along the edge of Black Bayou.

Start: Trailhead between campground and picnic area
Distance: 3.6-mile double loop
Approximate hiking time: 2 to 2.5 hours
Difficulty: Moderately easy, wet spots could slow you down
Trail surface: Leaf-covered bottomland
Seasons: Fall through spring
Other trail users: Hikers only
Canine compatibility: Leashed dogs permitted

Land status: State park
Nearest town: Hollandale
Fees and permits: Park entrance fee required
Schedule: Open year-round
Maps: Leroy Percy State Park nature trails; USGS maps: Swan Lake NW
Trail contacts: Leroy Percy State Park, P.O. Box 176, Hollandale, MS 38748; (662) 827-5436; http://home.mdwfp.com/parks.aspx

Finding the trailhead: From the intersection of U.S. Highway 82 and U.S. Highway 61 on the south side of Leland, head south on US 61 for 17.4 miles, then turn right onto Highway 12 west. Drive for 5.7 miles and turn right into the state park. Next, turn left into the camping entrance, but instead of turning into the campground, stay straight to immediately reach a parking area with picnic tables to your right. The campground will be just to your left. The trail starts to your left as you face the park lake. *DeLorme: Mississippi Atlas & Gazetteer:* Page 34 B3. GPS trailhead coordinates: N33 9' 55.52" / W90 56' 11.74".

The Hike

While walking toward Alligator Lake, note the spring flowing into it. As you stand near the spring, the trail starts to your left. Pass under a wooden archway. Cypress knees rise at your feet while you enter swamplands on a narrow footpath. You began circling the upper end of Alligator Lake in the margin between water-tolerant cypress trees and the bottomland hardwoods. Large oaks rise from drier ground. Vines—including poison ivy—drape over everything. Span a short boardwalk before crossing

Alligator Lake as seen from the trail

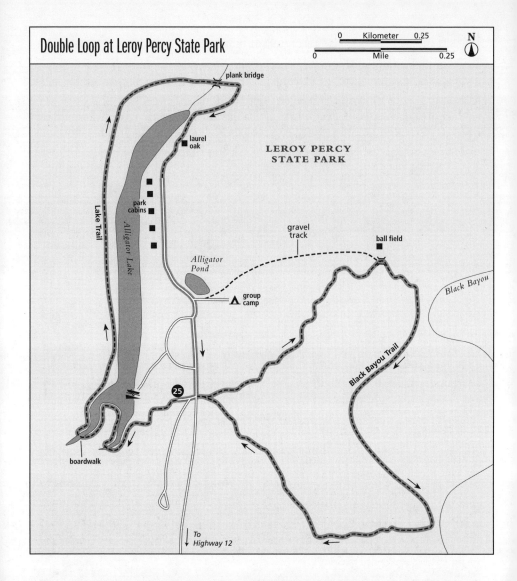

0   Kilometer   0.25

0   Mile   0.25

N

plank bridge

laurel oak

LEROY PERCY STATE PARK

park cabins

Lake Trail

Alligator Lake

gravel track

ball field

Black Bayou

Alligator Pond

group camp

Black Bayou Trail

25

boardwalk

To Highway 12

a longer one over the head of the lake. Duck moss overspreads the lake shallows. You are now on the far side of the lake from the park's developed facilities. The groomed nature of the park facilities contrasts with the more natural aspects of the forest through which you hike. Look for bigger cypress trees in the adjoining sloughs.

The level path widens as it joins an old, slightly raised roadbed rambling underneath tall forest with many hackberry trees. This forest type covered much of the Delta before farmers first grew crops in this area. Imagine the giant old-growth timber that had to be cut down to clear the fields that now are in this fertile land. Curve around the lower end of the natural lake.

Mississippi is the southerly range of the hackberry. They are more common in the Midwest, extending all the way to North Dakota. Easterly they head as far as New England. Its gray smooth bark, covered in corky warts, is its most identifiable feature. The smallish leaves are long and narrow. Hackberry grows in river valleys and moist areas. Its name was purportedly corrupted from the Scottish term "hagberry," referring to cherries grown in Scotland. Hackberry trees have small reddish berries favored by birds that visually resemble a cherry. They are also known as sugarberry trees in these parts.

After crossing a feeder stream, leave right off the raised roadbed, heading south. The drop of just a foot or two puts you in pure bottomland. Note the softer bed of the trail and how much more it is apt to be muddy, despite its once also being a roadbed—you can see vestiges of crumbled pavement here. Look for a massive laurel oak before emerging onto the paved road, passing the park cabins. Join the road then reach Alligator Pond, which has observation overlooks and is a big park attraction with its reptiles.

As you near the trailhead, look left for the Bayou Trail. It starts across the road from the picnic area. This trailhead is also part of the park disc golf course, hole #12. Mississippi state parks have many disc golf courses. The trail then leaves hole #12 on a narrower path straddling an old wire fence line in bottomland woods heavy with hackberry. The forest floor is very irregular here, with humps and low, wetter spots. Notice the saw palmetto lightly scattered in the woods. This is about as far north as this "underground palm" grows. You'll also see Spanish moss here. Continue winding through trees with bark covered in moss. Come along Black Bayou. The silent slough comes back into view just before the trail travels south, leaving the old roadbed. The footing becomes irregular, but is very doable. Check with the park before hiking this trail in spring, as it may be muddy or even inundated. You will soon hear the cars of Highway 12; then turn west. A final ramble leads you back to the trailhead.

Miles and Directions

0.0 Start at the parking area between the campground and the picnic area. To pick up the trail, walk toward Alligator Lake, then veer left when you get to the water.

0.4 After circling around the head of Alligator Lake, traverse a long boardwalk and begin curving north along the west side of Alligator Lake.

0.6 Pass under a transmission line. The park boat ramp is visible across the lake.

1.2 Curve around the upper end of Alligator Lake to cross a tributary on a plank bridge. Soon leave the roadbed you have been following and turn right, southbound.

1.5 Join a paved road and keep south, passing cabins to your right.

1.7 Reach the Alligator Pond on your left. Elevated observation areas allow you to see the reptiles. Just beyond here a gravel track leads left, connecting to the Bayou Trail. Continue walking down the park road.

1.9 The Bayou Trail leaves left away from the picnic area across from the trailhead. Pass under a ranch-style gate entering bottomland hardwoods at the same spot as disc golf hole #12.

2.4 Reach the bridge that crosses over to the old ball field. If you cross the bridge and turn left, you can follow the gravel track back to the Alligator Pond. This loop does not cross the bridge but turns right, southeasterly, toward Black Bayou.

2.5 Make a sharp right turn upon reaching Black Bayou.

3.1 Black Bayou Trail leaves Black Bayou and turns west, roughly paralleling Highway 12, before angling northwest, still in bottomland.

3.6 Arrive back at the trailhead after completing second loop.

More Information

Local Information
Greenville/Washington County Convention and Visitors Bureau, 216 S. Walnut Street; (800) 467-3582; www.thedelta.org.

Local Events/Attractions
Highway 61 Blues Museum, 400 N. Broad Street, P.O. Box 251, Leland, MS 38756, (662) 686-7646, www.highway61blues.com. This museum, located in Leland, chronicles many of the over one hundred famed blues musicians from within 100 miles of here, deep in the Delta.

26 Blue Lake Nature Trail

This is the only hiking trail in Mississippi's Delta National Forest, and it is a good one. Set deep in the swamps of the Yazoo basin in the Blue Lake Recreation Area, the trail cruises the edge of a brooding bayou for much of its length. Interpretive signage placed along the trail helps you learn about the flora and fauna of the region. Combine this hike with camping or boating (all three activities can be done from the trailhead).

Start: Blue Lake Recreation Area
Distance: 1.0-mile loop
Approximate hiking time: 1 to 1.5 hours
Difficulty: Easy
Trail surface: Pea gravel
Seasons: Fall through spring
Other trail users: Hikers only
Canine compatibility: Leashed dogs permitted

Land status: National forest
Nearest town: Rolling Fork
Fees and permits: No fees or permits required
Schedule: Open year-round
Maps: USGS maps: Red Rock
Trail contacts: Delta National Forest, 20380 Highway 61, Rolling Fork, MS 39159; (601) 965-1600; www.fs.fed.us/r8/mississippi/delta

Finding the trailhead: From Yazoo City, take Highway 16 west/Highway 149 north. After 12.3 miles stay left as Highway 16 west turns left. After 28.7 miles from Yazoo City, turn left on Forest Road 703 at the sign stating WORK CENTER, FISH LAKE, LOST LAKE, BLUE LAKE, BARGE LAKE. Take FR 703 for 1.6 miles, then turn right on Forest Road 715. After 1.6 miles reach Blue Lake Road. Turn right and follow it a short distance to the recreation area boat launch. The trail starts here. (Alternate directions from Rolling Fork to FR 703: take Highway 16 for 8 miles to FR 703, on your right.) *DeLorme: Mississippi Atlas & Gazetteer:* Page 34 F4. GPS trailhead coordinates: N32 49' 16.7" / W90 48' 36.9".

This bottomland hardwood is big enough for beast—or man—to enter

The Hike

This trail is located within the Sunflower Wildlife Management Area, part of the Delta National Forest. Note the dispersed campsites along the way in. They are numbered and each one has a picnic table, grill, and lantern post. Leave the boat launch area and head south along Blue Lake. This body of water is part of the greater Howlett Bayou, which connects the Little Sunflower River and the Big Sunflower River. Blue Lake is a beautiful little bayou lined with cypress trees and offers dark water boating and fishing. Sweetgums and ash trees rise tall over the pea gravel track. Hackberry trees, also known as sugarberry in these parts, dot the woods. Massive willow oaks stand overhead as well. Immediately reach a trail junction. Here the path begins its loop, as your return route leaves right toward the picnic area. Interpretive signs identify bald cypress, persimmon, nutall oaks, red maple, and other species. Note the wood duck nesting boxes in Blue Lake to your left. Look for violets at your feet in spring.

Vines climb among the trees, seemingly tying them together. Some of the persimmon trees here reach gargantuan sizes—for persimmons. They may not stand out as they are smaller than your average mature oak. No matter the size, wildlife appreciate the fruit they bear. Persimmons are a favorite for everything from birds to deer to squirrels and even the occasional black bear that rumbles through these woods. By the way, only the female persimmon tree bears fruit. The Louisiana black bear is federally protected in Mississippi as a threatened subspecies. The Magnolia State's bear population is largest here in the Delta.

The level track makes walking easy. Saw palmetto keeps the forest floor green even in winter. Virginia creeper vines climb the trees. Sweetgum balls line the trailbed. You will feel them under your feet. Signs have been placed at the base of some trees to help you identify them. Other interpretive signs get into the complexities of the ecosystem. Of particular interest is the Delta ecosystem sign, which naturally details the importance of wetlands, which filter pollution, among other things.

You may have trouble with mosquitoes in summer—I recommend this hike during the three other seasons. Birds appreciate the waters of Blue Lake, among the other wetlands of the Delta National Forest, as it is in the heart of the Mississippi flyway, connecting Canada to parts south.

Blue Lake Recreation Area has a picnic area, free campground, restroom, and boat launch as well as the Blue Lake Nature Trail. Consider staying overnight on your hiking adventure. The campground is set in a deep, bottomland forest. Two shady sites are directly by the boat ramp under large trees. Other sites are farther off the water and offer more private camping. A wooden fence separates the camping area from the rest of the recreation area.

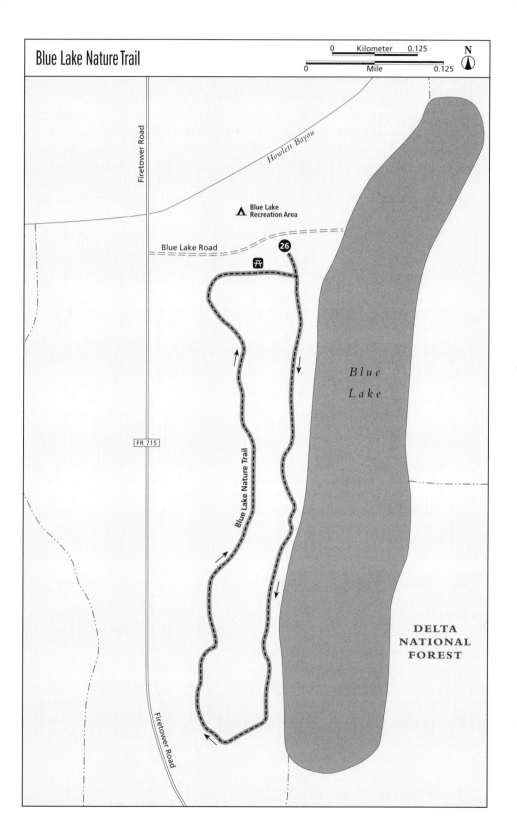

Blue Lake Nature Trail

N

0   Kilometer   0.125
0   Mile   0.125

Firetower Road

Howlett Bayou

▲ Blue Lake
   Recreation Area

Blue Lake Road

🚻   26

Blue Lake Nature Trail

FR 715

Blue Lake

Firetower Road

DELTA
NATIONAL
FOREST

Notice how the land rises from the bayou, creating a separation of water and earth. Duck moss covers portions of the bayou. The trail curves away from Blue Lake and begins its journey north. Another smaller wetland now parallels the trail to the west. More bird nesting boxes of all sorts are found along the water's edge and even in the water rising from posts. At 0.75 mile a boardwalk begins, spanning a wetland. Note the bat house located here. We don't often think of bats as being part of the ecosystem—we are usually hiking trails by day and don't see them or consider their forest function.

A large, partially broken off upright tree to the left of the trail stands near a resting bench. A large cavity lies within it. On a hike here a pair of deer shot out from the cavity, startling me. A person can easily walk inside. Try it. The trail curves right, passing through the picnic area, and completes the loop. If you want to explore more, a closed forest road leads north from the parking area. It is open to foot travel only.

Trailside interpretive information will grab your attention. They help you put together the forest mosaic and understand the web of life in these bottoms. One interesting sign details the edible items in the Delta National Forest, which include not only persimmons but also seeds and insects. Omnipresent oak acorns are very valuable as a good source of fat and protein, especially during the winter season, when other foods are scarce.

Miles and Directions

0.0 Start at Blue Lake Recreation Area near the boat ramp. Follow the loop clockwise.

0.5 Trail turns back north, away from Blue Lake.

0.9 Pass through the recreation picnic area.

1.0 Arrive back at the trailhead, completing the loop.

More Information

Local Information
Yazoo County Economic Development, 212 E. Broadway Street, P.O. Box 172, Yazoo City, MS 39194; (662) 746-1273; www.yazoochamber.org.

Local Events/Attractions
Yazoo County Fair, 332 N. Main Street, Yazoo City, MS 39194, (800) 381-0662, www.yazoo.org. Rides, canning demonstrations, crafts, and catfish cookery attract residents and visitors each fall.

27 Natchez Trace at Choctaw Boundary

This section of the Natchez Trace National Scenic Trail offers a variety of settings as it travels southwesterly along the Natchez Trace Parkway. The path alternates between hilly woods, bottomlands where sluggish streams flow, and open fields that offer extensive vantages of this preserved ribbon of natural Mississippi. The path ends at the historic Choctaw Boundary, where a line of trees marks a nearly 200-year-old delineation of Choctaw lands. A short loop nature trail here adds interpretive information. This is a there and back hike; however, you can use a car shuttle if desired.

Start: Yockanookany Picnic Area
Distance: 3.0 miles one way, total 5.9 miles
Approximate hiking time: 2.5 to 3 hours there and back
Difficulty: Moderate, mostly level
Trail surface: Leaves, pine needles
Seasons: Year-round
Other trail users: Equestrians
Canine compatibility: Leashed dogs permitted

Land status: National park
Nearest town: Ridgeland
Fees and permits: No fees or permits required
Schedule: Open year-round
Maps: Natchez Trace National Scenic Trail; USGS maps: Farmhaven
Trail contacts: Natchez Trace Parkway, 2680 Natchez Trace Parkway, Tupelo, MS 38804; (800) 305-7417; www.nps.gov/natr

Finding the trailhead: From exit 105A on Interstate 55 just north of Jackson, head northbound on the Natchez Trace for 29.5 miles to Yockanookany Picnic Area, located at milepost 130.9 on the Parkway. *DeLorme: Mississippi Atlas & Gazetteer:* Page 36 H5. GPS trailhead coordinates: N32 39' 47.34" / W89 45' 40.86"

The Hike

This section of the Natchez Trace National Scenic Trail is lightly used, and it is the northernmost trailhead for a 26-mile segment of the path that extends toward Jackson. The farther south you go the more it is utilized. It is marked with white paint blazes on trailside trees. The beginning can be confusing as no trail or trail sign is evident from the Yockanookany Picnic Area. Leave the parking area and walk through a field southbound to pass through a pine grove and another small field. The signed trail starts on the far side of this field.

Pines dominate the trailside forest, though laurel oaks come in a close second place. Maple, other oaks, and ever-present sweetgum round out the forest composition. The Natchez Trace Parkway stands off to your left and is visible through the trees. Climb a hill as pines increase in number. Keep southwesterly on the soft trailbed of pine needles. The trail continues rolling to span Dancing Rabbit Creek. The sluggish stream is about 8 feet wide. The trail opens to cross a hay field and continues in bottomlands to bridge a second stream. The trail opens onto the field again. It is hard to figure out the exact path of the trail in these meadows. Stay along the edge of the woods and keep a general southwesterly direction and you won't get lost.

The fields are divided by occasional small woodland areas. The grass can be somewhat thick and slows your trekking, especially if it hasn't been cut in a while. The track remains level in the woods and fields. Since the path travels through open areas, it's a good one for people who are nervous about being in the woods by themselves. These fields are also conducive for a good cold winter day hike, as you will be walking in the sun.

Beyond the grassy areas, the path enters bottomland oak woods. This area could be inundated during spring or other wet times, forcing a detour. You'll be glad to get back into higher drier terrain if the rains have been recent. Rise into pines. A few palmetto bushes and redbud trees also occupy these woods. Keep cruising in rolling piney forest. Watch for a heavily used path running parallel to the trail you are on. This is the nature trail at the Choctaw Boundary road pull-off. Continue following the more lightly used Natchez Trace National Scenic Trail, which spills into a field near the road pull-off parking area for the Choctaw Boundary.

As a final treat, take the nature trail you saw earlier. The lightly graveled singletrack path offers interpretive signage to increase your knowledge about pine trees, which are prevalent along the Natchez Trace. From here, it is 2.9 miles back to Yockanookany Picnic Area. If you are interested in using a car shuttle, the Choctaw Boundary is located at milepost 128.4 on the Natchez Trace Parkway.

The line of trees just south of the informational sign marks the spot where the Choctaw Boundary was made, dividing lands ceded between this spot and the Mississippi River. To the north and east remained Choctaw lands with the Chickasaw Indians occupying what is now north Mississippi. Some Choctaw lands extended into what is now Alabama. Later, the Choctaw were forced to cede the lands carved out with the boundary, as American settlers moved ever westward.

Miles and Directions

0.0 Start at the trail sign south and out of sight of the picnic area. Walk through a grove of pines, then a small field to reach the trailhead. Enter woods and climb a hill.

0.3 Top a wooded hill and descend.

0.5 Cross a farm road that crosses the Trace connecting to private property.

0.8 Bridge Dancing Rabbit Creek on a wooden span.

1.3 Pass through oak copse in between fields.

1.6 Reach and cross Grown Williams Road. Continue southwesterly in fields.

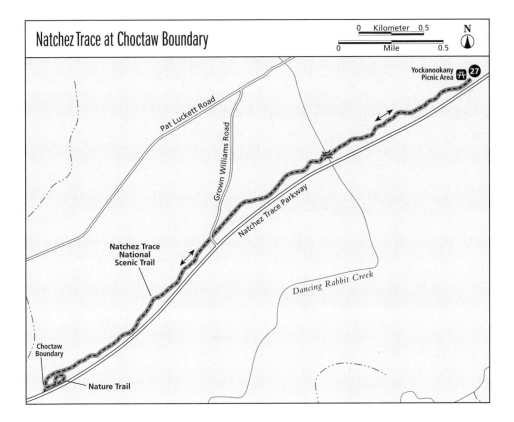

Natchez Trace at Choctaw Boundary

0   Kilometer   0.5
0   Mile   0.5

N

Yockanookany
Picnic Area   27

Pat Luckett Road

Grown Williams Road

Natchez Trace Parkway

Natchez Trace
National
Scenic Trail

Dancing Rabbit Creek

Choctaw
Boundary

Nature Trail

1.8 Reenter woods in potentially muddy bottomland forest.

2.2 Come very near the Trace Parkway.

2.8 Come alongside heavily used nature trail. Stay with the path you are on to open into a field.

2.9 Reach Choctaw Boundary informational area. Begin nature trail loop.

3.0 Return to Choctaw Boundary informational area. Begin backtracking on Trace hiking trail.

5.9 Arrive back at the Yockanookany Picnic Area and the trailhead.

More Information

Local Information

Madison County Chamber of Commerce, 618 Crescent Boulevard, Suite 101, Ridgeland, MS 39157; (601) 605-2554; www.madisoncountychamber.com.

Local Events/Attractions

Mississippi Museum of Natural Science, 2148 Riverside Drive, Jackson, MS 39202, (601) 354-7303, http://museum.mdwfp.com/. See ever-changing exhibits, including a 100,000-gallon aquarium displaying the biological diversity of the Magnolia State. It's very worth your time.

28 Natchez Trace/Cypress Swamp

The Natchez Trace Parkway is the setting for a hike combining a there-and-back trek along the Natchez Trace National Scenic Trail with a short loop on an adjacent nature trail. First, take the Trace as it winds through hilly woods and fields, then retrace your steps to the trailhead. Next, cruise a mellow pea gravel track in an attention-grabbing wetland. A picnic area stands nearby on the Parkway, so consider packing lunch before you hit the trail.

Start: Cypress Swamp trailhead on Natchez Trace Parkway
Distance: 4.4-mile lollipop
Approximate hiking time: 2.5 to 3 hours
Difficulty: Moderate
Trail surface: Leaves, pea gravel
Seasons: Fall through spring
Other trail users: Equestrians on Trace, none on Cypress Swamp Trail
Canine compatibility: Leashed dogs permitted

Land status: National park
Nearest town: Canton
Fees and permits: No fees or permits required
Schedule: Open year-round
Maps: Natchez Trace National Scenic Trail; USGS maps: Sharon SE
Trail contacts: Natchez Trace Parkway, 2680 Natchez Trace Parkway, Tupelo, MS 38804; (800) 305-7417; www.nps.gov/natr

Finding the trailhead: The trail starts at milepost 122 on the Natchez Trace, about 20 miles north of Jackson, at the Cypress Swamp pullover. *DeLorme: Mississippi Atlas & Gazetteer:* Page 42 B4. GPS trailhead coordinates: N32 34' 47.4" / W89 52' 11.88".

The Hike

You can choose to walk the Cypress Swamp Loop first or upon your return. I recommend it after hiking the Trace. The Trace access trail starts directly across the road from the parking area for the Cypress Swamp. Cross the road and walk just a short distance to access the Natchez Trace National Scenic Trail. You can go left or right—go right toward River Bend. Begin trekking northbound through mixed pine-oak woods on a narrow singletrack path marked with white blazes. Note the dogwoods in the forest. The moister hollows will have not only wildflowers in spring but also species such as buckeye, along with ferns and cane. The Natchez Trace Parkway will be on your right as you travel.

Violets, trillium, and mayapple are among the wildflowers you may see. The understory buckeye trees, many looking bush-like, may be blooming as well. Shortly cross the first little drainage at 0.3 mile. These drainages separate the hills over which you roll. Oaks, some draped with vines, climb high from the forest floor. Bisect a small gas line clearing at 0.4 mile.

Ahead, a 20-foot wooden bridge spans an intermittent streambed, very near the parkway. Turn away from the parkway. Another bridge spans a hollow full of beech trees. At 0.8 mile, the River Bend Picnic Area is visible through the woods to your right. It is located on the shores of Ross Barnett Reservoir, which is an impoundment of the Pearl River and provides drinking water for the nearby city of Jackson. A faint trail leads to the picnic area. Just ahead, a defunct water tower rises from a small

Phlox brightens the spring woods along the Natchez Trace

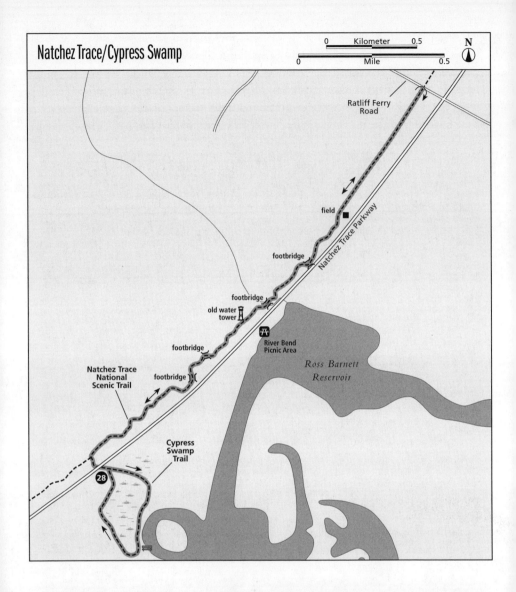

Natchez Trace/Cypress Swamp

0   Kilometer   0.5

0   Mile   0.5

N

Ratliff Ferry Road

field

Natchez Trace Parkway

footbridge

footbridge

old water tower

River Bend Picnic Area

footbridge

Ross Barnett Reservoir

Natchez Trace National Scenic Trail

footbridge

Cypress Swamp Trail

28

clearing. The trail then splits. An old road used to access the tower leaves right to the picnic area. Stay left here, still on singletrack path.

Come along a perennial stream cutting deeply into the land to your left. The Trace is visible to the right. This rich wildflower area has phlox and mayapple aplenty. At 1.0 mile, a bridge spans the gullied stream. Come near the Trace again at 1.2 miles, bridging a smaller stream. At 1.4 miles, open to a field bordered by cedar. Keep forward, running parallel to a power line. The open, green meadow will be lush in the warm season and provide contrast to the thick woods through which you have been hiking. Bisect a line of woods before opening into a second field. Reach Ratliff Ferry Road at 2.0 miles. This is a good place to turn around and backtrack. If you are feeling feisty, the Natchez Trace National Scenic Trail continues 5 miles farther to Choctaw Boundary.

The Cypress Swamp Trail leaves the parking area down steep steps to a boardwalk over a slough, an oxbow created by the Pearl River, which has changed course since it ran below the bluff where the Trace stands. Note the widely buttressed stumps of the cypress and tupelo trees rising from the black water. Turn south along the slough on a level path lined with pea gravel. This is alligator country—you may see one peering from the depths or sunning itself. A bench overlooks the now-dammed Pearl River at the far end of the nature trail. Bridge a small slough on your return, watching for beaver dams, as they have been here in the past. Rejoin the river bluff and return to the trailhead after completing the 0.4-mile loop, making for a total hike of 4.4 miles.

Miles and Directions

0.0 Start at Cypress Swamp pullover on the Natchez Trace. Cross the road and join the Natchez Trace National Scenic Trail.

0.3 Span the first footbridge.

0.4 Bisect a gas line clearing.

0.8 Pass the River Bend Picnic Area to the right.

1.0 Bridge a deep gullied stream.

1.4 Enter an open field, traveling parallel to a power line.

2.0 Reach Ratliff Ferry Road. Backtrack.

4.0 Return to the trailhead and begin Cypress Swamp Nature Trail.

4.4 Complete loop on Cypress Swamp Nature Trail, returning to the trailhead.

More Information

Local Information

Madison County Chamber of Commerce, 618 Crescent Boulevard, Suite 101, Ridgeland, MS 39157; (601) 605-2554; www.madisoncountychamber.com.

Local Events/Attractions

Mississippi Museum of Natural Science, 2148 Riverside Drive, Jackson, MS 39202; (601) 354-7303; http://museum.mdwfp.com/. See ever-changing exhibits, including a 100,000-gallon aquarium displaying the biological diversity of the Magnolia State. It's very worth your time.

29 Shockaloe Trail

This trail makes the longest single loop in the state—nearly 23 miles of trekking pleasure. The mostly level path winds through remote woodlands of east-central Mississippi. Be apprised this trail is shared with horses, which turns some hikers off. However, the Bienville National Forest keeps it in good shape, making it doable for hikers as well. Backpackers enjoy the loop, and day hikers can make a long day trip or divide the hike into segments, as the Shockaloe occasionally crosses roads. Two campgrounds—one at the trailhead—can serve as hiker base camps.

Start: Shockaloe Base Camp 1
Distance: 22.5-mile loop
Approximate hiking time: 9 to 12 hours
Difficulty: Difficult due to length
Trail surface: Pine needles, leaves, dirt
Seasons: Fall through spring
Other trail users: Equestrians
Canine compatibility: Leashed dogs permitted
Land status: National forest

Nearest town: Forest
Fees and permits: No fees or permits required
Schedule: Open year-round
Maps: USFS Shockaloe Trail; USGS maps: Pulaski, Hillsboro
Trail contacts: Bienville National Forest, 3473 Highway 35 South, Forest, MS 39074; (601) 469-3811; www.fs.fed.us/r8/mississippi/bienville

Finding the trailhead: From exit 88 on Interstate 20, Raleigh/Forest/Highway 35, take Highway 35 north for 1.8 miles to the town of Forest, then turn left on U.S. Highway 80 west. Travel for 5.3 miles on US 80 to turn right on Forest Road 513. Head north on FR 513, immediately crossing railroad tracks. Travel for 0.2 mile, then turn right into Shockaloe Base Camp 1 (if the trailhead road is closed, as it is in winter, park outside). Keep going to reach a fenced area with a picnic shelter and restroom. The loop trail starts here. *DeLorme: Mississippi Atlas & Gazetteer:* Page 43 E7. GPS trailhead coordinates: N32 21' 56.58" / W89 33' 43.98".

The Hike

▶ **This loop makes for a first-rate backpacking destination. To ensure water you can either cache some near a forest road crossing, or you can camp near Shockaloe Creek, which is the only guaranteed source of water in fall and other dry times.**

The singletrack trail overlays a 6-foot-wide bed with drainages on either side, which keep the path in great shape. I recommend doing this loop in a clockwise direction as most equestrians go counterclockwise. This way you will see horses coming at you rather than behind you. The trail explores mostly level terrain beneath tall pines and shorter hickories. Periodic prescribed burnings keep the understory low and brushy. However, after crossing forest roads you may notice the understory being a different height and age. The Forest Service often uses roads as a barrier when using prescribed fire. You may also see occasional milepost signs.

Pine-oak-hickory woods dominate the woodland. The pines are widespread in most places. However, when the canopy thickens—especially in an oak wood—the Shockaloe Trail travels under vegetation tunnels. Occasional culverts bisect the path, helping to drain these mostly level woods. Some of the bigger culverted streams will

Fall flowers flank the Shockaloe Trail

flow well into summer and after thunderstorms. In fall, these will mostly be dry. Low areas near the culverts may be muddy after rains. But it is along the streams where the most flora species diversity occurs, whereas pine is king elsewhere. These bottomland hardwood areas will have colorful leaf displays in late October/early November.

Occasional woodland ponds provide drinking opportunities for wildlife. This is one element of the enhancements done here in the Bienville Wildlife Management Area. The path will bisect sporadic unnumbered forest roads closed to the public that are used to maintain the wildlife areas.

Lush woods thrive beyond Base Camp 2, rising to an impressive area of mature pines, then dipping to hardwoods, aiming for Shockaloe Creek. You will see beech and laurel oaks in these parts. The path circles around private property and makes its final northbound push, sometimes through sparse woodland. The trailbed will be grassy where the canopy is limited. Varied forests include high pines, smaller younger pines, and areas of maples and sweetgum where the trail is close to the water table.

▶ **The white-banded trees you see along the trail are red cockaded woodpecker habitats, trees where they have nested. This endangered species only nests in old-growth longleaf pines, at least one hundred years old. The banded trees will have sap dripping from the nest hole areas; the woodpeckers do this to protect the entrance to their nests from predators such as rat snakes.**

The path turns south in bottomland after crossing Shockaloe Creek. The adjacent bottoms may be quite wet—and scenic—in spring. Beyond the second crossing of County Road 538, pines once again dominate, including a stand of impressive mature pines at a forest road crossing at 18.1 miles. Head into the Tallabogue Creek watershed before curving southwest for Base Camp 1. The end is near when you can see the tracks of the Kansas City Southern Railroad off to your left. Make a final push through young dense woods, completing the loop at 22.5 miles.

Miles and Directions

0.0 Start the hike as you face the picnic shelter area. Pick up the trail that passes to the left of the picnic shelter and astride Base Camp 1 campground, skirting a couple of campsites.

0.7 Reach and cross gravel Clifton Road, FR 513.

1.4 Shockaloe Trail angles left, slightly northwest, and begins a long and obvious straightaway, altering its winding course.

2.5 Cross paved Hillsboro Road, CR 538. Reenter pine-oak-hickory wood in a northerly direction.

3.5 Pass a grassy meadow on your left. This is a wildlife clearing, providing more food opportunities for deer and turkey.

4.0 Pass small wildlife pond on trail left.

4.6 Cross gravel Forest Road 536. Leave young woods, still heading northbound.

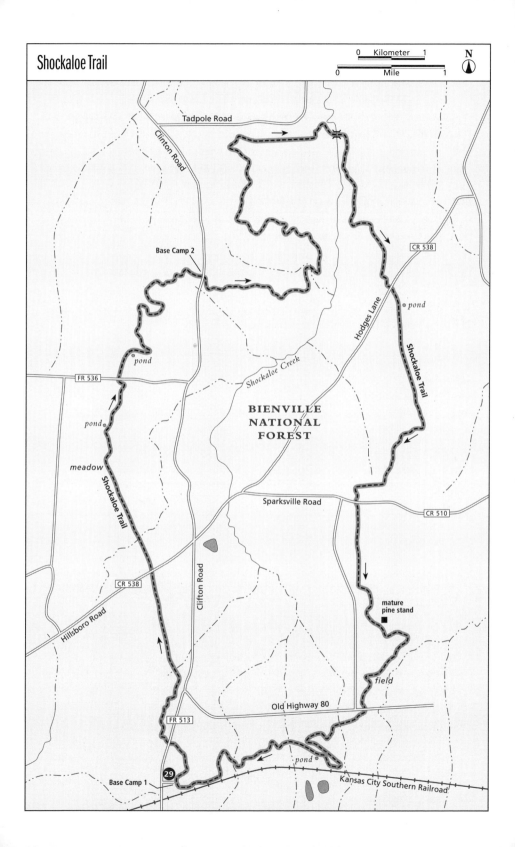

Shockaloe Trail

0 Kilometer 1
0 Mile 1

N

Tadpole Road

Clinton Road

Base Camp 2

CR 538

pond

Hodges Lane

pond

Shockaloe Creek

FR 536

Shockaloe Trail

pond

BIENVILLE
NATIONAL
FOREST

meadow

Sparksville Road

CR 510

Shockaloe Trail

CR 538

Clifton Road

Hillsboro Road

mature
pine stand

field

Old Highway 80

FR 513

29

Base Camp 1

pond

Kansas City Southern Railroad

4.9 Pass a pond on trail right. In the next 0.7 mile the trail winds around quite a bit in a real mix of forest types and areas, from open sunny spots to thick hardwoods to high pines.

6.8 Reach Base Camp 2, an alternate trailhead. It offers a shaded picnic and camping area, water, and restrooms. Immediately cross paved FR 513 and head east.

8.4 Come within a quarter-mile of Shockaloe Creek before turning north and west, curving along open private property.

11.0 The trail begins a long due east direction, again aiming for Shockaloe Creek.

12.2 Come alongside Shockaloe Creek. Note the abundance of beech and musclewood trees. Potential backpack camping area. Cross the stream on a low-water bridge.

14.0 Cross gravel CR 538. Keep south in pines.

16.8 Cross paved Sparksville Road, County Road 510.

18.1 Cross gravel forest road in mature pine stand.

18.8 Pass a field divided from the trail by a thin screen of young pines.

19.1 Cross old US 80, barely discernable as a former major road. Shockaloe Trail aims southwest for Base Camp 1.

20.9 Pass a small pond on your left.

22.5 Arrive back at Base Camp 1, completing the loop.

More Information

Local Information
Forest Area Chamber of Commerce, P.O. Box 266, Forest, MS 39074; (601) 469-4332; www.forestmschamber.com.

Local Events/Attractions
Wing Dang Doodle Festival, www.forestmschamber.com. This cooking and eating event is all about chicken wings. It includes cooking contests and is held at Gaddis Park in September.

30 Bonita Lakes

If only other cities had parks as fine as this one! The Bonita Lakes Park is a 3,300-acre ensemble of water and land recreation, with trails for bikers, hikers, and equestrians. It also offers picnic pavilions and picnic areas in a generally gorgeous swath on the south side of Meridian. The park and trail avail a quick entry into nature for nearby residents as well as those from afar.

Start: Trailhead near boat ramp
Distance: 4.7-mile loop
Approximate hiking time: 2.5 to 3 hours
Difficulty: Moderately difficult due to many hills
Trail surface: Pea gravel
Seasons: Year-round
Other trail users: Hikers only
Canine compatibility: Leashed dogs permitted
Land status: City park

Nearest town: Meridian
Fees and permits: No fees or permits required
Schedule: Open year-round
Maps: Bonita Lakes Trails; USGS maps: Meridian South
Trail contacts: City of Meridian, 2412 7th Street, Box 1430, Meridian, MS 39302; (601) 485-1920; www.meridianms.org

Finding the trailhead: From exit 154A on Interstate 20 on the south side of Meridian, take Highway 19 south for 0.4 mile, then turn right into Bonita Lakes Park. Enter the park and immediately turn left and continue 0.5 mile to the upper lake and a T intersection. Turn right, cross the dam of the upper lake, then veer left to park. The paved boat ramp parking area is on your left and on your right is the gravel equestrian parking area. On nice weekends try to park in the gravel area as cars with boat trailers will be parked in the paved boat ramp area. *DeLorme: Mississippi Atlas & Gazetteer:* Page 45 E6. GPS trailhead coordinates: N32 21' 20.5" / W88 39' 43.9".

The Hike

This description follows the Bonita Lakes Recreation Trail, a wide pea gravel track that meanders through the heart of the park and circles the main lake, as well as the smaller impoundments that are part of the overall water scheme here. But it's not all water—you will be surprised at the steepness of the terrain and hills. There's even a vista at one high point!

Maps and brochures are posted at the trailhead. Scattered trailside benches allow for contemplation or relaxation opportunities. Leave the boat ramp area and the upper lake, passing around a wooden gate. Fitness equipment has been installed at various places along the trail. You will immediately pass the first blue-blazed single-track bike path. It offers a natural-surfaced narrow trail.

The trail immediately climbs away from the lake in pines. The hills here will surprise—they are quite sharp in places. From these high points you can look deeply into the hollows. You will be especially pleased with the westerly vista that can be had

▶ Bonita Lakes Park has over 20 miles of horse trails and more miles of bicycle trails. The hiking, biking, and equestrian trails are interconnected with multiple loops and junctions that make the possibilities nearly limitless. After you experience the seemingly innumerable trail junctions, you may want to consider staying with the Bonita Lakes Recreation Trail on your first go-round and then developing some loops of your own.

from a big hill near a picnic table at 0.8 mile. Who knew such views could be had in east-central Mississippi?

It isn't long before the path makes a dive for the lake on a northbound ridge. When you reach the water, a picnic table awaits. A small island is just offshore. Cruise along the lake on a level track. A sharp left turn precedes your first dam crossing. You can see the small lake above you and the main lake below. The upper lakes will sometimes be muddier than the main lake, especially after rains.

Tall ridges divide the embayments of Bonita Lake. The beautiful woods may distract you from all the huffing and puffing you are doing to surmount these ridges. It isn't long before you drop down to the second dam and just as quickly climb again. The third embayment comes after another downgrade. A pea gravel track leads left beyond this third embayment but you stay straight, climbing through woods to join a park road. Here, you will trace the paved road back down to the dam holding back the main lake. A short walk beyond the dam leads you back to the trailhead.

Waterfowl gather on Bonita Lake

Bonita Lakes

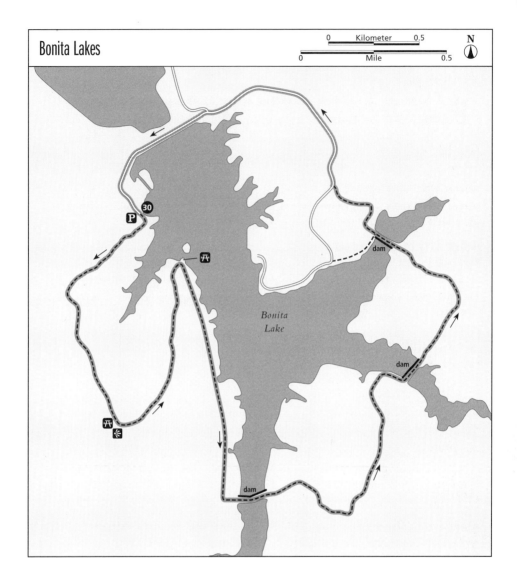

Miles and Directions

0.0 Start near the boat ramp parking area. Pass around a gate and join a wide pea gravel track heading uphill, with the lake to your left.

0.8 Reach a picnic table and westerly vista after climbing a big hill.

1.3 Reach the lake and a picnic table near a small island. The trail now turns right and keeps generally along the lakeshore.

2.1 Cross the first dam after a sharp left turn. The trail then ascends a high ridge between another arm of Bonita Lake.

2.9 Cross the second dam. Ascend again, entering dense pines.

3.5 Cross the third dam. Just beyond the third dam a spur trail leads left along the shore to reach a park road. This loop continues forward and climbs.

3.7 Reach a park road and join it, heading right. The road eventually curves back to the left and downhill.

4.3 Begin crossing the dam holding back the main lake. Stay with the road.

4.7 Arrive back at the trailhead.

More Information

Local Information

Meridian/Lauderdale County Tourism Bureau, P.O. Box 5313, Meridian, MS 39302; (888) 868-7720; www.visitmeridian.com.

Local Events/Attractions

Highland Park/Dentzel Carousel/Jimmie Rogers Museum, www.meridianms.org. The latter two are located at Highland Park. The carousel, in operation since 1909, is a National Historic Landmark. The Jimmie Rogers Museum chronicles the life of the country singer.

31 Lefleur's Bluff State Park

A green oasis on the banks of the Pearl River in Jackson, this state park offers a rewarding walk on a series of nature trails, leading from one end of the park to the fine facility that is the Mississippi Museum of Natural Science, where you can combine your trek with some indoor learning at one of the Magnolia State's educational jewels.

Start: Lakeland Terrace entrance of Lefleur's Bluff State Park

Distance: 3.1-mile lollipop

Approximate hiking time: 1.5 to 2 hours

Difficulty: Moderate

Trail surface: Gravel, leaves, dirt, roots, asphalt, pea gravel

Seasons: Year-round

Other trail users: Hikers only

Canine compatibility: Leashed dogs permitted

Land status: State park

Nearest town: Jackson

Fees and permits: Park entry fee required

Schedule: Open year-round

Maps: Lefleur's Bluff State Park trail map; USGS maps: Jackson

Trail contacts: Lefleur's Bluff State Park, 2140 Riverside Drive, Jackson, MS 39202; (601) 987-3923; http://home.mdwfp.com/parks .aspx

Finding the trailhead: From exit 98B on Interstate 55, take Highway 25, Lakeland Drive, east. You'll be tempted to turn right on Highland Drive, but don't. Instead continue 0.7 mile on Lakeland Drive to Lakeland Terrace, turning right at the Shell station. Once on Lakeland Terrace, you'll soon reach the park gatehouse. Pass the gatehouse, then veer left to soon reach the day use parking area on the right, below the camp store, which is on pilings. The trail starts to the right of the camp store as you face it. *DeLorme: Mississippi Atlas & Gazetteer:* Page 42 E1. GPS trailhead coordinates: N32 19' 47.5" / W90 8' 50.6".

The Hike

The trail system meanders along the greater Pearl River floodplain and bluffs above it, connecting state park sections to the Mississippi Museum of Natural Science. This museum, the crown jewel of natural history in the Magnolia State, offers ever-changing exhibits, life-size habitats displaying Mississippi's biodiversity, a huge aquarium, and an open building encouraging the meshing of the outdoors and indoors, along with open-air and indoor auditoriums. You can access the museum by auto as well, following the above directions but turning onto Highland Drive from Highway 25 instead of Lakeland Terrace.

Leave the day use parking area on the gravel path signed NATURE TRAIL, passing picnic pavilions along the way. Immediately reach Mayes Lake. The state park campground stands across the water. Bear right and begin walking the lakeshore on an ever-narrowing peninsula, with an unnamed body of water to your right. Docks extend into the water, availing water access to the old oxbows where the Pearl River once flowed.

View of Pearl River from trailside overlook

Sizable oaks grow between these bodies of water. Cane crowds the trailway. Reach a trail junction. If you continued straight, you would follow a trail that curves to pass a boat ramp and then reaches the campground access road. This hike, however, turns right, following a purple-blazed path, traveling cypress swamps and wetlands, using a boardwalk at one point. The landscape seems more water than land in places. Spur trails lead to these water features, including the Pearl River at times. You're walking atop a 15-foot bluff above the Pearl. Take one of these unmarked and short spur trails to see Mississippi's watery heart pulsing down the center of the state. A sandbar stands across the river inside a bend. Meander through the bottoms where sweetgums and oaks rise high overhead and brush crowds the track.

Span a boardwalk at 0.75 mile. The sloughs, swamps, and lakes are all interconnected, especially when the water rises. Ahead, a spur trail leads left through bottomland to the Pearl River. Blue-eyed grass blooms here in profusion in spring, mixing with flood litter to create an odd mosaic of splendor and unsightliness. Emerge on the river's edge just upstream of a low head dam. A bridge is visible downstream.

The main route leads to a long concrete bridge spanning Eubanks Creek. Wind through rich woods in an area known as the Swamp Terrace, as it is surrounded by water. Cross a slough then reach Lefleur's Bluff. While climbing the bluff, turn right on the Blue Trail. A rare sound for central Mississippi—a waterfall—reaches your ears. However, before you get overly excited, realize the sounds are from two pipes emitting water down the bluff. There may have been a true waterfall here in the past. Cruise the margin between the steep bluff and a swamp below. Pass an observation deck leading swampside. The bluff becomes so sheer as to force the building of a hiker walkway. Note the beech tree integrated into the walkway, among many bluffside beech trees. Curve onto a backbone ridge, now aiming for the Mississippi Museum of Natural Science. The manicured state of the golf course contrasts with the natural characteristics of the preserved bluff. Reach a trail junction—the Yellow Trail leaves left and right. Stay right and pass by the Mississippi Museum of Natural Science. Join a boardwalk and walk until you approach a water fountain, an outdoor amphitheater, and an overlook with wintertime views into the dropoffs below. Pass the amphitheater, joining the Green Trail and enjoying the bluff edge. Descend an expensive boardwalk—it protects the unique character of the bluff. Complete the loop portion of the hike, then backtrack to the Lakeland Terrace Day Use Area.

Miles and Directions

0.0 Start at the camp store at Lefleur's Bluff State Park, Lakeland Terrace Day Use Area. Follow gravel path marked NATURE TRAIL.

0.9 Span Eubanks Creek on a concrete bridge. (FYI: Trillium bloom here by the hundreds in late March and early April.)

1.2 Begin loop portion of hike on bluff rising to Mississippi Museum of Natural Science.

1.9 Complete loop portion of hike. Leave the bluff and begin backtracking toward trailhead.

3.1 Return to trailhead at camp store.

Lefleur's Bluff State Park

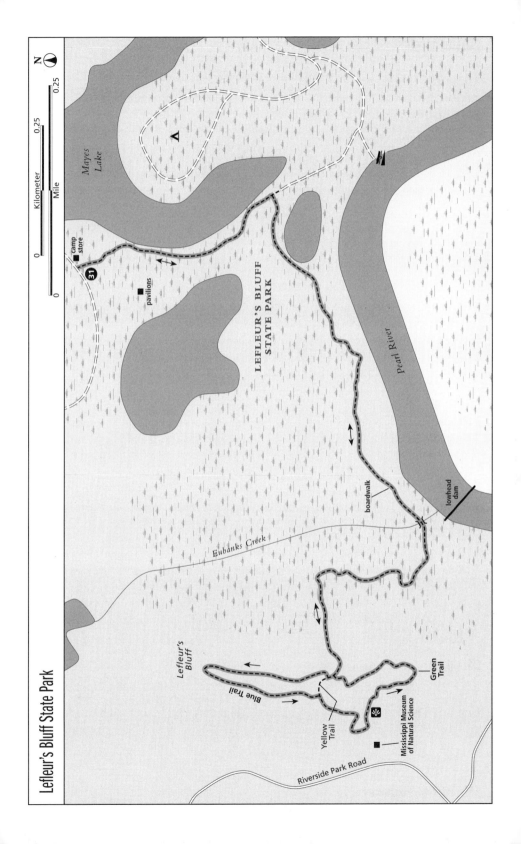

N

Kilometer
0   0.25

Mile
0   0.25

camp store

31

pavilions

Mayes Lake

△

LEFLEUR'S BLUFF
STATE PARK

Eubanks Creek

boardwalk

Pearl River

lowhead dam

Lefleur's Bluff

Blue Trail

Yellow Trail

Green Trail

Mississippi Museum of Natural Science

Riverside Park Road

More Information

Local Information
Jackson Convention and Visitors Bureau, 111 E. Capitol Street, Suite 102, Jackson, MS 39201; (800) 354-7695; www.visitjackson.com.

Local Events/Attractions
Mississippi Museum of Natural Science, 2148 Riverside Drive, Jackson, MS 39202; (601) 354-7303; http://museum.mdwfp.com/. See ever-changing exhibits, including a 100,000-gallon aquarium displaying the biological diversity of the Magnolia State. This hike travels by the museum.

32 Roosevelt State Park

Roosevelt State Park offers numerous recreation opportunities, one of which is hiking. The trail system here rolls through the hills and hollows and mixes in a little human and natural history. This particular hike takes you from the park entrance into hill country, where you can see some old Civil War earthworks as well as a petrified wood outcrop. Consider combining your hike with camping, fishing, boating, or swimming.

Start: Park entrance station
Distance: 3.0-mile lollipop
Approximate hiking time: 2 hours
Difficulty: Moderate with hills
Trail surface: Pine needles, leaves
Seasons: Year-round
Other trail users: Hikers only
Canine compatibility: Leashed dogs permitted
Land status: State park

Nearest town: Morton
Fees and permits: Park entry fee required
Schedule: Open year-round
Maps: Roosevelt State Park trails; USGS maps: Morton
Trail contacts: Roosevelt State Park, 2149 Highway 13 South, Morton, MS 39117; (601) 732-6316; http://home.mdwfp.com/parks .aspx

Finding the trailhead: From exit 77 on Interstate 20, take Highway 13 north for 0.6 mile to the state park entrance, on your left. Continue into the park to reach the entrance station. Upon leaving the entrance station, make a U-turn as if you were leaving the park and park near the entrance station. *DeLorme: Mississippi Atlas & Gazetteer:* Page 33 E8. GPS trailhead coordinates: N33 30' 52.49" / W88 29' 46.53".

The Hike

This is one of the original Mississippi state parks, first developed by the Civilian Conservation Corps. It has been updated through the years, however. The road splits just beyond the park entrance station. Here, the Lakeview Trail heads left and the Muscadine Trail heads right. Take the Muscadine Trail, walking under a cedar archway to immediately enter the hilly woods with pines, dogwood, oak, hickory, cherry, and sweetgum all draped in a healthy dose of muscadine vines. Look also for beech and maple trees.

Muscadines are a grape native to the southeastern states, extending from Delaware to the Gulf of Mexico and westward to Oklahoma. The wild vines grow generally from 60 to 100 feet in length. They typically need a lot of sun and thus grow atop trees, seeking the light. This was the first grape to be cultivated by American colonists. Purportedly very good for you, muscadines are making a comeback as a gourmet food.

Come very near a gas line clearing while still winding along the hillside. The trail levels out and tree-covered hills drop off around you. The path then drifts toward the old campground, coming directly behind site #33. If campers are grilling hot dogs, see if you can bum one. The path brightens while passing through a power line clearing to reach the Rolling Hills Trail and the loop part of the hike. Just a little farther is a junction with Civil War Trail, which will be your return route. True to its name the Rolling Hills Trail immediately rolls downhill to cross an intermittent streambed. Note the ferns and bay trees in this moist hollow. Alternate between drier hills and moist hollows, almost always in thick woods.

▶ Roosevelt State Park has numerous springs that have a combined capacity of around 3,000 gallons of water per day. These streams feed the 160-acre park impoundment, known as Shadow Lake, which is divided from another smaller impoundment called Upper Shadow Lake.

The sound of I-20 hums in the distance, quite a contrast from the days when the park was founded and interstates were nonexistent. Just as the heart of Mississippi has undergone a metamorphosis, so has Roosevelt State Park. The facilities have changed dramatically over the years, though the original CCC infrastructure areas still remain. Continue in hilly terrain, dropping to a streambed at 0.9 mile. The hollows will most often be dry, so you have few wet-footed worries for your hike. Keep your eyes peeled here as the trail is much more indistinct than it was. You never know where this trail's going to go. It's hard to predict.

Top a hill and reach dug-out earthworks from Civil War doings. The trail descends past more entrenchments. Imagine Civil War soldiers slaking their thirst from the area springs while waiting for battle.

Drop a bit to find a sign indicating a rock outcropping as petrified wood. The wood grains are easily visible in the stone. The trail then travels on and off old roadbeds, but paint blazes and signs will keep you on the right path. Descend into a deeply desiccated drainage to reach a swampy wetland. Continue down along the drainage,

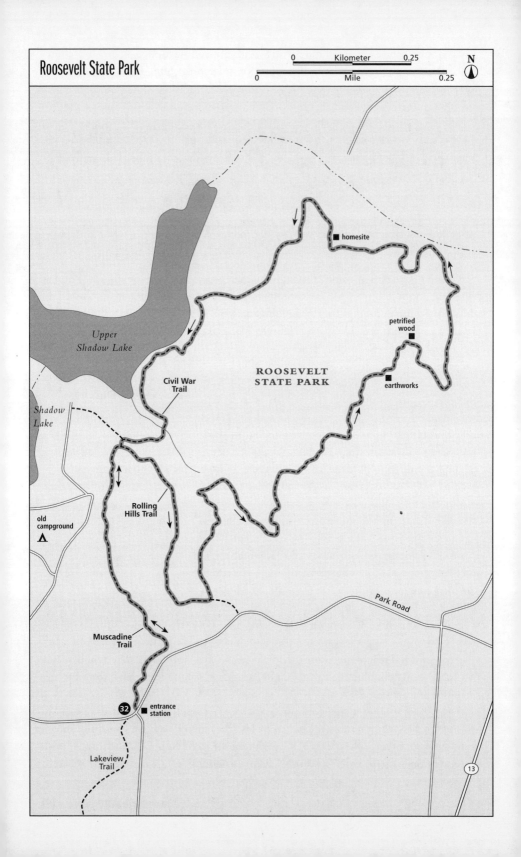

Roosevelt State Park

0 Kilometer 0.25

0 Mile 0.25

N

Upper
Shadow Lake

■ homesite

petrified
wood ■

ROOSEVELT
STATE PARK

Civil War
Trail

■ earthworks

Shadow
Lake

old
campground
⛺

Rolling
Hills Trail

Park Road

Muscadine
Trail

32

■ entrance
station

Lakeview
Trail

13

spanning small streamlets on sturdy board bridges. Note the preponderance of straight-trunked tulip trees in this moist area.

Upper Shadow Lake is more swamp than lake, with tupelo trees rising from its waters. Travel through moist bottomlands, eventually heading up one of the spring branches that feed the lakes. This gorgeous flat is full of bay trees, laurel oaks, and tulip trees. Shortly complete the Civil War Trail, then backtrack to the trailhead.

Miles and Directions

0.0 Start on the Muscadine Trail, very near the park entrance station.

0.3 Come beside the old campground. Trail then crosses clearing under transmission line.

0.4 Reach junction with the Rolling Hills Trail. Turn right here.

0.8 The Rolling Hills Trail dips to a junction. This loop turns left, joining the Civil War Trail, while the remainder of the Rolling Hills Trail climbs to the park entrance road.

1.4 Reach trail's high point after a steep climb. Look around for Civil War entrenchments. Descend from hill.

1.5 Pass sign indicating rock as petrified wood. Look for the fine grains that make it easy to see it once was wood.

1.6 Come very near the park boundary, which is marked with white paint bands around trees.

1.7 Pass small swamp in hollow after a descent.

2.0 The Civil War Trail reaches an old homesite. Note the stones and large cedar trees.

2.3 Reach the shores of Upper Shadow Lake.

2.6 Complete the Civil War Trail to meet the Muscadine Trail. Turn left here and backtrack.

3.0 Emerge near the entrance station to complete hike.

More Information

Local Information
City of Morton, Mississippi, 97 W. First Avenue, P.O. Box 555, Morton, MS 39117-0555; (601) 732-6252.

Local Events/Attractions
Wing Dang Doodle Festival, Forest Area Chamber of Commerce, P.O. Box 266, Forest, MS 39074; (601) 469-4332; www.forestmschamber.com. This cooking and eating event is all about chicken wings. It includes cooking contests and is held at Gaddis Park in September.

33 Dunn's Falls

The natural setting, where the Chunky River makes a big bend while flowing over noisy, rocky shoals, where Dunn's Falls splashes even louder over a rock face, and where steep wooded bluffs drop down to the water's edge, makes for a good destination to not only glimpse Mississippi history but also hike a pair of short loops in this beautiful part of Lauderdale County.

Start: Trailhead near Dunn's Falls
Distance: 1.3-mile double loop
Approximate hiking time: 1 to 1.5 hours
Difficulty: Easy due to short length
Trail surface: Natural surface, some steps
Seasons: Year-round
Other trail users: Hikers only
Canine compatibility: Leashed dogs permitted
Land status: State water park

Nearest town: Meridian
Fees and permits: Entry fee required
Schedule: Open year-round Wednesday through Sunday from 9:00 a.m. to 5:00 p.m.
Maps: USGS maps: Stonewall
Trail contacts: Dunn's Falls Water Park, 6890 Dunn's Falls Road, Enterprise, MS 39330; (601) 655-8550

Finding the trailhead: From exit 142 on Interstate 59 south of Meridian, turn right onto Burrage Road and travel just a short distance. Next, turn left on Meehan-Savoy Road East and follow it for 0.3 mile, then turn left on Dunn's Falls Road. Follow Dunn's Falls Road for 3.3 miles to reach the falls parking area on your right. *DeLorme: Mississippi Atlas & Gazetteer:* Page 44 F4. GPS trailhead coordinates: N32 13' 41.21" / W88 49' 16.44".

The Hike

Dunn's Falls Water Park is a must for Mississippi trail trekkers. The centerpiece is a 65-foot waterfall created by an Irishman named John Dunn. He diverted a stream, changing its course to fall over a bluff into the Chunky River. Astride the bluff he built a mill and a three-story wooden building. Right about that time the Civil War broke out and the Confederacy confiscated his mill and used its water power to make clothing and other supplies for the Rebel soldiers. After the war was over, Dunn resumed his operation, grinding flour and cornmeal among other things. Later, ol' Dunn disappeared and so did the mill. Eventually, another mill was brought to the spot and the area was restored to what you see today.

After paying your entry fee, you might as well go straight to the falls and take a peek. It's quite a drop to the Chunky River below. Now begin the south loop, the first of two loops here, following Old Dunn's Falls Road. The grassy track heads uphill just a short distance before surmounting a berm to enter a beautiful wooded bluff stretching steeply down to the Chunky River. The trail is but a narrow thread winding between smooth bark beech trees and mountain laurel, which enjoys this cool, northeast-facing hillside. The watercourse below chatters over rocky shoals. Pay close attention to the painted blazes as the trail is narrow and somewhat faint. Shortly reach a junction with the loop going back right, upstream toward the falls. Another path angles down for the river then peters out. The trail system here could use some work, but it is what it is. You can walk down to the river and then backtrack back up to the junction. At one time I suspect a hiking trail went along the river, but seems to have been abandoned.

Either way, return to the falls and explore the area. Hear the cranky old water-wheel. Enter the Richardson/Carroll Mill. It was moved here from Georgia. Check out the machinery inside the wooden millhouse. Grab a view of the Chunky River from the windows. The Chunky is a fine canoeing waterway.

Long steps lead down to the base of the falls. The churning water has washed the bluff bare. Now join the hiking loop heading upstream along the Chunky River in thick woods ranging from tupelo and sycamore beside the stream to pines, oaks, cedar, and, as usual, sweetgum, which should be the state tree of Mississippi in my opinion, since it is so widespread.

(The state tree is actually the magnolia. Before 1938 when the legislature officially designated the magnolia, Mississippi had no state tree. Prior to this, the director of forestry persuaded the schoolchildren of Mississippi to vote for a state tree, and the magnolia was the overwhelming winner.)

Dunn's Falls flows into the Chunky River

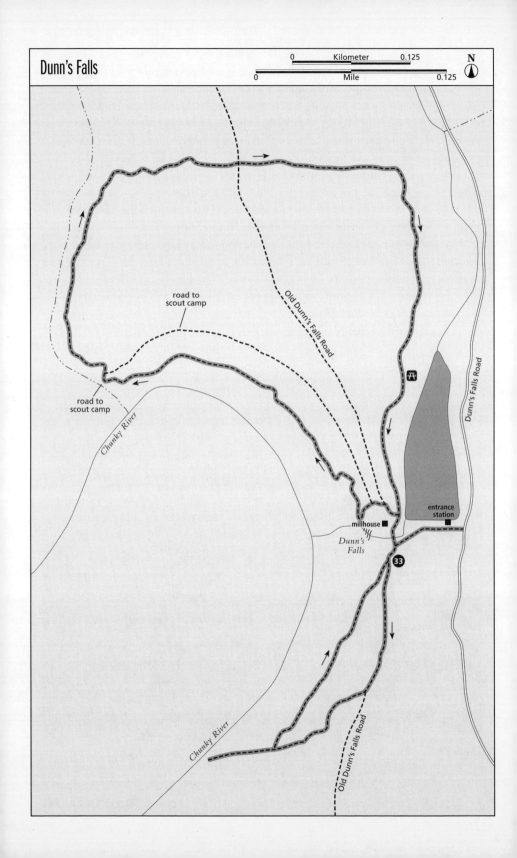

Dunn's Falls

0   Kilometer   0.125

0   Mile   0.125

N

road to scout camp

road to scout camp

Chunky River

Old Dunn's Falls Road

Dunn's Falls Road

entrance station

millhouse

Dunn's Falls

33

Chunky River

Old Dunn's Falls Road

▶ **Dunn's Falls Water Park also offers primitive camping, a rental cabin, paddleboat rentals, and a picnic area. It is operated by the Pat Harrison Water District.**

Magnolias are present along this part of the trail. Watch for occasional rock outcrops both in the river and on the land. This trail is one of the most beautiful in the state, but it could use a little more TLC as it will likely have blowdowns and is subject to landslides, as you will see.

After reaching the Boy Scout camp, head up a gorgeous hollow created by water and time. Holly trees proliferate among the beech and the laurel oaks. The path becomes quite steep before crossing Old Dunn's Falls Road at the top of a hill. Come alongside the stream feeding Dunn's Falls and begin angling back toward the mill area. First pass through a beech grove and picnic area, then come alongside the small fishing lake before completing the loop.

Miles and Directions

0.0   Start near the falls. As you face the river, look left for a sign indicating the hiking trail. It heads up Old Dunn's Falls Road, which is now but a grassy track left to us hikers.

0.4   Return from the south loop to explore the millhouse. Take the steps leading down to the base of the falls.

0.7   Reach the Boy Scout camping area after cruising alongside the Chunky River. At this point a dirt road accessing the camp comes in. Also a bridge leads over a ravine. Do not take this as it crosses the ravine merely to reach another camping area. Instead, look for the yellow blazes and a faint track leaving uphill away from the river, roughly paralleling the ravine to your left.

0.9   Cross Old Dunn's Falls Road after a steep climb. Immediately descend.

1.2   Reach the picnic area and small fishing pond.

1.3   Arrive back at the trailhead.

More Information

Local Information
Meridian/Lauderdale County Tourism Bureau, P.O. Box 5313, Meridian, MS 39302; (888) 868-7720; www.visitmeridian.com.

Local Events/Attractions
Highland Park/Dentzel Carousel/Jimmie Rogers Museum, www.meridianms.org. The latter two are located at Highland Park. The carousel, in operation since 1909, is a National Historic Landmark. The Jimmie Rogers Museum chronicles the life of the country singer.

34 Marathon Lake Loop

The Marathon Hiking Trail, despite its name, is actually a short path that cruises around Marathon Lake, named for the Marathon Lumber Company, which once operated in this area and built the lake. The trail circles the fifty-acre impoundment, and includes a wetland boardwalk and good views from many places. Hiking is but one element of the Marathon Lake recreation experience, which includes fishing, camping, picnicking, boating, and bicycling.

Start: Marathon Lake Recreation Area boat ramp
Distance: 2.0-mile loop
Approximate hiking time: 1 to 1.5 hours
Difficulty: Easy, mostly level
Trail surface: Grass, boardwalk, leaves, dirt
Seasons: Year-round
Other trail users: Hikers only
Canine compatibility: Leashed dogs permitted
Land status: National forest

Nearest town: Forest
Fees and permits: Entry fee required
Schedule: Open year-round unless winter weather forces closure
Maps: USGS maps: Clear Springs
Trail contacts: Bienville National Forest, 3473 Highway 35 South, Forest, MS 39074; (601) 469-3811; www.fs.fed.us/r8/mississippi/bienville

Finding the trailhead: From exit 88 on Interstate 20, Forest/Raleigh, take Highway 35 south for 6.8 miles to the town of Homewood, then turn left on Morton-Marathon Road. Travel for 9.2 miles, then turn right on Smith County Road 520. Travel for 0.3 mile, then turn left into the Marathon Lake Recreation Area. Continue past the entrance station to bear left at 0.4 mile following the directions to the boat ramp. The trail starts near the boat ramp. *DeLorme: Mississippi Atlas & Gazetteer:* Page 43 G9. GPS trailhead coordinates: N32 11' 59.31" / W89 21' 31.65".

The Hike

The Marathon Hiking Trail starts near the boat ramp, beside a small dock. Turn left and head north as you face the lake. The campground is to your left behind a thin screen of trees. Short paths connect the campsites to the lake. You are actually walking the grassy margin between fifty-acre Marathon Lake and the wooded campground. Campers and other visitors may be bank fishing from the grassy shore. Tall pine trees shade the shore in the afternoon. The path soon enters woods, passing the last few campsites before leaving the campground entirely. You are now circling around the uppermost part of the lake, gaining the east side of the lake via a 200–plus–foot boardwalk. The water around the boardwalk is more creek/swamp-like at this point.

A grassy area runs parallel to the lake's east side, but the Marathon Lake Trail enters woods. You can see where other hikers or anglers choose to stay along the lake in the grassy margin. The forest is thinner here, with sporadic tall pines rising above

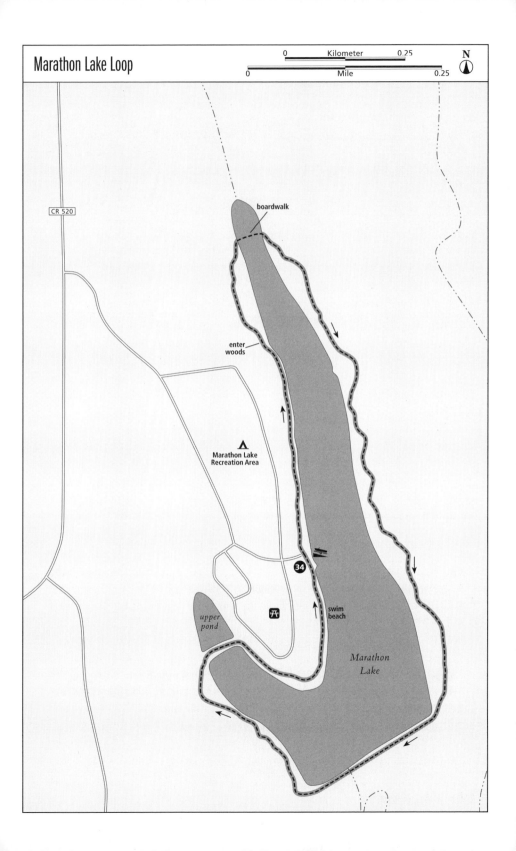

Marathon Lake Loop

0   Kilometer   0.25

0   Mile   0.25

N

CR 520

boardwalk

enter
woods

Marathon Lake
Recreation Area

34

swim
beach

upper
pond

Marathon
Lake

Marathon Lake Recreation Area is a fine destination in the Bienville National Forest. A large picnic area with a picnic shelter and many attractive sites overlooks Marathon Lake. A well-kept and maintained thirty-four-site campground is located astride the lake as well, in a mix of pine and oak woods. The bathhouses have flush toilets and warm showers. Each campsite has electricity and water, as well as a tent pad, picnic table, upright grill, and fire ring. These are deluxe campsites by national forest standards. Loop B has lakefront sites that are among the most desirable camps.

younger pines and oaks. Small grassy clearings and sweetgums round out the vegetation. The trail remains level and the hiking easy as you cruise about 50 or so feet back from the water, though some sections of the trail get farther away from the shore. The Forest Service is trying to keep a 40- to 50-foot grassy area for bank fishermen. The lake offers angling for bream, catfish, and largemouth bass.

The open area atop the lake dam avails another vista point. You can see up the lake and—closer by—to the swim beach and picnic area. Pine woods below the dam contrast with the open waters of Marathon Lake. Curve north beyond the dam, staying with the lake rather than a woods road leading away from the water. Shortly reach a second dam, this one much smaller, which separates a smaller pond from the main lake. The upper pond has little land peninsulas where you can bank fish.

Upon crossing this dam you can either cruise through the recreation area on the paved road or continue to walk the margin of the lake, passing the swim beach along the way. I recommend walking the margin along the lake for more watery views until you return to the boat ramp and conclude the hike. Since this trail is somewhat short, consider combining your hike with other activities here: swim, picnic, boat, fish, or camp. The quiet paved recreation area roads make for fun recreational biking.

Miles and Directions

0.0 Start at the boat ramp on the west side of Marathon Lake. Head north, keeping the lake to your right and the recreation area campground to your left.

0.3 Leave the grassy lakeside area for the woods and keep northbound on a true trail under the trees.

0.4 Trail reaches the boardwalk crossing the uppermost part of the lake. Good views can be had to the south.

1.1 Pass a large clearing, then turn right, cruising atop the lake dam.

1.4 Reach the far side of the dam. The hiking path turns right here; stay along the water's edge.

1.6 Cross a small dam, dividing an upper pond from the main lake.

2.0 Reach the recreation area boat ramp and complete the loop.

More Information

Local Information
Forest Area Chamber of Commerce, P.O. Box 266, Forest, MS 39074; (601) 469-4332; www.forestmschamber.com.

Local Events/Attractions
Wing Dang Doodle Festival, www.forestmschamber.com. This cooking and eating event is all about chicken wings. It includes cooking contests and is held at Gaddis Park in September.

35 Historic Trace near Rocky Springs

This out-and-back hike travels along portions of the actual Natchez Trace as it travels northeasterly. Pass through the Little Sand Creek drainage before rolling through forested wetland to reach the Gees Creek drainage. First, explore the town site of Rocky Springs, where you can see evidence of early pioneers.

Start: Rocky Springs
Distance: 6.0 miles out-and-back
Approximate hiking time: 2.5 to 3 hours there and back
Difficulty: Moderate, some undulations
Trail surface: Leaves, dirt, pine needles, maybe mud
Seasons: Fall through spring
Other trail users: Equestrians
Canine compatibility: Leashed dogs permitted

Land status: National park
Nearest town: Vicksburg
Fees and permits: No fees or permits required
Schedule: Open year-round
Maps: Natchez Trace National Scenic Trail; USGS maps: Carlisle
Trail contacts: Natchez Trace Parkway, 2680 Natchez Trace Parkway, Tupelo, MS 38804; (800) 305-7417; www.nps.gov/natr

Finding the trailhead: From the town of Port Gibson, take Highway 18 east a short distance to reach the Natchez Trace Parkway. Head north on the parkway for 15 miles. The trail is at the Rocky Springs Site, located off milepost 54.8 on the Natchez Trace. Upon reaching Rocky Springs, continue on the paved road, passing the spur roads to the campground and picnic area to reach a loop. The trailhead is on the right-hand side of the loop. *DeLorme: Mississippi Atlas & Gazetteer:* Page 40 H4. GPS trailhead coordinates: N32 5' 19.0" / W90 48' 33.1".

The Hike

Before you start your hike, drive around the loop to the upper trailhead for the short walk through the town of Rocky Springs, a once thriving rural community founded in the late 1790s. It is now hard to believe that over 2,000 people lived around this watery upwelling and its outskirts just prior to the Civil War. Take a segment of the Old Trace and begin the town site loop. The old church is still being used. Only relics are left elsewhere. Interpretive signs help you enjoy the trail. The Civil War, yellow fever, and finally the boll weevil did in Rocky Springs.

Now, return to the lower trailhead and begin the historic Trace. The poignant inscription at the trailhead reads as follows: THIS IS THE NATCHEZ TRACE. FOR MANY YEARS IT SERVED MAN WELL, BUT AS WITH MANY THINGS WHEN ITS USEFULNESS PAST, IT WAS ABANDONED. OVER THE YEARS, THIS TIME WORN PATH HAS BEEN A SILENT WITNESS TO HONOR AND DISHONOR. IT BEARS THE PRINTS OF COUNTLESS MEN. WALK DOWN THE SHADED TRAIL—LEAVE YOUR PRINTS IN THE DUST, NOT FOR OTHERS TO SEE BUT THE ROAD TO REMEMBER.

Follow the sign's directive and begin the Trace. Time and the elements have eroded the path into a ravine of sorts. The bases of trees stand well above you. This wearing down of the path wasn't done during the heyday of the Trace, but is a result of decades upon decades of storms. The park service occasionally dumps gravel here to retard the undermining of the road. The sunken nature of the Trace adds to its haunting mystery. Cane, ferns, basswood, red maple, magnolia, beech, and pines grow astride the track. This is one of the longest stretches of the original Trace still preserved in the south end of the entire Parkway, which extends from Natchez, Mississippi, to Nashville, Tennessee. The Trace isn't always sunken. Sometimes it is but a foot or two below where it should be. But the land all around has sunken and eroded from poor farming practices of the past, when cotton brought wealth to the greater Rocky Springs area.

In some places, the Trace cuts an incredibly deep track as it heads downhill, nearly 20 feet below the former soil line. Water bars have been installed to check erosion. At some point in the past it was even paved, but all that remains are a few crumbling bits of asphalt. Cross feeder branch of Little Sand Creek. The Trace descends into the Little Sand Creek drainage, passing a horse trail and a spur path to the recreation area campground before crossing Little Sand Creek, its waters flowing crystalline over a grainy bed.

Imagine the quagmires of 200 years ago when fall rains would turn this bottom into a mucky mess that made the journey all the more difficult. The Trace leaves the bottom as it should and comes to Old Port Gibson Road. Return to piney woodland after briefly going along the road. This trail, just like the original Trace, tries to stay on the ridgelines as much as possible, but in this desiccated area it just doesn't last long and you are down by a streambed in a quarter mile. Continue riding the roller coaster in thick, vine-draped woods to reach Midway Road.

Beyond Midway Road the Natchez Trace Parkway is visible off to the right. The singletrack trail, which parallels the Parkway, traverses ravines in very dense woods with a thick understory of pine and sweetgum. The path here is eroded in places much like the original Natchez Trace, except on a smaller scale. Atop the ravines, the trail is in fine shape however. Make a final descent for Gees Creek. This is a good spot to turn around.

Historic Trace near Rocky Springs

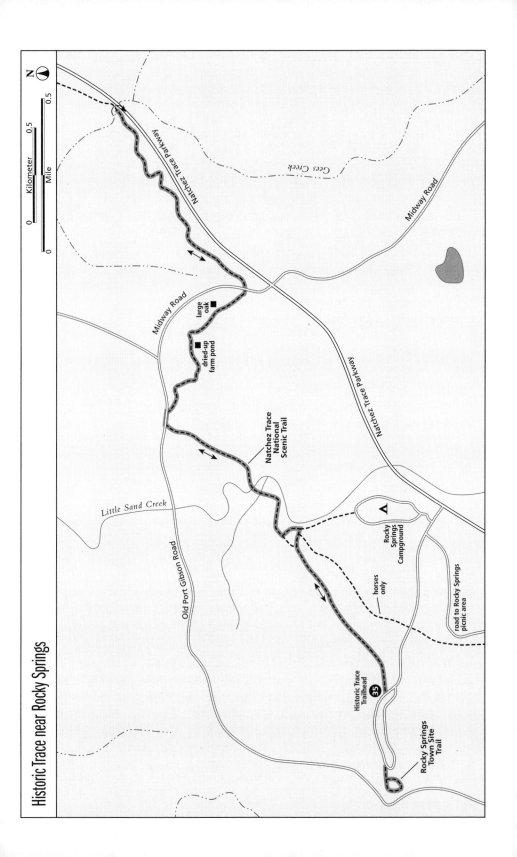

N

Kilometer
0   0.5
0   0.5
Mile

Natchez Trace Parkway

Gees Creek

Midway Road

Midway Road

large oak

dried-up farm pond

Natchez Trace National Scenic Trail

Little Sand Creek

Old Port Gibson Road

Natchez Trace Parkway

Rocky Springs Campground

horses only

road to Rocky Springs picnic area

Historic Trace Trailhead 35

Rocky Springs Town Site Trail

Miles and Directions

0.0   Start on the historic Trace at the upper loop at Rocky Springs Site.

0.6   Reach a three-way intersection, passing a horse-only trail, then a little path to Rocky Springs Campground. Shortly cross a tributary of Little Sand Creek. The trail turns to a singletrack path, bordered by many cedars, before crossing Little Sand Creek. Raised circular steps give you a chance to keep your feet dry.

1.4   Reach Old Port Gibson Road after climbing away from Little Sand Creek on another portion of the historic Trace. Turn right on the paved road and briefly follow it, looking for a singletrack trail entering woods downhill and to your right from the road.

1.6   Step over a normally dry streambed. Continue undulating, passing a dried-up farm pond.

1.9   Pass a particularly large oak to left of the trail.

2.0   After a final climb, reach and bisect paved Midway Road. Continue on a narrow singletrack path through dense woods. Parkway is to right of the trail.

3.0   Emerge onto grassy area adjacent to Natchez Trace Parkway. Natchez Trace Trail uses the Parkway bridge to span Gees Creek. This is a good spot to turn around.

6.0   Arrive back at the trailhead.

More Information

Local Information

Chamber of Commerce of Port Gibson, P.O. Box 491, Port Gibson, MS 39150; (601) 437-4351; www.portgibsononthemississippi.com.

Local Events/Attractions

Grand Gulf Military Park, www.grandgulfpark.state.ms.us/. This park is dedicated not only to the history of the Civil War in Claiborne County, but also to other aspects of a past shaped by the Mississippi River. Visit the museum and also see old buildings from pioneers' houses to moonshine-making operations.

36 Owens Creek Falls

This hike travels the Natchez Trace National Scenic Trail from Rocky Springs Recreation Area, rolling over hills along the Natchez Trace Parkway to end at a pair of waterfalls. The first waterfall is a tributary of Owens Creek, while the second, a larger falls, is on Owens Creek. For maximum flow and drama, try to hike this trail during winter or spring or after heavy rains, otherwise it may be less fulfilling. I suggest combining your hike with at least a picnic or even a campout. Rocky Springs Recreation Area offers free primitive camping, with water and restrooms, just off the Natchez Trace.

Start: Rocky Springs Picnic Area
Distance: 5.6 miles out-and-back
Approximate hiking time: 2.5 to 3 hours
Difficulty: Moderate due to a few hills
Trail surface: Leaves, dirt, roots
Seasons: Year-round
Other trail users: Equestrians
Canine compatibility: Leashed dogs permitted
Land status: National park

Nearest town: Port Gibson
Fees and permits: No fees or permits required
Schedule: Open year-round
Maps: Natchez Trace National Scenic Trail;
USGS maps: Carlisle
Trail contacts: Natchez Trace Parkway, 2680
Natchez Trace Parkway, Tupelo, MS 38804;
(800) 305-7417; www.nps.gov/natr

This waterfall is but a trickle in autumn

Finding the trailhead: From the town of Port Gibson, take Highway 18 east a short distance to reach the Natchez Trace Parkway. Head north on the parkway for 15 miles. The trail is at the Rocky Springs Recreation Area, located off milepost 54.8 on the Natchez Trace. Upon reaching Rocky Springs, keep forward on the paved road, then turn left and follow the road leading to the Rocky Springs Picnic Area. The trail starts at the turnaround. *DeLorme: Mississippi Atlas & Gazetteer:* Page 40 H4. GPS trailhead coordinates: N32 5' 1.08" / W90 48' 13.68".

The Hike

Leave the picnic area, joining a spur of the Natchez Trace National Scenic Trail, dropping into classic pine-oak woodland. Needles and cones line the track. Ferns and cane are prominent underbrush elements. Cross a couple of small drainages and then ascend a hill. Reach the Natchez Trace National Scenic Trail. Stay left, southbound. The path comes alongside private timbered lands on the park boundary, to soon bridge a stream. Notice the thick, foot-high concrete trail markers alongside the path. You will undoubtedly notice the paint blazes on the trees indicating property lines. Bridge a second stream. Southern magnolias intersperse the woods here.

Dogwoods are as common in this Mississippi forest as they are most places in the area. Oak and sweetgum dominate the drier areas. Many are draped with Spanish moss. Beeches thrive along the gullies. At 0.7 mile, the path nears the Parkway to skirt a drainage, then turns back into the woods. Shortly return again to the Parkway, bridging a gully. The trail is routed this way to avoid building bridges over the sharp chasms. At 1.2 miles, ford another gully at the confluence of two streams. Paradoxically, this ford may be challenging when you want to see the falls at their best, which is flowing strongly. Unfortunately, I haven't been able to catch Owens Creek Falls after a heavy rain. Parts of the trail could be muddy and/or sandy when crossing washes. The upland areas will be generally drier, but the trail never stays high for long—invariably descending to wetter drainages. The historic Trace, which white settlers used, followed an old Indian path that attempted to stay along the ridgelines as much as possible to avoid these wet bottoms and stream crossings. Of course, in this modern era, we must recognize property boundaries, which alter the laying out of the route of this national scenic trail.

At 1.8 miles, the trail makes a steep climb, then heads directly downhill. This is a likely good example of fitting the path into the current national park boundary lines versus the old travelers of the Trace going where it best suited them, where the route availed the easiest travel. Climb yet again—Old Port Gibson Road comes into sight on your right. The path winds amid mountain laurel and cedar trees in the area before reaching Whitaker Road at 2.0 miles. Old Port Gibson Road intersects Whitaker Road within sight. Bear left and climb sharply from Whitaker Road to enter mixed cedar-oak forest.

Watch for a hilltop graveyard on trail left, circled by remnant fencing, though much of the site is being overtaken by trees. Most markers indicate service in the Confederate Army. This hilltop was a good final resting spot as it was not subject

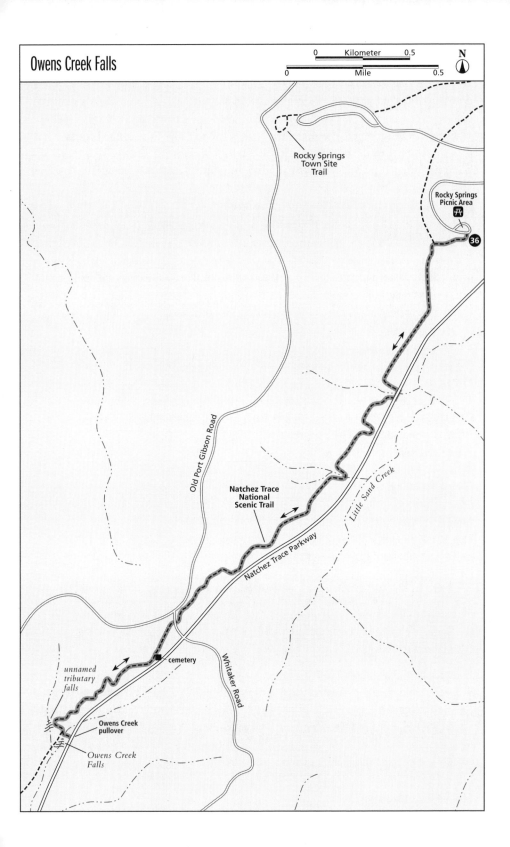

Owens Creek Falls

0   Kilometer   0.5

0   Mile   0.5

N

Rocky Springs
Town Site
Trail

Rocky Springs
Picnic Area

36

Old Port Gibson Road

Natchez Trace
National
Scenic Trail

Natchez Trace Parkway

Little Sand Creek

cemetery

Whitaker Road

unnamed
tributary
falls

Owens Creek
pullover

Owens Creek
Falls

to the flooding so rampant among the streams here. The path becomes incredibly steep here—you'll be surprised such inclines exist in the Magnolia State. Note the saw palmetto and beech trees in these declivitous ravines. This section of the Trace is downright challenging as it continues its undulations. At 2.7 miles, reach a tributary falls near Owens Creek. Curve toward the Parkway beyond the first falls, passing a small picnic area before reaching Owens Creek Falls, adjacent to the Parkway. This falls drops into a much larger amphitheater over a rock overhang. Sand gathers at the bottom of the pool. The base of the falls will be cooler in summer due to the waterfall cooling the air. This was a landmark for early Natchez Trace travelers, and is a stopping point for modern Parkway drivers and hikers.

Miles and Directions

0.0 Start at Rocky Springs Picnic Area. (FYI: Note the blackened tree trunks. The National Park Service uses prescribed burning to preserve the natural characteristics of the landscape.)

0.4 Come very near the Parkway.

1.2 Descend into a gully and ford at confluence of two small streams.

1.8 Begin a hilly section.

2.0 Cross Whitaker Road.

2.2 Pass a hilltop cemetery on trail left. Note the Confederate graves.

2.7 Reach a falls on a tributary of Owens Creek. (FYI: You will hear the falls before you see them. They drop about 15 feet into a circular amphitheater over a rock lip, forming a plunge pool. The trail offers a good vantage of these unnamed falls.)

2.8 Reach Owens Creek Falls and Parkway. Backtrack.

5.6 Arrive back at the trailhead.

More Information

Local Information
Chamber of Commerce of Port Gibson, P.O. Box 491, Port Gibson, MS 39150; (601) 437-4351; www.portgibsononthemississippi.com.

Local Events/Attractions
Grand Gulf Military Park, www.grandgulfpark.state.ms.us/. This park is dedicated not only to the history of the Civil War in Claiborne County, but also to other aspects of a past shaped by the Mississippi River. Visit the museum and also see old buildings from pioneers' houses to moonshine-making operations.

37 Clarkco State Park

This hiking loop circles Ivy Lake, the centerpiece of Clarkco State Park. As you might have guessed, this destination is in Clarke County. Developed by the Civilian Conservation Corps (CCC), the park offers numerous amenities from cabins to camping to swimming. The nature trail here circles the south side of Ivy Lake, where an observation tower allows a grand view. Circle the north end of the lake on a park road.

Start: State park lodge
Distance: 2.9-mile loop
Approximate hiking time: 1.5 to 2 hours
Difficulty: Easy, a few hills
Trail surface: Grass, leaves, some dirt, pavement
Seasons: Year-round
Other trail users: Hikers only
Canine compatibility: Leashed dogs permitted

Land status: State park
Nearest town: Quitman
Fees and permits: Entry fee required
Schedule: Open year-round
Maps: USGS maps: Quitman
Trail contacts: Clarkco State Park, 386 Clarkco Road, Quitman, MS 39355; (601) 776-6651; http://home.mdwfp.com/parks.aspx

Finding the trailhead: From Enterprise, Mississippi, just off Interstate 59, take Highway 513 south for 1.2 miles to Highway 514 east. Turn left on Highway 514 east and follow it for 6.7 miles to U.S. Highway 45 south. Turn right onto US 45 and follow it for 5.9 miles to turn left on Highway 145 north. Follow Highway 145 north for 0.2 mile and turn right into the Clarkco State Park. Park at the lodge/office area. *DeLorme: Mississippi Atlas & Gazetteer:* Page 45 H6. GPS trailhead coordinates: N32 6' 7.6" / W88 42' 14.2".

The Hike

Clarkco State Park was hit hard by Hurricane Katrina. The trail system has been shortened since then, but will hopefully be restored to its full glory in the future. For now you can still do a nice loop hike utilizing park roads part of the way. Leave the lodge area and walk back up the entrance road to begin the hike. As you face the entrance station, leave left. The trails to the right are currently closed. Immediately pass under a transmission line, then veer left, following the red blazes on the wide track. These trails are in better shape but still have some debris.

Pass behind the park's sewage lagoon, then enter ragged woodland. The path can be quite brushy here. This doesn't last long, however, as the trail curves right at a junction and begins meandering between the majestic pines. After all, this is the Pine Belt. Yaupon, oak, wax myrtle, and sweetgum add variety to this forest. The park uses fire regularly to keep the understory

▶ During Hurricane Katrina, over nine hours of 110-mph winds toppled 2,000 trees, just over the paved park roads. During the storm park guests and personnel huddled in the lodge, which had its roof ripped off. All survived.

down. You may notice blackened trunks on the trees here. Just as you are appreciating the forest, it gives way to a wide-open timbered area.

Reach a junction in the middle of the clearing. Turn left here, tracing the double-track trail in more open land. The trail may be muddy at times as you climb a hill to reenter tall woods. After passing an intersection with a trail leading left to the cabins, the main loop comes near Ivy Lake, passing over wooded wetlands where bay trees, holly, and cane thrive. Ivy Lake is now in sight to your left through the woods. Reach the observation tower. Climb the steps for a great sweeping view of the length of the lake. The lodge, your starting point, is visible way in the distance. Peer into the forest below. Note the buttressed trunks of the trees growing lakeside. This is to withstand periodic flooding. Rejoin a built-up roadbed before bridging the upper end of the unnamed stream feeding Ivy Lake. It is a tributary of Moore's Mill Creek. Notice the woods around you are subject to periodic flooding.

▶ Park visitors like to bicycle the old paved scenic route across Moore's Mill Creek and onto the old CCC camp location. The road is closed to vehicles and makes a good walking venue as well.

Ivy Lake is the centerpiece of Clarko State Park

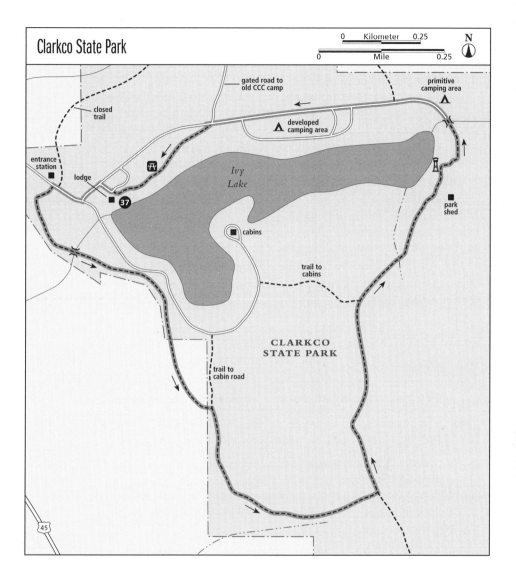

The trail opens into the primitive camping area. From here, trace the park road closest to the lake back to the lodge. Take note of the picnic pavilion. It is a rustic relic of the CCC, and it contrasts mightily with the modern plastic-based playground equipment nearby. You will see water recreation is easy at Clarkco State Park. Pass a boat launch, a fishing pier, and a swim beach. The hike ends at the park lodge.

Miles and Directions

0.0 Start near the lodge. As you face the entrance station, head left and join a wide, grassy track after passing under a transmission line.

0.3 Cross a wooden footbridge overlaying pilings of an old road bridge. The bridge crosses the outflow of Ivy Lake.

0.8 Reach a trail junction near an old fence. To your left, a trail leads almost due north back to a park road. This loop turns right, heading south into tall pines.

1.3 Reach a trail junction in an open timbered area. The nature trail curves left here.

1.5 Reenter woods atop a hill.

1.7 Reach a trail junction in woods. Here a wide track leads left to the park cabins. This loop curves right on a wide shaded trail.

1.9 Follow a singletrack trail veering left. A park shed facility is visible in the distance at this turn. Reach the lake observation tower.

2.1 Span the stream feeding Ivy Lake. Enter the primitive camping area.

2.2 Closed nature trail leads right away from the park road. Stay straight, passing the developed campground on your left.

2.6 Stay left along Ivy Lake. To your right is the closed scenic road leading to the old CCC camp.

2.9 Arrive back at the park lodge.

More Information

Local Information
Clarke County Chamber of Commerce, 100 S. Railroad Avenue, P.O. Box 172, Quitman, MS 39355; (601) 776-5701; www.netpathway.com/~clarkech/.

Local Events/Attractions
Archusa Creek Water Park, 540 County Road 110, Quitman, MS 39355-9562; (601) 776-6956; www.phwd.net/parks. This water park, part of the Pat Harrison Waterway District, features a 450-acre lake. This impoundment is a popular fishing, boating, swimming, and waterskiing venue. It also offers picnicking and camping.

38 Tree Tops Trail at Chautauqua Park

Tree Tops Trail is a unique hike. Here at historic Chautauqua Park, you can enjoy the 1,500 feet of elevated boardwalk—the Tree Tops Trail—which gives you a high-rise view of the forest amid spring-filled hollows and tree-covered hills. But this park has more than just the boardwalk. Other hiking trails add up to make a worthwhile loop, though you may consider doing the Tree Tops Trail twice, a "victory lap," if you will. Also bring a picnic and enjoy the rustic facilities in this attractive setting.

Start: Visitor center

Distance: 1.3-mile loop

Approximate hiking time: 1 to 1.5 hours

Difficulty: Easy but does have hilly sections

Trail surface: Dirt, leaves, pine needles, wooden boardwalk

Seasons: Year-round

Other trail users: Hikers only

Canine compatibility: Leashed dogs permitted

Land status: City park

Nearest town: Crystal Springs

Fees and permits: No fees or permits required

Schedule: Open year-round

Maps: Chautauqua Park Trails; USGS maps: Crystal Springs, Terry

Trail contacts: City of Crystal Springs– Parks & Recreation, P.O. Box 473, Crystal Springs, MS 39059; (601) 892-0007; www.csparksandrec.com

Finding the trailhead: From exit 72, North Crystal Springs/Utica, on Interstate 55, take Highway 27 south for 0.4 mile to the four-way stop and intersection with U.S. Highway 51. Turn right at the four-way stop and travel south on US 51 for 1 mile. Turn right into Chautauqua Park, then make an immediate left and park at the visitor center. *DeLorme: Mississippi Atlas & Gazetteer:* Page 48 B40. GPS trailhead coordinates: N31 59' 57.18" / W90 21' 40.43".

The Hike

Chautauqua Park, today known for the Tree Tops Trail, has been through many incarnations through the years. In the late 1800s it was a Methodist camp retreat. Later, Lake Chautauqua was added by the Illinois Central Railroad to provide water for the steam locomotives that traveled between Memphis and New Orleans. Crystal Springs was already an important stop for the railroad as they shipped the rich agricultural bounty, notably, tomatoes that came from Copiah County, of which Crystal Springs is the seat. Later, during the Great Depression, the Works Progress Administration labored on many of the stone buildings you see today. The locale is now run by the city of Crystal Springs, and you can not only hike the Tree Tops Trail but also enjoy the other more conventional paths that wind through the seventy-four-acre preserve.

Trail maps and interpretive information are available inside the visitor center. Leave the visitor center and walk the visitor center access road to cross the main park road, joining a wide gravel path to soon meet a path with one of the all-time great names—the Trail of Tranquility. A large archway leads to the T of T; enter pine-oak woodland typical of the heart of Mississippi. The natural setting is fine, but auto sounds are audible with US 51 on one side of the park and I-55 on the other. However, don't let that distract you.

Meet the Barred Owl Trail, which travels over a quaint arched bridge, then dead-ends. At one time, the Chautauqua Park trail system here had extravagant interpretive information and signage. But the ground trails and developed mini-ecosystems have been neglected somewhat. That being said, the Tree Tops Trail itself is being kept in superlative shape since it is the number one trail drawing card at Chautauqua Park. Continue in deep bottomland along a transparent spring branch flowing over rock outcrops. Sycamores are among the trees thriving down here. Short boardwalks cross intermittent branches. On a summer morning it may be 10 degrees cooler here than on the hilltops. Leave the clear stream, passing some sizable beech trees before topping out beside the park's outdoor classroom. Turn right and pass the outdoor classroom, taking the wide gravel track downhill.

You will finally meet the Tree Tops Trail, leading left at the next junction. But don't take it yet; keep going straight and then take the Tree Tops Trail leading right. Here, follow the boardwalk right as it heads toward Chautauqua Lake. Travel at mid-tree level, gaining a "squirrel's eye view" of the forest around you. The boardwalk descends to its low point above Clear Creek, which emerges from Chautauqua Lake. It winds among the treetops, where you can gain a different perspective of the woods that are all around you. Not only does the Tree Tops Trail—a massive boardwalk—go up and down, it also travels side to side as it works its way through the forest. Eventually, you will hear what you think is a waterfall but is just simply the outflow of Chautauqua Lake, dropping from a pipe. But it is pleasant sounding no matter the source.

Emerge onto the thirty-five-acre lake that was originally created to water steam engines but is now a recreation destination. After working your way back, join the second section of the Tree Tops Trail, enjoying more of the unique perspective this exclusive trail gives. Watch for the covered springhouse below. It emits reddish-iron water that is not too tasty looking. The elevated boardwalk passes by some very large beech trees. Other big trees include oaks and hickories. At times the boardwalk is near the ground and other times it is well elevated as it cuts across ravines. Consider the money and time it took to build this trail. It cost $170,000 to erect, using state taxpayer money, as well as individual and business donations from local sources. Beyond the boardwalk, the trail opens to a clearing then soon reaches the main park road near the playground/picnic area. Look at the stonework of the facilities around here. This area is quite scenic. Note the PTA was founded here by some concerned citizens wanting to improve their local schools. Folks from outside the state would never guess that the organization was begun right here in Mississippi!

Miles and Directions

0.0 Start at the visitor center. Walk road leading from the visitor center to cross the entrance road, joining a wide gravel track.

0.1 Leave the gravel track and keep going, passing under arch to join the Trail of Tranquility.

0.3 Reach a junction after a steep descent. The short Barred Owl Trail crosses an arched bridge over one of the many spring branches in this park. Stay left with the Trail of Tranquility, traveling alongside the spring branch.

0.4 Meet the gravel track, stay right, passing by outdoor classroom.

0.5 Trail leads right to lower lake. Keep going over a spring branch, then climb to the first junction with the Tree Tops Trail. Keep going here (stay to the right) on gravel track, then turn right at the second junction with the Tree Tops Trail.

0.8 Emerge onto Lake Chautauqua at boat ramp and alternate parking area. Backtrack on Tree Tops Trail, briefly join the gravel track, then veer right on the other half of the Tree Tops Trail.

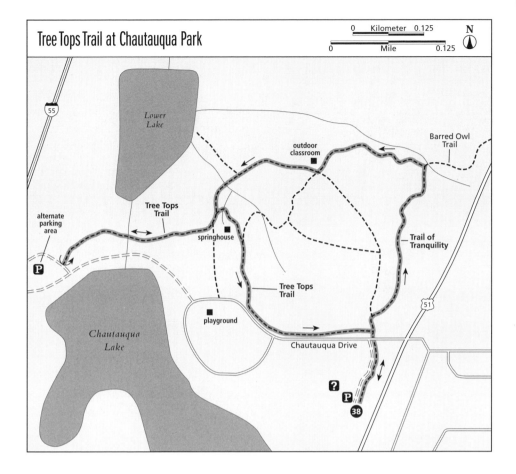

Tree Tops Trail at Chautauqua Park

1.1 Open onto the main park road near the playground. Turn left here and follow the main park road, then turn right on the road toward the visitor center.

1.3 Arrive back at the trailhead after walking the main park road.

More Information

Local Information
Crystal Springs Chamber of Commerce, P.O. Box 519, 210 E. Railroad Avenue, Crystal Springs, MS 39059; (601) 892-2711; www.crystalspringsmiss.com.

Local Events/Attractions
Crystal Springs Tomato Festival. Crystal Springs' nickname is "Tomatopolis," so many of the red delights are grown in these parts. They have vendors, parades, races, and a lot of tomatoes. Y'all come! It is sponsored by the Crystal Springs Chamber of Commerce, noted above, and is held annually on the last Saturday in June.

South Mississippi

39 Longleaf Trace near Prentiss

This rail trail extending 40 miles from Prentiss to Hattiesburg is the pride of South Mississippi. The stretch from Prentiss to Carson described here is arguably its most scenic. Start in a quaint park in downtown Prentiss, then leave the town for serene countryside on a paved track that is used by not only hikers but also joggers, walkers, and bicyclists. The one-way trek ends in Carson, where you can set up a car shuttle or hike back to Prentiss.

Start: Gateway Park in downtown Prentiss
Distance: 6.8 miles one way, 13.6 miles out-and-back
Approximate hiking time: 3 hours one way
Difficulty: Moderate despite the distance
Trail surface: Asphalt
Seasons: Year-round
Other trail users: Bicyclists, joggers, in-line skaters
Canine compatibility: Leashed dogs permitted

Land status: Public rail trail
Nearest town: Prentiss
Fees and permits: No fees or permits required
Schedule: Open year-round
Maps: Longleaf Trace; USGS maps: Prentiss East
Trail contacts: Longleaf Trace, P.O. Box 15187, Hattiesburg, MS 39404; (601) 450-5247; www.longleaftrace.org

Finding the trailhead: From the intersection of U.S. Highway 84 and Highway 13 near Prentiss, take US 84 west for a half mile, then turn right on Front Street and follow it for 0.2 mile to Gateway Park and the Longleaf Trace, which will be on your left. To get to the Carson trailhead from here, backtrack on Front Street 0.2 mile to US 84. Turn right and follow US 84 west for 0.8 mile, then turn left on Highway 42 east. Follow Highway 42 for 6.1 miles to the Carson trailhead on your left, just past a church and the center of town. The parking area is on a right curve in the town of Carson. *DeLorme: Mississippi Atlas & Gazetteer:* Page 49 H9. GPS trailhead coordinates: N31 35' 51.66" / W89 51' 59.66".

The Hike

Gateway Park has a picnic area, gazebo, water fountain, and restrooms. Join the approximately 10-foot-wide asphalt path as it leaves southeast away from downtown. Thus begins the trail that extends 40 miles to Hattiesburg. The Longleaf Trace is part of the rails to trails effort in the United States and is a great example of turning an abandoned track into a recreational venue used by all Mississippians. Head along the old abandoned railway-turned-trailway. The trail is most often open overhead but is bordered by thick brush, kudzu, and trees, along with a grassy mown shoulder extending a few feet on either side of it. The trail is nearly level the whole way, and you will see how the bed was built up in low areas or cut through hills in others to make it level. The Longleaf Trace becomes canopied beyond the town and reaches its first bridge in a half mile. This wood and concrete structure spans White Sand Creek.

The Trace is delineated in mile marker increments to help you keep apprised of your whereabouts. Stop signs have been placed at road crossings, primarily for bicyclists who perhaps use the trail in greater numbers than hikers do. It is an ideal bicycling destination, and a bike trip can be just as rewarding as doing it by foot.

Trestle-turned-bridge spans White Sand Creek

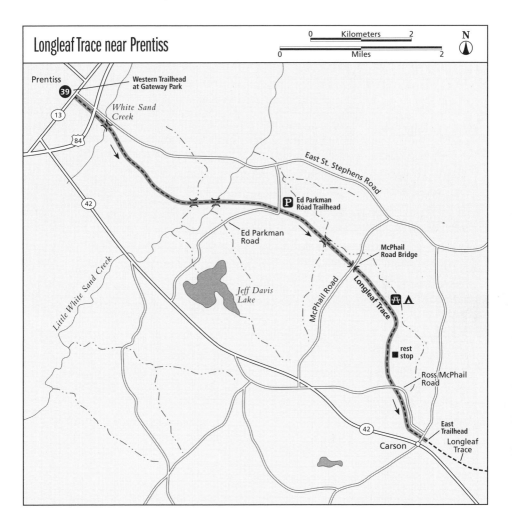

Longleaf Trace near Prentiss

Sometimes you will look down upon wetlands and swampy areas, featuring cypress and other moisture-loving vegetation. When the terrain is above the trailbed, pines will prevail. The trail as a whole heads in a southeasterly direction, aiming for Hattiesburg, but it does gently curve here and there. By 1.5 miles, you have left the little hustle and bustle there is in Prentiss and have now entered a distinctly rural landscape. Nature's sounds reign here, ironically as you travel over a route that once was perhaps the noisiest of them all in this area.

A trailhead and parking is available where Ed Parkman Road crosses the Trace at 3.2 miles. Make a 6.4-mile out-and-back if you turn around here. Beyond, the Longleaf Trace travels under mature pines that give way to a mix of field and forest, and pine plantations elsewhere.

The Trace even has a picnic/campsite at 4.9 miles. A couple of tent pads and a picnic table add value. The trail begins angling more southeasterly to get to Carson, a few houses appear, and you begin to hear the rumble of Highway 42. Reach the Carson Longleaf Trace parking area and the end of the hike. An information kiosk, parking area, and covered picnic shelter are located here.

Miles and Directions

0.0   Start at Gateway Park in downtown Prentiss.

0.3   Cross busy US 84 and begin to leave Prentiss.

0.5   Bridge White Sand Creek.

2.0   Bridge a tributary of Little White Sand Creek.

2.3   Bridge Little White Sand Creek on a long span with scenic overlook.

3.2   Cross Ed Parkman Road. Jeff Davis Lake is to the right and offers a picnic area, campground, and fishing.

3.9   Bridge tributary of Little White Sand Creek.

4.3   Cross paved McPhail Road, then a bridge.

4.9   Reach picnic/campsite to left of trail. Picnic table and tent pads available.

5.7   Reach rest stop deck overlooking forest below.

6.1   Cross Ross McPhail Road. A few houses stand about the area.

6.8   Reach the Carson trailhead with an information kiosk, parking, and covered picnic table.

13.6   Arrive back at the Prentiss trailhead if you are completing the out-and-back hike.

More Information

Local Information
Prentiss Community Development Association, 1025 3rd Street, Prentiss, MS 39474; (601) 792-5903.

Local Events/Attractions
Longleaf Trace Birthday Challenge. For information contact the Prentiss Community Development Association, noted above. The challenge, held the second Saturday in November, is to run, walk, bike, in-line skate, or wheelchair your age in kilometers on the Longleaf Trace.

40 Longleaf Trace near Hattiesburg

This section of Mississippi's longest rail trail—the Longleaf Trace—is the pride of Hattiesburg and the University of Southern Mississippi. The paved path leaves west along a wooded corridor from the university through urban and suburban areas before finally ending at quiet Clyde Depot, which makes for a good turnaround point. The trail is accommodating to hikers, with benches and rest areas strategically located along the path. Bicycles can be rented at the USM trailhead if you are so inclined.

Start: University of Southern Mississippi

Distance: 7.4 miles one way, 14.8 miles out-and-back

Approximate hiking time: 3 to 3.5 hours one way

Difficulty: Moderate

Trail surface: Asphalt

Seasons: Year-round

Other trail users: Bicyclists, joggers, in-line skaters, walkers

Canine compatibility: Leashed dogs permitted

Land status: Public rail trail

Nearest town: Hattiesburg

Fees and permits: No fees or permits required

Schedule: Open year-round

Maps: Longleaf Trace; USGS maps: Hattiesburg, Hattiesburg SW

Trail contacts: Longleaf Trace, P.O. Box 15187, Hattiesburg, MS 39404; (601) 450-5247; www.longleaftrace.org

Finding the trailhead: To reach the USM gateway from exit 65 on Interstate 59, take U.S. Highway 98 east (Hardy Street) for 0.3 mile to the second traffic light, 38th Avenue. Turn left on 38th Avenue and follow it for 0.7 mile, then turn right onto 4th Street. Follow 4th Street for 0.8 mile and then turn left into the signed Longleaf Trace parking area, located near the University of Southern Mississippi water tower. To reach the Clyde Depot end of the hike from the USM gateway, take 4th Street West (4th Street becomes old U.S. Highway 42/Sumrall Road) for 8 miles to Railroad Avenue and a sign for the Longleaf Trace. Turn right on Railroad Avenue and follow it for 0.2 mile, then turn right again into the parking area for Clyde Depot. *DeLorme: Mississippi Atlas & Gazetteer:* Page 57 C9. GPS trailhead coordinates: N31 19' 58.7" / W89 19' 54.4".

The Hike

Pick up the Trace at the Jerry Ryan Outdoor Center. Here you can rent bikes, or use the restroom and covered picnic facilities in the midst of the University of Southern Mississippi. The Longleaf Trace leaves west from the Outdoor Center in the urban/suburban area of Hattiesburg. A screen of trees divides you from the apartments and houses on either side of the Trace, populated with USM students. The trail extends about 12 feet wide and is nearly level. Soon you'll pass through a short tunnel under a local road. Ahead, reach a deck and bench overlooking a patch of woods.

Since the USM area is busy with traffic, the Trace tunnels under a second road then passes over I-59 on a bridge. This way Trace travelers don't have to worry about cars so much. However, at 1.6 miles you must cross West Hills Drive. Use care at road crossings. Trees draw closer and the trail narrows to 10 feet beyond West Hills Drive. In keeping its westerly direction, the Trace will sometimes cut through hills or be built up above flats. (FYI: Between Prentiss and Hattiesburg the Longleaf Trace drops 125 feet over 40 miles for an average elevation change of 3 feet per mile.)

At 3.0 miles you are more or less beyond Hattiesburg, but suburban housing developments are sprawling out this way, which makes the Trace all the more valuable as a natural resource. These neighborhoods have connectors to the Trace. Reach the Jackson Road Depot at 4.1 miles. If you are not using a shuttle, this might be a good place to turn around. Bicyclists will have an easier time covering the entire out-and-back distance of this trek. The going is as pleasant as ever as you cruise the wooded corridor. Take time to absorb the nature around the Trace. A good opportunity occurs at 5.8 miles, where a deck overlooks a wood-encircled pond. The trail continues westerly under the trees in the Cross Creek valley. When traveling the Trace east to west you have the slightest uptick, but you probably won't even notice it. Reach Clyde Depot on your left and the end of this hike. The wooden structure was built by the Bond family, who live nearby. It is now owned and operated by the Longleaf Trace. Note the rustic artifacts under the shelter, which also has a picnic table. From here the Trace continues for 32 miles west to Prentiss.

▶ The Trace travels through five towns on its journey: Prentiss, Carson, Bassfield, Sumrall, and finally Hattiesburg.

Miles and Directions

0.0 Start at the University of Southern Mississippi gateway. (FYI: Not only can you rent bikes here, but you can also store your bike for a nominal fee.)

0.3 Pass rest area with benches and deck overlooking woods.

1.2 Bridge I-59.

Longleaf Trace near Hattiesburg

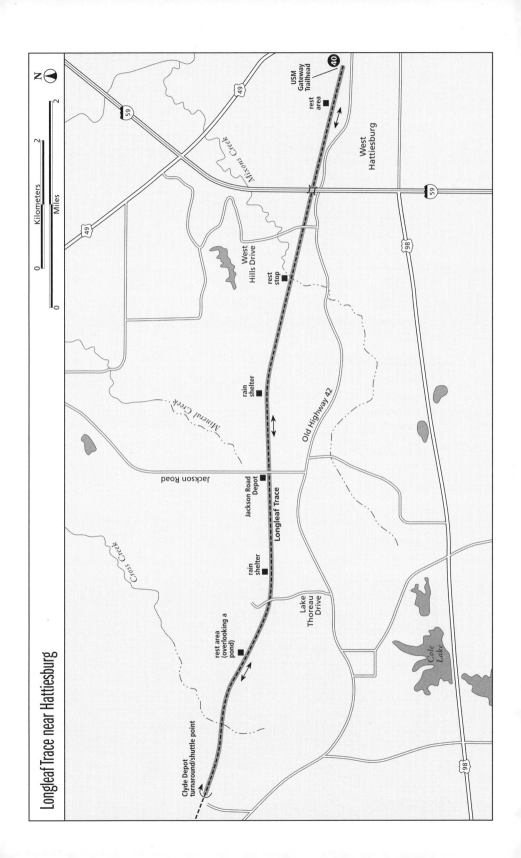

N

Kilometers
0   2

Miles
0   2

59
49
49

Nixons Creek

USM Gateway Trailhead
40
rest area

West Hattiesburg

59

98

West Hills Drive
rest stop

Mineral Creek

rain shelter

Old Highway 42

Jackson Road

Jackson Road Depot

Longleaf Trace

Cross Creek

rain shelter

Lake Thoreau Drive

rest area (overlooking a pond)

Clyde Depot turnaround/shuttle point

Cole Lake

98

1.6 Cross West Hills Drive. Use caution.

2.1 Bridge Mixons Creek.

3.2 Reach a rain shelter with a picnic table underneath it.

4.1 Reach the Jackson Road Depot. A parking area, vending, restrooms, and water are located here.

5.0 Reach a rain shelter just after passing a gas line clearing.

5.3 Cross quiet Lake Thoreau Drive.

5.8 Reach a rest area overlooking a pond in quiet woods.

7.4 Reach Clyde Depot with restrooms, water, and shelter.

14.8 Arrive back at USM gateway. (FYI: Hundreds of people have traveled the entire 40 miles of the Trace, most bicycling, though some have hiked or jogged the entire route.)

More Information

Local Information
Hattiesburg Convention and Visitors Bureau, Five Convention Center Plaza, Hattiesburg, MS 39401; (800) 638-6877; www.hattiesburg.org.

Local Events/Attractions
University of Southern Mississippi sports, www.southernmiss.cstv.com. See the Golden Eagles take on Conference USA opponents in football and basketball among other sports. Top rivals include University of Memphis and UAB. The football and basketball venues are located within walking distance of the Trace.

41 Richardson Creek/Mills Branch Loop

This trek rambles along the southern section of the Clear Springs Recreation Area, combining the Richardson Creek Trail and the Mills Branch Trail with a little stretch of the Tallys Creek Trail thrown in to create a rewarding loop that passes by streamside bluffs, small falls, and secluded forest scenery. The trails of this area were the second phase of the Clear Springs Trail Complex construction, first laid out in the late 1980s. This second portion was finished in the 1990s. The terrain is carved with many hills and hollows and the hike reflects it, with numerous undulations, sometimes winding "worser than a snake." Consider combining this loop with the Tallys Creek Loop for a multi-night backpacking trip. Overnighting at Clear Springs Lake Campground is a second option.

Start: Clear Springs Recreation Area trailhead

Distance: 10.5-mile loop

Approximate hiking time: 5.5 to 6.5 hours

Difficulty: Difficult

Trail surface: Roots, dirt, leaves, concrete riprap

Seasons: Year-round

Other trail users: Mountain bicyclists

Canine compatibility: Leashed dogs permitted

Land status: National forest

Nearest town: Meadville

Fees and permits: Recreation area parking fee

Schedule: Open year-round

Maps: Clear Springs Trail Complex; USGS maps: Meadville, Knoxville

Trail contacts: Homochitto National Forest, 1200 Highway 184 East, Meadville, MS 39653; (601) 384-5876; www.fs.fed.us/r8/mississippi/homochitto

Prescribed fire improves woodpecker habitat

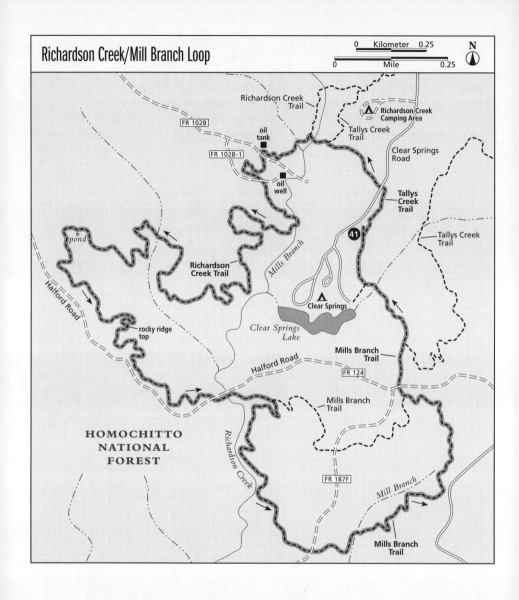

Richardson Creek/Mill Branch Loop

Richardson Creek Trail

FR 102B

oil tank

FR 102B-1

oil well

Richardson Creek Camping Area

Tallys Creek Trail

Clear Springs Road

Tallys Creek Trail

Tallys Creek Trail

41

Richardson Creek Trail

Mills Branch

pond

Halford Road

rocky ridge top

Clear Springs

Clear Springs Lake

Mills Branch Trail

Halford Road

FR 124

Mills Branch Trail

HOMOCHITTO NATIONAL FOREST

Richardson Creek

FR 187F

Mill Branch

Mills Branch Trail

Finding the trailhead: From Meadville, take U.S. Highway 84 west for 6 miles to Clear Springs Road. Turn left on Clear Springs Road and follow it 3.9 miles to the Clear Springs trailhead, on your left, just before passing the campground entrance kiosk. *DeLorme: Mississippi Atlas & Gazetteer:* Page 54 B3. GPS trailhead coordinates: N31 25' 47.00" / W90 59' 0.34".

The Hike

Leave the Clear Springs trailhead to meet the Tallys Creek Trail. Curve left beneath the parking area to shortly bisect paved Clear Springs Road. Slice downward through a drainage to meet the Richardson Creek Trail at 0.8 mile. Turn left and follow spring branches a short distance where they join Richardson Creek. A sheer bluff rises from Richardson Creek just above the confluence with the spring branches, which form small falls as they tumble into the bigger stream. Turn downstream along Richardson Creek to span it on a sturdy iron truss bridge. Turn left here, heading downstream as the upper part of the Richardson Creek Trail heads upstream. Bridge a feeder branch of Richardson Creek.

Notice blackened trunks on many trailside trees. The Forest Service keeps this area under a three-year prescribed burn cycle, to maintain the characteristics of a natural forest and to improve red cockaded woodpecker habitat. A few decades ago, woodpecker habitat had shrunk and the Homochitto National Forest began to manipulate the forest to improve habitat, including using prescribed burns. The number of red cockaded woodpecker nesting "clusters" has more than doubled as a result.

The trail winds away from Richardson Creek, reaching a clearing at 1.0 mile. An oil tank stands above the path, which reenters nearly pure pine woods. You may hear an engine running in the woods before crossing Forest Road 102 B-1. The engine is running a nearby oil well. Mississippi is doing its part for American energy independence—more than 75 percent of the national forest oil wells of the Magnolia State are in the Homochitto. (FYI: Mississippi ranks thirteenth by state in oil production. This includes offshore drilling as well as on terra firma, in places like the Homochitto National Forest. Over 4,000 wells are in operation.)

Join streamside bluffs above Richardson Creek after crossing a forest road leading to the aforementioned oil well. Straddle a berm between Richardson Creek to the left and an overflow slough to the right, under beech and mountain laurel. When hiking, take your time to gaze from the bluffs down to the scenic stream as it winds between sandbars. All too soon turn away from Richardson Creek, tracing a feeder branch westerly.

The trail continues winding in the hills and hollows on the west side of Rich-ardson Creek, finally returning at 2.6 miles to the main stream by a high bluff. Immediately traverse a costly curved bridge. You are very close to the Clear Springs Recreation Area—it is just across Richardson Creek yet out of sight. Here, the trail leaves the creek to make a large loop, winding through hills and ultimately keeping westerly, bisecting deep, ravine-like tributaries where vegetation grows lush in sum-mer, forming mini ecosystems in their cool depths. Smaller bluffs allow good views into these ravines. Cruise the edge of young pines to pass a small pond at 4.6 miles. Reach a most westerly point before turning east where Halford Road, Forest Road 144, comes into view. Roughly parallel the road, passing through a red cockaded woodpecker nesting area.

At 5.5 miles, the path nearly doubles back on itself on a steep hill. Note the exposed boulders here on this hilltop, unusual for the Homochitto. Snake between shallow intermittent drainages, emerging onto Halford Road at 6.5 miles. Turn left here and cross Richardson Creek on the road bridge. Beyond the bridge the trail leads right as a singletrack path, crossing a clear stream then climbing to intersect the Mills Branch Trail at 6.8 miles. Here, you have two choices: Stay left and shortcut the loop, or turn right for the longer, more scenic route. It's worth it. Continue on singletrack now on the blue-signed Mills Branch Trail, which nearly curves back on itself. You'll see where you were hiking several minutes earlier.

Return to Richardson Creek. The waterway has gained size and volume since you last saw it and is quite alluring. The bottoms are lush with musclewood. Leave the scenic waterway for good at 7.5 miles, climbing into laurel oak, sparkleberry, and pine. Sparkleberry is a shrubby tree that also needs controlled burns for best habitat. Top out to cross Forest Road 187F at 8.0 miles. Descend away from the forest road to cross the upper reaches of Mills Branch, still keeping easterly; enter an area of widely spaced mature pines extending their large green crowns skyward. The wide-open understory can be brushy if it hasn't been subject to a burn in a few years. The trail stays in big pines as it turns north. Reach the other end of the Mills Branch Trail at 9.5 miles, then come to Halford Road. Turn right and briefly follow Halford Road before crossing it.

The Mills Branch Trail keeps north to meet the Tallys Creek Trail at 9.8 miles. To complete the loop, join the Tallys Creek Trail, which continues along a piney ridge. Dip into a wet area where the path bridges feeder branches flowing into Clear Springs Lake. Pass a spur trail leading left to the campground before beginning your final ascent. The trailhead comes into sight as the path levels off. Complete the loop at 10.5 miles.

Miles and Directions

0.0 Start at Clear Springs Recreation Area trailhead. Follow trail leading away from parking area.

0.8 Meet the Richardson Creek Trail after crossing Clear Springs Road.

1.0 Pass by a hilltop oil tank in a clearing.

2.6 Come alongside Richardson Creek at a bluff. Traverse a costly wooden bridge.

4.6 Pass a trailside pond near most westerly point of loop.

5.5 Pass interesting exposed boulders atop a hill.

6.5 Use Halford Road Bridge to cross Richardson Creek.

6.8 Intersect the Mills Branch Trail. Stay right for longer, more scenic loop.

7.5 Leave Richardson Creek for good, climbing into pines.

8.0 Cross Forest Road 187F.

9.5 Intersect the other end of the Mills Branch Trail to soon cross Halford Road a second time.

9.8 Join Tallys Creek Trail.

10.5 Complete the hiking loop and immediately arrive back at the trailhead.

More Information

Local Information

Franklin County Economic Development, P.O. Box 663, Meadville, MS 39653; (601) 384-2453; www.meadvillems.com.

Local Events/Attractions

Homochitto River. This river flows through the heart of the Homochitto National Forest. Ernest Herndon, in his book *Canoeing Mississippi,* calls the 7-mile float from Eddiciton to Bude "the prettiest on the river . . . with water so clear at times it's like floating on air." However, beware the shifting sands on the river. Yet, the large sandbars that form make for good camping spots. Herndon's book details put-ins and take-outs the length of the Homochitto and is a great resource for paddling not only this river, but also all the significant waterways of the Magnolia State.

42 Tallys Creek Loop

This is the longest loop in the Clear Springs trail system, based in the Homochitto National Forest. Be prepared for a hilly and adventurous trek, as this loop dips into sandy spring drainages nestled between pine–oak hills. After leaving the recreation area and the other trails, the Tallys Creek Trail strikes out on its own, looping through remote forest terrain. Backpackers can do this as an overnight loop or combine other trails in the Clear Springs Trail Complex to do a multi–night loop.

Start: Clear Springs Recreation Area trailhead
Distance: 11.1-mile loop
Approximate hiking time: 6 to 7 hours
Difficulty: Difficult
Trail surface: Roots, dirt, leaves, concrete riprap
Seasons: Fall through spring
Other trail users: Mountain bicyclists
Canine compatibility: Leashed dogs permitted
Land status: National forest

Nearest town: Meadville
Fees and permits: Recreation area parking fee
Schedule: Open year-round
Maps: Clear Springs Trail Complex; USGS maps: Meadville
Trail contacts: Homochitto National Forest, 1200 Highway 184 East, Meadville, MS 39653; (601) 384-5876; www.fs.fed.us/r8/mississippi/homochitto

Finding the trailhead: From Meadville, take U.S. Highway 84 west for 6 miles to Clear Springs Road. Turn left on Clear Springs Road and follow it 3.9 miles to the Clear Springs trailhead, on your left, just before passing the campground entrance kiosk. *DeLorme: Mississippi Atlas & Gazetteer:* Page 54 B3. GPS trailhead coordinates: N31 25' 47.00" / W90 59' 0.34".

The Hike

The trailhead has a mountain bike wash, map station, and large parking area. Immediately join a short spur that connects to the Tallys Creek Trail loop. Continue on an old roadbed beneath pines, oaks, and a few scattered tulip trees, descending a rocky ridge into moist drainages. Occasional plastic and more concrete riprap is laid across wet areas.

> Umbrella magnolia trees grow in the moist drainages of the Clear Springs hill country. Unlike Mississippi's state tree, the Southern magnolia, umbrella magnolias lose their leaves each year. They both produce copious, fragrant blooms. The white flowers of the umbrella magnolia range from 7 to 10 inches in size, and stand out in a spring forest. Clear Springs lies near the umbrella magnolia's southwesterly limit.

Pass a spur trail leading to Clear Springs Lake Campground. A boardwalk spans waters flowing into the recreation area lake, just downstream. These clear, sandy streamlets flowing between steep-sided ridges highlight southwest Mississippi's beauty. Sweetgums find their places in these hills, as they do throughout the Homochitto National Forest. Cane is a prominent understory throughout the forest here, even on the hillsides. Tallys Creek Trail joins a ridgeline to reach a trail junction at 0.8 mile. After seemingly searching out the most convoluted terrain, Tallys Creek Trail curves back north to pick up a long abandoned roadbed, judging by the size of the trees growing atop it. Descend to use three bridges spanning sandy streams. These watercourses are what cut these valleys and make it such a pretty place. At 1.9 miles, the path climbs into high pines. The Tallys Creek Trail mercifully levels off, making a ridgeline forest cruise.

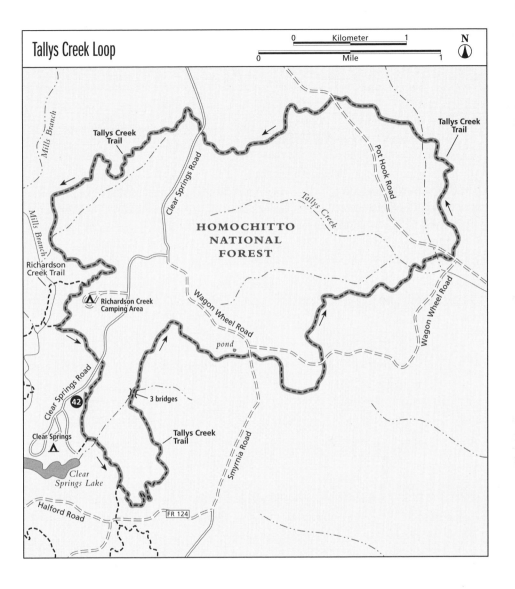

0   Kilometer   1

0   Mile   1

N

Tallys Creek
Trail

Mills Branch

Clear Springs Road

Pot Hook Road

Tallys Creek

Tallys Creek
Trail

HOMOCHITTO
NATIONAL
FOREST

Mills Branch

Richardson
Creek Trail

Richardson Creek
Camping Area

Wagon Wheel Road

Wagon Wheel Road

pond

Clear Springs Road

42

3 bridges

Tallys Creek
Trail

Smyrnia Road

Clear Springs

Clear
Springs Lake

Halford Road

FR 124

Reach a high point—nearly 400 feet—then turn easterly. The easy ridge walking is interrupted as the trail dives to bridge yet another sandy stream. Of course, this is followed by a climb. Watch for a pond on trail left then cross Smyrnia Road at 3.0 miles. Make Wagon Wheel Road at 3.7 miles. Span a curved trail bridge before coming alongside sandy Tallys Creek. Sandbars along the watercourse open the canopy overhead and brighten the woods. Emerge onto gravel Pot Hook Road at 5.1 miles. Ascend from the bottoms to do a little ridge running, undulating through low hills, meandering northwesterly into sizable pines.

Reach and cross Pot Hook Road for a second time at 6.6 miles. Undulate westerly, shortly bridging a small stream on a narrow singletrack path. A young forest then closes tightly on the trail. A clearing to the right of the path contrasts with the darker woods through which you travel. Hard work went into building this snaky trail section. Cross paved Clear Springs Road, the road upon which you drove to access the trailhead, at 7.7 miles.

Come alongside a tributary of Mills Branch and parallel it downstream. Look for mountain laurel and holly in this watershed. At times you travel a bluff well above the stream, an eye-pleasing vantage. All too soon climb away from the picturesque rivulet, only to shortly lose elevation you just gained, bridging more alluring spring branches, for which this area is named. Reach your first junction with Richardson Creek Trail at 10.1 miles. Dip to another clear spring branch, then reach the second junction with the Richardson Creek Trail. Climb along one last creek to bisect Clear Springs Road at 10.8 miles. Roughly parallel the road to make the entire Tallys Creek Loop. A final few backtrack steps complete the hike.

Add to your outdoor experience with a camping trip at Clear Springs Recreation Area. It offers a twenty-two-site developed campground, along with a second primitive camping area for tent campers. A shower house at the developed camp area is an oasis of cleanliness after a long hike. Clear Springs Lake also has a swim area and picnic shelter. A short, hiking-only trail circles the lake. The Richardson Creek/Mills Branch Loop, part of the Clear Springs Trail Complex, is also in this area.

Miles and Directions

0.0   Start at Clear Springs Recreation Area trailhead. Follow trail leading away from parking area.

0.8   Mills Branch Trail leads right. Stay left here on Tallys Creek Trail, signed in yellow, as the Mills Branch Trail, signed in blue, continues forward. Here, the Tallys Creek Trail splits away from the trail complex and begins its large loop into a remote area of the national forest.

3.0   Cross Smyrnia Road. The singletrack path resumes in an easterly direction. Forest Road 186B, Wagon Wheel Road, is visible in the distance. You will soon be crossing it, but first must bisect a deep drainage. This streamlet, like most others, has an alluring camping flat beside it.

3.7   Cross Wagon Wheel Road. Enter pine-dominated woodland while aiming for Tallys Creek. Laurel oaks increase in number as you enter the Tallys Creek valley.

5.1   Cross Pot Hook Road. (FYI: This is the low point of the loop. Bridge a second stream just after the road. Note the tupelo trees at the water's edge.)

6.6   Cross Pot Hook Road a second time.

7.7   Cross Clear Springs Road. Resume singletrack travel, zigzagging southwesterly through typical ridgetop pine-oak woods, now in the Mills Branch drainage. The ridge along which Clear Springs Road travels marked the dividing line.

10.1 Reach first intersection with Richardson Creek Trail. Tallys Creek Trail keeps forward, climbing. Top out below Richardson Creek primitive camping area. Spur trails lead up to it.

10.8 Cross Clear Springs Road a second time.

11.1 Arrive back at the trailhead.

More Information

Local Information
Franklin County Economic Development, P.O. Box 663, Meadville, MS 39653; (601) 384-2453; www.meadvillems.com.

Local Events/Attractions
Homochitto River. This river flows through the heart of the Homochitto National Forest. Ernest Herndon, in his book *Canoeing Mississippi,* calls the 7-mile float from Eddiciton to Bude "the prettiest on the river . . . with water so clear at times its like floating on air." However, beware the shifting sands on the river. Yet, the large sandbars that form make for good camping spots. Herndon's book details put-ins and take-outs the length of the Homochitto and is a great resource for paddling not only this river, but also all the significant waterways of the Magnolia State.

43 Magnolia Trail at Saint Catherine Creek National Wildlife Refuge

This hiking trail, composed of three loops, meets one of the stated goals of Saint Catherine Creek National Wildlife Refuge "to provide opportunities for wildlife oriented recreation and environmental education." Here, you can enjoy a gravel track that winds through hills extending toward the Mississippi River. It explores varied environments, including cypress ponds, bluffs, and creeks. At one point it leads to a photography blind, where you can observe waterfowl. Interpretive signage enhances the experience.

Start: Magnolia Trail parking area
Distance: 3.6-mile double loop
Approximate hiking time: 1.5 to 2 hours
Difficulty: Moderate
Trail surface: Gravel
Seasons: Fall through spring
Other trail users: Hikers only
Canine compatibility: Leashed dogs permitted
Land status: National wildlife refuge

Nearest town: Natchez
Fees and permits: No fees or permits required
Schedule: Open year-round
Maps: USGS maps: Buck Island
Trail contacts: Saint Catherine Creek National Wildlife Refuge, P.O. Box 217, Sibley, MS 39165; (601) 442-6696; www.fws.gov/saintcatherinecreek

Finding the trailhead: From the intersection of U.S. Highway 61 and U.S. Highway 84 in Natchez, take US 61 south for 11.6 miles to the signed right turn onto York Road. Follow York Road for 2 miles to Pintail Lane. Turn left on Pintail Lane. Keep going for 1.6 miles to reach the trailhead parking on your left. *DeLorme: Mississippi Atlas & Gazetteer:* Page 53 B8. GPS trailhead coordinates: N31 20' 40.0" / W91 25' 26.9".

The Hike

This trail system may be expanded by the time you get here, connecting to the relocated refuge headquarters, north of the trail's most northerly loop. From the main trailhead, begin hiking on a wide gravel track bordered by grass. Soon reach your first junction. Stay right here. The other way will be your return route. The path shortly becomes shaded. Pass the cypress overlook—it is an observation area to the right of the trail where you can peer into a swampy wetland.

The trailside trees have signs identifying them. Stay right at the next junction, climbing into the Loess Hills. Another junction comes; if you stay right here, it dead-ends but leads to a bluff view west, toward the Mississippi River. The third junction splits right to the trailside photography blind. The wooden structure with small observation slits overlooks a pond. This is a tangible part of the refuge's stated goal—providing an opportunity for wildlife-oriented recreation. The refuge's other goals are: "Provide and maintain optimum habitat for migratory waterfowl in the Mississippi Flyway; provide habitat and protection for endangered species including the bald eagle; and provide habitat for a natural diversity of wildlife and plant species."

The waterfowl observation area has signage with pictures of what waterfowl you may see. Friends of Saint Catherine Creek National Wildlife Refuge are partially responsible for the construction of this trail and interpretive information, so give them a thank you. Backtrack to the main loop, now turning north on an elevated track beside a sometimes-submerged wetland to make yet another junction. Stay right, enter loblolly pines, and begin undulating in hills, bridging dry washes.

You are nearly back to the trailhead. However, if you've come this far you might as well enjoy the entire hike. So turn right yet again, now on a level track. The forest changes to almost exclusively hardwoods in this section. Flora identification signs continue. The hills continue as well. Occasional contemplation benches are situated throughout the trail system, not only for rest but to observe wildlife. Sometimes, it is best to be still and let wildlife come to you. The trail comes very near Pintail Lane and reaches the northern loop of the hike. Cruise near the former refuge headquarters before turning away and curving to dip into bottomland. The Fish and Wildlife Service has installed a trailside rope to help hikers navigate the steep descent. You may see a few Southern magnolias here. Oddly enough, there aren't many magnolias on this trail despite the name. Come alongside a tributary of the Homochitto River, which flows into the Mississippi River on the south side of the refuge. Bridge the tributary and make up the elevation you just lost. Level out to enjoy an upland

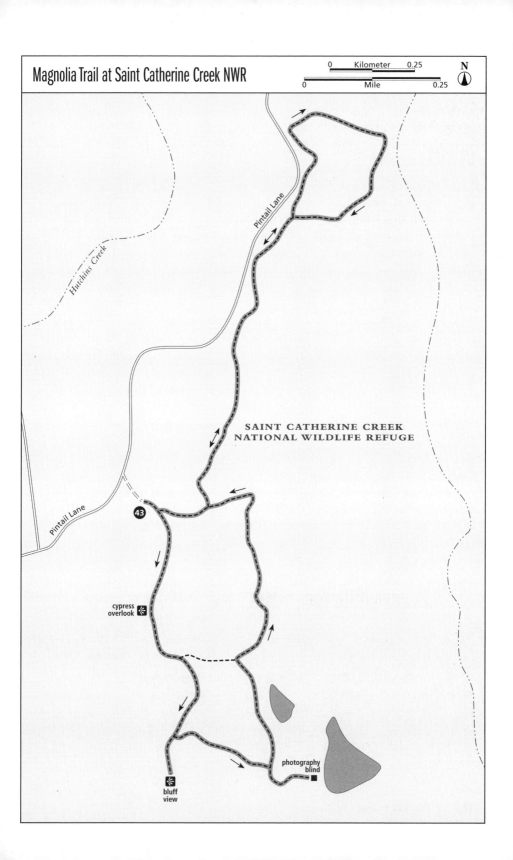

Magnolia Trail at Saint Catherine Creek NWR

0   Kilometer   0.25

0   Mile   0.25

N

Pintail Lane

Hutchins Creek

SAINT CATHERINE CREEK
NATIONAL WILDLIFE REFUGE

Pintail Lane

43

cypress
overlook

photography
blind

bluff
view

hardwood cruise. Scattered clearings create wildlife openings—they enhance the possibility of seeing nature's beasts. This truly is a wildlife refuge—I've seen deer and turkey while here on the trail. After completing this last, most northerly loop, backtrack to the trailhead. While here, consider checking out some of the other parts of this 24,000-plus-acre refuge, including visiting Wildlife Drive.

Miles and Directions

0.0   Start at Magnolia Trail parking area. Follow gravel track southeast. Stay right at immediate junction.

0.4   Reach junction and stay right. Climb into hills.

0.5   Trail leading right dead-ends but offers westerly views toward Mississippi River.

0.9   Spur trail leading right heads to wildlife photography blind.

1.3   Stay right at junction.

1.7   Complete the lower loop. Stay right again, now heading north into woodland.

2.3   Reach northern loop near Pintail Lane.

3.0   Complete northern loop. Backtrack toward the trailhead.

3.6   Stay right here, arriving back at the parking area.

More Information

Local Information
The Natchez Convention & Visitors Bureau, 640 S. Canal Street, Box C, Natchez, MS 39120; (601) 446-6345; www.visitnatchez.com.

Local Events/Attractions
Antebellum Homes of Natchez. The architecturally significant antebellum homes are a primary attraction of this historic city founded in 1716. This Mississippi River town has a long history. Especially appealing to us hikers, many of the historic attractions in downtown are within walking distance of one another.

44 Bogue Chitto Water Park

This hike travels through the woods and wetlands along the Bogue Chitto River with waterfalls, swamps, and vistas all packed into one trek. It consists of two loops, one of which travels on bluffs overlooking the Bogue Chitto and another which bisects wetlands, including one stretch that offers numerous boardwalks. The loops have multiple cross trails and junctions, but the whole area is small, so even if you get lost you won't be lost for long. The cross trails provide additional hiking opportunities if you want to extend your mileage on this relatively short trek.

Start: Bogue Chitto River boat ramp
Distance: 1.7-mile lollipop
Approximate hiking time: 1 to 1.5 hours
Difficulty: Easy
Trail surface: Dirt, leaves, roots
Seasons: Year-round
Other trail users: Hikers only
Canine compatibility: Leashed dogs permitted

Land status: State water park
Nearest town: McComb
Fees and permits: Entry fee required
Schedule: Open year-round
Maps: USGS maps: Holmesville
Trail contacts: Bogue Chitto Water Park, 1068 Dogwood Trail, McComb, MS 39648; (601) 684-9568; www.boguechittowaterpark.com

Fall leaves color wetland boardwalk

Finding the trailhead: From exit 15 on Interstate 55, take U.S. Highway 98 east for 12.6 miles to reach Connerly Drive. You'll pass through the town of McComb on the way. Turn right on Connerly Drive and pass numerous river outfitters to end after 1.2 miles at Bogue Chitto Water Park. Pass the park entrance station and continue forward for 0.2 mile to a stop sign and left toward the boat ramp. The trail starts on the downstream side of the river under an archway. *DeLorme: Mississippi Atlas & Gazetteer:* Page 55 E10. GPS trailhead coordinates: N31 9' 45.8" / W90 16' 44.3".

The Hike

On the way in you will see various signs pointing you toward nature trails here at the park—there are multiple trailheads—but head to the boat ramp for the longest possible loop. You will follow the Connector Trail a short distance to the River Trail, then cross a park road and join the Billie Jane Trail double loop. Seemingly just for confusion's sake, there are two trailheads at the boat ramp. Both have a trail map at their access and archways that lead to the main trail system. Start at the one with the map that is the farthest away from the river. Pass under the trailhead gate. The Bogue Chitto River is off to your left. You are atop a bluff overlooking the waterway. In summer, many tubers, kayakers, and canoers will be floating by.

Pass an outdoor amphitheater to shortly reach a tributary of the Bogue Chitto, which cuts off the bluff. This side stream is falling steeply and loudly as it bisects the bluff, following gravity's orders. The Connector Trail turns up the stream and you can see as well as hear these cascades—nothing big really, but music to the ears of trail travelers in this part of the state. Meet a spur trail leading right toward the park's covered pavilion. Stay left here and immediately bridge that noisy feeder branch you've been traveling alongside.

The River Trail offers two different environments in its loop—river bluff and hurricane-affected woodland. Stay right here on the River Trail and travel on the grassy track through a forest of oaks, dogwood, maple sweetgum, and tall pine, with numerous intact trees standing proud among the toppled ones. The trail canopy will be renewed over time and the trailbed will revert from grass to duff fallen from the canopy-creating trees.

The path then joins the Billie Jane Trail. This is an alternate trailhead and also has restrooms. If all the junctions prove confusing, stay right and you will do the longest loop. Note the wetland off to your right on the Billie Jane Trail. Cross several boardwalks before leaving the wetland in storm-damaged forest. You'll see many toppled trees in this area, too. After rejoining the River Trail you will travel under lush intact woodland, then come to a bluff overlooking the Bogue Chitto. A large waterside sandbar shines brightly through the screen of trees. Occasional open overlooks avail a view of this clear stream 30 feet below. You will soon again be hearing the tributary branch as it noisily drops to meet the Bogue Chitto River. Complete the River Trail and meet the Connector Trail. The sight and sounds of these falls are a bonus for hikers. Bridge the tributary and return to the trailhead. Thank the Pike County Board of Supervisors and the Pearl River Basin Development District for developing these paths.

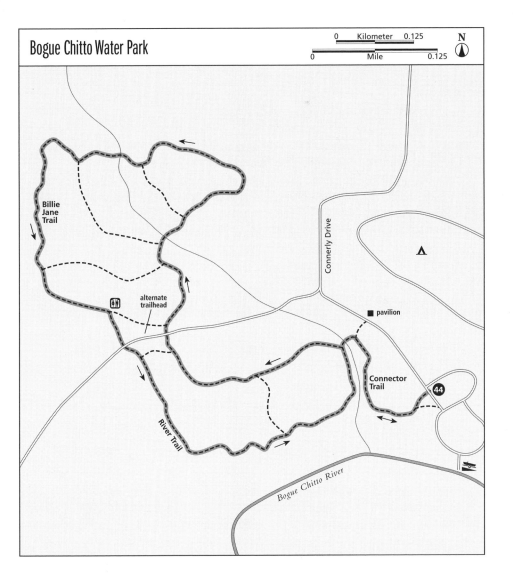

Bogue Chitto Water Park

Billie Jane Trail

Connerly Drive

alternate trailhead

pavilion

Connector Trail

44

River Trail

Bogue Chitto River

Bogue Chitto Water Park also has a campground. You can get campsites with hookups or primitive sites located in a well-shaded forest of laurel oaks and sweetgums. You can also picnic, swim, or fish. However, canoeing the Bogue Chitto is the most popular pastime. See the outfitter information below if you are interested in combining your hike with a canoe trip.

Miles and Directions

0.0 Start at the boat ramp. Two archways soon connect and you begin to follow the Connector Trail on a bluff above the Bogue Chitto River.

0.2 Intersect the spur trail leading right to a covered pavilion. Cross a feeder branch then intersect the River Trail. Stay right on the River Trail.

0.3 Pass a junction on your left, which cuts the River Trail in half.

0.4 River Trail loop cuts left just before this hike crosses the park road. Keep forward beyond park road and pass under an archway, now on the Billie Jane Trail.

0.5 Pass first junction shortcutting Billie Jane Trail, then cross several boardwalks over streams and swamp. Pass multiple junctions as the Billie Jane Trail has three shortcut paths bisecting its loop.

1.1 Reach a trail junction near restrooms. This is the end of the Billie Jane loop. Trail leading left goes to the alternate trailhead. Take the trail leading right to cross the park road and rejoin the River Trail.

1.3 After traveling through rich woods, the trail comes out atop the bluff above the Bogue Chitto River. Decent views can be had as spur trails extend to the edge of the bluff.

1.4 Pass the cross trail bisecting the River Trail. Soon curve away from the river along tributary with waterfalls along it.

1.5 Complete the River Trail. Cross the bridge over the tributary and backtrack to the trailhead.

1.7 Arrive back at the trailhead and boat ramp, completing the hike.

More Information

Local Information

Pike County Chamber of Commerce, 112 N. Railroad Boulevard, McComb, MS 39648; (601) 684-2291; www.pikeinfo.com.

Local Events/Attractions

Paddle the Bogue Chitto River, Ryals Tube and Canoe Rental, 1053 Dogwood Trail, McComb, MS 39648; (601) 684-4948; www.ryalscanoe.com. Multiple outfitters are stationed outside the water park, which abuts the Bogue Chitto River. You can even start your river trip from the very same spot as the hike trailhead!

45 Ethel Vance Natural Area Trails

Ethel Vance Natural Area is located on the banks of the West Fork Amite River in the extreme southwest portion of the state. Run by the city of Liberty, the seat of Amite County, this park features 10 miles of singletrack trails, popular with mountain bikers and hikers, traveling along the river and adjacent floodplains, as well as along the bluff above the river. Be apprised that the trail network is very convoluted and potentially confusing.

Start: Ethel Vance Natural Area trailhead
Distance: Approximate 10-mile loop
Approximate hiking time: 4.5 to 5 hours
Difficulty: Moderate
Trail surface: Dirt, leaves, roots, sand, mud
Seasons: Fall through spring
Other trail users: Mountain bicyclists
Canine compatibility: Leashed dogs permitted

Land status: City park
Nearest town: Liberty
Fees and permits: No fees or permits required
Schedule: Open year-round
Maps: USGS maps: Liberty
Trail contacts: City of Liberty, 160 Clinic Drive, Liberty, MS 39645; (601) 657-8077

Finding the trailhead: From Liberty, take Highway 24 west and go for 2 miles, then turn left into Ethel Vance Natural Area Park. If you cross the West Fork Amite River on Highway 24, then you have gone too far. Follow the recreation area road, passing the campground and livestock pavilion on your right. You will see the trailhead on your right marked with a post upon which stands a mountain bike. The trail starts at the edge of the woods. *DeLorme: Mississippi Atlas & Gazetteer:* Page 54 E4. GPS trailhead coordinates: N31 9' 28.9" / W90 50' 12.5".

The Hike

The trail system was laid out by and for mountain bikers. However, Mississippi hikers would be remiss to not pay this park a visit. The natural area, 700 acres in size, offers numerous components of a riverine ecosystem. For starters, there is the West Fork Amite River itself. It flows south toward Louisiana to meet the East Fork Amite River just before entering the Bayou State. The West Fork is a classic sandy coastal plain stream. It moves fast, shifts on occasion, and is choked with deadfall. Intrepid canoers occasionally float it but have to work around the logjams, which you will see on your hike, as a significant portion of the trail travels along the river.

Sloughs and bottoms stretch away from the Amite, and are the most common environment through which the trail system travels. Here, the silent and slow-moving black water is home to cypress and tupelo trees, bordered by taller oaks that grow in drier margins. The trail itself travels alongside these wetlands, bridging sloughs where needed and otherwise running back and forth among these water features.

West Fork Amite River has deadfall and sandbars aplenty

There is far more forest than water here, though water is a constant companion. Beyond the bottoms a tall bluff rises to the developed area of the park. The woods grow thick overhead, with heavy underbrush that adds to the confusion you may feel your first time or two here—it seems as if you are going in circles, and you nearly are. This is because the mountain bikers who laid out the trail system simply wanted to maximize the trail mileage within the parameters of the natural area. I can almost guarantee that you will get lost on your first trip. But don't let this be a deterrent. It's hard to stay lost for long here—you have the Amite River to your west and the main park road to your east separated by only a half-mile-wide area where this trail system lies. Furthermore, a roadbed runs through the trail system and can be a good hiking destination of its own or simply an "out route" if you get tired of winding back and forth.

The following description will get you started and down into the West Fork Amite River bottoms. After that, once you get into the maze, you are on your own. The westbound trail begins at the edge of the woods, a singletrack that immediately crosses the dry wash in dry, pine-oak woods with sparkleberry understory. After meandering through woods, it curves behind the livestock pavilion and campground. Needles and rocks and roots form the trailbed. Occasional beech and magnolia join the vegetational fray. Circle behind the campground along a steep bluff, dropping toward the Amite River to reach a junction. Here, a trail leads forward, dropping off the bluffs, but the main loop keeps curving around the campground before turning back west.

► Make a weekend of it at Ethel Vance. A campground is located within walking distance of the trailhead. It offers twenty campsites with water, electricity, and upright grills.

Come fairly close to Highway 24, skirting between a ball field and the highway. Parallel a power line before turning left into the woods, reaching the Amite River bottoms. Come along an old river meander from which rise tupelo and cypress trees. Bridge the meander, looking for bay trees. The evergreens are mostly bush size here and are found throughout the bottoms. This tupelo-cypress complex is among the ecosystems where bay trees are found.

Continue wandering through the bottom. If you are wondering where this trail is going, it is trying to make the most of the natural area and not going anywhere in particular. It seems you have entered a maze as the trail works around a profusion of sloughs. This

► Ernest Herndon, in his book *Canoeing Mississippi,* says the following about the Amite River: "I've floated it countless times but wouldn't recommend it to anyone since there's probably one log jam per 50 yards . . . there are a number of possible trips if you can stand the toil." He goes on to recommend various put-ins and take-outs, mentioning this particular section of river as "bordering the beautiful Ethel Stratton Vance Natural Area."

area is subject to sporadic flooding and needs the occasional overflows to remain in its natural state. You'll know when you reach the Amite River, as opposed to the other meanders. Its flow is much stronger than the other watery features. Sandbars stand on its edges and bends. It's a little over 3 miles before you come alongside the river. Travel downstream along the Amite, a favorite stretch of trail at Ethel Vance. Notice fallen trees across the river, which make this stretch of river tough for paddlers.

▶ Amite County borders Louisiana, and actually once tried to withdraw from the state of Mississippi and join the state of Louisiana in a dispute over locating the state university in Oxford. But it stayed in the Magnolia State and thus is part of this book.

You travel along a bluff above the river, but the riverbed has shifted. Therefore, the trail curves along an old, cypress-filled meander before returning to the flowing West Fork Amite. By now you have come alongside and/or crossed a mown roadbed that roughly parallels the watercourse. This is your exit in case you get tired of the convolutions or simply want to shortcut your hike.

You are on your own from here. Along the way you will repeatedly see other sections of the trail no more than 10 or 15 feet away running parallel to where you are currently hiking. When you see this, know that you were just there or you will soon be there. Again, if you become troubled or sick of it, just head east through the woods, or join the roadbed.

Miles and Directions

0.0   Start at Ethel Vance Natural Area trailhead. Follow singletrack path at the edge of the woods.

0.4   Reach junction and stay right, curving around the park campground.

1.2   Pass beside old ball field before reentering woods in bottomland.

3.2   Come alongside West Fork Amite River.

4.1   Turn away from river and hike along cypress slough.

4.5   Leave the Amite River for good. More trail convolutions lie ahead.

10.0 Arrive back at the trailhead if you successfully traverse all the trails once without doubling back.

More Information

Local Information

Amite County Economic Development Organization, P.O. Box 250, Liberty, MS 39645.

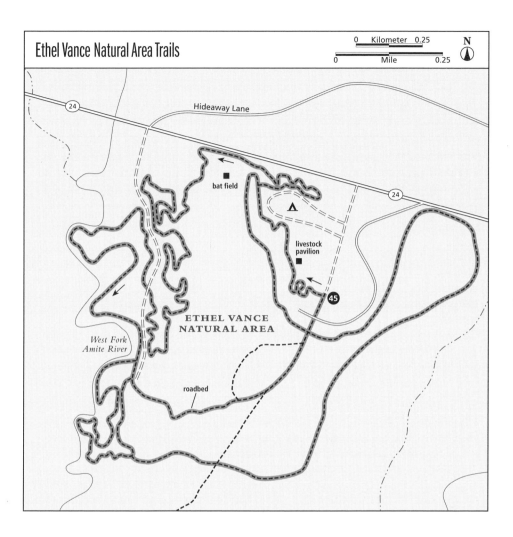

Ethel Vance Natural Area Trails

0   Kilometer   0.25

0   Mile   0.25

N

24

Hideaway Lane

bat field

24

livestock
pavilion

45

ETHEL VANCE
NATURAL AREA

*West Fork
Amite River*

roadbed

Local Events/Attractions

McComb Railroad Museum, 108 N. Railroad Boulevard, P.O. Box 7220, McComb, MS 39649-7220; (601) 684-2291; www.mcrrmuseum.com. Located in a refurbished circa 1901 train depot, this museum details the relationship between the railroads of southwest Mississippi and the founding of McComb. Includes oral and visual history displays, a model train, and more.

▶ Amite County's courthouse, located in Liberty, is the oldest continuously used courthouse in the state. It was finished in 1841.

46 Clark Creek Natural Area Loop

Clark Creek Natural Area is one of Mississippi's most special places. Located in the Tunica Hills just east of the Mississippi River, this 700-acre park is where Clark Creek and its tributaries offer over fifty waterfalls. The deep woodland is also home to state champion trees, such as the hop hornbeam and Mexican plum. Make a loop through the natural area, traveling incredibly steep trails past some of these waterfalls and also along spindly ridges and astride clear sandy streams. There's even a view or two from atop the ridges. Forewarning: This may be some of the toughest hiking in the entire state.

Start: Clark Creek Natural Area trailhead
Distance: 4.8-mile lollipop, plus side trails
Approximate hiking time: 4 to 4.5 hours
Difficulty: Difficult due to numerous steep climbs and descents
Trail surface: Gravel, dirt, leaves, roots, sand
Seasons: Fall through spring
Other trail users: Hikers only
Canine compatibility: No dogs allowed

Land status: State park
Nearest town: Woodville
Fees and permits: Parking fee required
Schedule: Open year-round
Maps: USGS maps: Fort Adams
Trail contacts: Clark Creek Natural Area, 366 Ft. Adams Pond Road, Woodville, MS 39669; (601) 888-6040; http://home.mdwfp.com/parks.aspx

Finding the trailhead: From the intersection of U.S. Highway 61 and Highway 24 in Woodville, take Highway 24 west a short distance to turn left at the signed turn for Pond, on Woodville-Pond Road. Follow Woodville-Pond Road for 14 miles to turn right onto the paved Fort Adams–Pond Road, immediately crossing a cattle guard, passing the Pond Store. Follow Fort Adams–Pond Road for 0.3 mile, then turn left to reach the trailhead. *DeLorme: Mississippi Atlas & Gazetteer:* Page 53 F7. GPS trailhead coordinates: N31 4' 18.4" / W91 30' 42.9".

The Hike

This loop first follows the Improved Trail for 1.4 miles, then picks up a narrow, natural surface footpath, the extremely rugged and aptly named Primitive Trail. Trail signs have been posted at important junctions along the trail system. Leave the parking area; follow the gravel road leading down to the right past a kiosk rather than the foot trail heading left. Enter a gate. The wide road-like track travels a narrow ridge to pass an overlook with a bench swing. Precipitous ravines below this oak-covered ridgeline will surprise. The trail descends. Steps have been installed beside the track on the steepest parts. Travel a second set of stairs on another sharp section to reach a stream and bridge at 0.5 mile. Here, the Primitive Trail leaves left—your return route.

Stay with the gravel path. Be vigilant as user-created spur trails split off the main track here. The Improved Trail spans another bridge and climbs steeply to reach the

One of many falls in Clark Creek Natural Area

first spur trail at 0.6 mile. Falls are audible from the junction. Drop 0.1 mile to these falls, which tumble 15 to 20 feet into a circular loess amphitheater. Wood steps lead down to the base of the falls. Continue on the Improved Trail to reach the second spur trail at 0.7 mile. Turn left here, making a precipitous descent to another cascade. Elaborate steps have been built here too, including an access to the top and bottom of the cataract. Note the sheer bluff below the falls and an amazing and massive rock garden through which the stream flows.

Continue on the now-undulating Improved Trail, among ferns, saw palmetto, vines, and a riot of vegetation. Clark Creek Natural Area is a place where "if it ain't movin' something's growin' on it." Pass the third spur trail leading left at 0.8 mile. It leads a quarter-mile to a Clark Creek tributary. The Improved Trail circles around a steep hill in junglesque woodland, before picking up a westbound ridgeline where you can look into the canopy of trees beyond. Reach a little storm shelter at 1.2 miles. An abundance of cedars grow here. A stilled hiker will hear waterfalls spilling from Clark Creek north of the ridge. The vast majority of cascades here are either completely off trail or accessed via unmaintained, user-created paths that can be slippery and often treacherous. The Improved Trail narrows into a rocky spine, finally reaching stairs entering a deep, lush chasm through which Clark Creek flows. Upon reaching the bottom at 1.4 miles, arrive at a small falls where the stream

▶ **This most pristine of Mississippi state parks was established in 1978. Several entities came together to preserve the tract, including not only the state but also International Paper Company, which donated most of the land. The Nature Conservancy also helped with acquisition.**

cuts deeper into the floor day by day. This is a confusing area, as trail conditions go instantly from ultra-maintained to barely followable. To join the Primitive Trail and continue the loop, stay on the east side of the creek and begin heading downstream. Under normal conditions the stream is as clear as mountain waters of the Southern Appalachians or Ozarks. Many hikers head directly down the gravel creekbed. Take stream levels into account before doing this part of the trail. And don't get caught in a thunderstorm here, either. A faint trail runs astride the creek, but travels over fallen trees and irregular terrain.

At 1.7 miles, reach the confluence of Clark Creek with an unnamed major tributary. Beech trees thrive here. Posted land is just downstream. The Primitive Trail keeps forward, crossing the tributary and heading straight up the far bank. Look for white paint blazes on trees. The path becomes easier to follow while climbing away from the stream, then merges into a singletrack, clambering an insanely sheer slope to reach a storm shelter encircled by cane at 2.1 miles. From this vantage you can look south beyond the trees. During the warm season expect a symphony of birdsong to accompany you while hiking.

Clark Creek Natural Area Loop

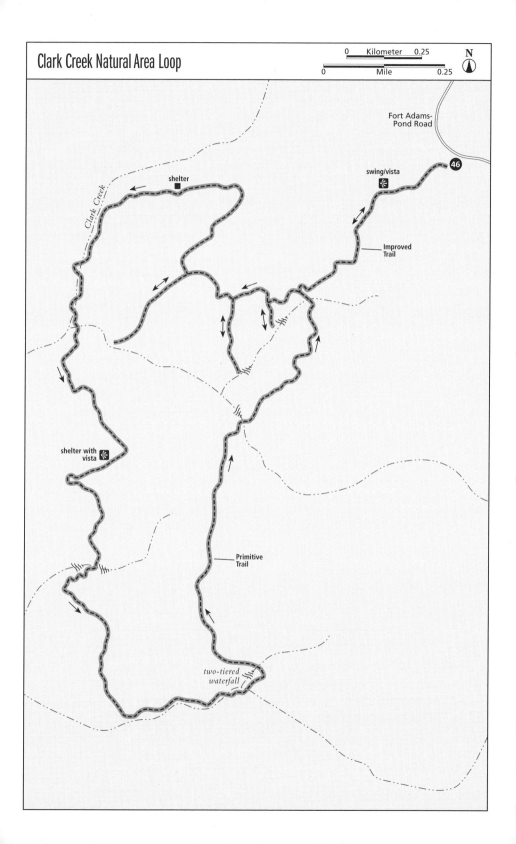

0 Kilometer 0.25
0 Mile 0.25

N

Fort Adams-
Pond Road

46

swing/vista

shelter

Clark Creek

Improved
Trail

shelter with
vista

Primitive
Trail

two-tiered
waterfall

Dim ranks of dense cane trace the descending path. At Clark Creek, neither the land nor the trails ever stay level for long. Eventually drop to water to make a waterfall at 2.4 miles—a vertical ribbon drop. A second falls just downstream plummets into a rock gorge. Keep scrambling south, descending to another tributary at 2.8 miles. Travel east on a sheer loess bluff overlooking one of Clark Creek's largest tributaries. Beech flats border the stream beyond the bluff. The Primitive Trail crisscrosses this tributary, keeping upstream. Your travel will take you through beech flats or in the creekbed. If you're like most hikers, you will use both. Reach a point where a tributary splits right and the trail traces a steep eroded incline. Level off as a path leads forward to posted land, while the Primitive Trail drops left to the top of a waterfall at 3.2 miles. The reason this trail climbs so much and then drops is to get around this fern-draped, two-tier cascade. Unfortunately, it is hard to gain a good look at this falls without endangering yourself.

The trail mostly climbs from the falls—no surprise—and surmounts a slender cane-crowded ridgeline. At 3.8 miles, reach a stream and a heard-before-seen waterfall. This is the father of all trailside waterfalls at Clark Creek Natural Area. It drops about 30 feet over a rock lip into a half-cathedral where scattered rocks and gravel lie below. The cathedral down here will be quite cool in the warmer months.

The Primitive Trail crosses the stream just above the big falls, rising hand over fist before evolving into your average Clark Creek lung-buster climb. Amazingly, it levels off for once, before meeting the Improved Trail. Complete the loop portion of the hike at 4.3 miles. From here it is a half-mile uphill backtrack to the trailhead.

Miles and Directions

0.0 Start at Clark Creek Natural Area trailhead. Follow gravel track leading downhill from parking area. (FYI: A picnic area and restrooms are located at the trailhead, but overnight camping is not allowed.)

0.5 Reach a stream and the Primitive Trail. Stay on the gravel path.

0.6 Spur trail leads left to a falls.

0.7 Second spur trail leads left to another falls.

0.8 Third spur trail leads left to tributary.

1.2 Pass small wooden storm shelter.

1.7 Leave Clark Creek at the confluence with a tributary.

2.1 Reach second storm shelter with southerly view through the trees.

2.4 Pass above a pair of waterfalls.

3.2 Pass above a two-tiered waterfall.

3.8 Reach a 30-foot superlative waterfall.

4.3 Complete Primitive Trail; backtrack toward trailhead on the Improved Trail.

4.8 Arrive back at the trailhead.

More Information

Local Information

Woodville/Wilkinson County Main Street Association, P.O. Box 1546, Woodville, MS 39669; (601) 888-3998.

Local Events/Attractions

Pond Store, 182 Fort Adams–Pond Rd, Woodville, MS 39669; (601) 888-4426. Located just 0.3 mile from the Clark Creek trailhead, historic Pond Store has been an area landmark since 1881. A trip into the wooden structure takes you back in time, when this spot was part of a cotton-hauling route. Livestock were watered at the built pond while pulling cotton over the steep hills from here to the Mississippi River. A store and post office was erected and has stood the test of time. Stop by and peruse. They also offer overnight cabin rental.

47 Black Creek Trail: Brooklyn to Moodys Landing

This hike covers a 4.2-mile section of the 41-mile Black Creek Trail. It runs along the course of the federally designated wild and scenic Black Creek, amid cypress swamps, by sugar white sandbars, and through hardwood forests. Caney tributaries feed Black Creek, and you will cross them by boardwalks and footbridges. High bluffs offer vantages to enjoy Black Creek. Other areas will reflect the damaged woodlands left after Hurricane Katrina.

Start: Forest Road 319 F-1 near Brooklyn
Distance: 4.2 miles one way, 8.4 miles out-and-back
Approximate hiking time: 2 to 3 hours one way
Difficulty: Moderately difficult due to rugged terrain and trailside brush
Trail surface: Leaves, needles, sand
Seasons: Fall through spring
Other trail users: Hikers only

Canine compatibility: Leashed dogs permitted
Land status: National forest
Nearest town: Brooklyn
Fees and permits: No fees or permits required
Schedule: Open year-round
Maps: Black Creek De Soto National Forest; USGS maps: Bond Pond, Janice
Trail contacts: De Soto National Forest, 654 West Frontage Road, Wiggins, MS 39577; (601) 528-6160; www.fs.fed.us/r8/mississippi

Finding the trailhead: From the main intersection in Brooklyn, head east on Main Street, immediately crossing railroad tracks. Continue for 0.3 mile, then stay right at the split, now on Ashe Nursery Road (the left split is Brooklyn-to-Janice Road, which you use to reach Moodys Landing). Continue on Ashe Nursery Road for 0.9 mile, then turn left on now paved Pete Anderson Road, FR 319 F-1. Follow Pete Anderson Road for 0.7 mile, then veer left on gravel Forest

Road 319-I and follow it for 0.4 mile. Here, the Black Creek Trail leaves left. Look for the white plastic diamonds. To reach Moodys Landing, backtrack toward Brooklyn, this time turning right on Brooklyn-to-Janice Road, and follow it for 6 miles to the signed camping area and boat launch on your right. *DeLorme: Mississippi Atlas & Gazetteer:* Page 58 G2. GPS trailhead coordinates: N31 3' 59.9" / W89 9' 32.2".

Backpacker spans clear sandy tributary of Black Creek

The Hike

This section of trail begins its downstream trip in remote Mississippi woodlands. If you are interested in making this a one-way hike, be apprised that it requires a ford of Black Creek. You will know you're at Moodys Landing and the end of the hike when you see a large sandbar across the river from a high bluff you stand upon. An auto-accessible parking area will be above the sandbar. An 8.4-mile there-and-back trek can be done in one day, so the ford at Moodys Landing can be easily avoided. Along the way, make sure you stay with the white plastic diamonds as user-created forest trails and faint woods roads occasionally intersect the Black Creek Trail and may prove confusing.

Leave the forest road and aim easterly for Black Creek. After reaching the waterway the Black Creek Trail cuts across steep ravines divided by pine bluffs. Some of the promontories extend a good 50 feet above the river. The path will dip into some ravines, whereas others will be spanned with high bridges. The trail was cleared with heavy equipment—the only way after the hurricane—and it has become wide and brushy in many places. Briars can be troublesome in sunny spots. But give it time. It will improve and it needs hikers to help keep it open.

About halfway along the trek to Moodys Landing, the Black Creek experience is seemingly concentrated in one area. Here, you pass along a swamp to your right with the river to the left, then bridge a steeply cut ravine where a clear stream speeds below. Just beyond this the trail ascends sharply to a pine bluff where you can look upon Black Creek. It's hard to pack so many environments in one short distance but somehow this scenic area does it. Of course, just a few feet in elevation changes the forest types here.

The trail continues to stay close to Black Creek. The forest continues to stay brushy and scraggly as well. Hurricane Katrina did a good job. However, plenty of magnolias and other trees survived along the river and elsewhere along Black Creek. Beech trees are common also. Since much of the tree canopy was torn down, it is striking to see the surviving beech and magnolia standing tall and alone in sunny woods, as opposed to their natural environment in shadier situations. You will also see fallen trunks and limbs galore, as well as broken-off trunks still reaching skyward and waiting for the day when they will topple to decompose and become part of a future magnificent forest along this watercourse. But for now, the more open the forest the more brush with which you contend. The Forest Service will be working over this trail more in future years, and use by the public will help keep it open as well.

► Look for mountain laurel, with its pinkish-white April blooms, alongside the trail. This small tree or bush has reddish bark and waxy green leaves.

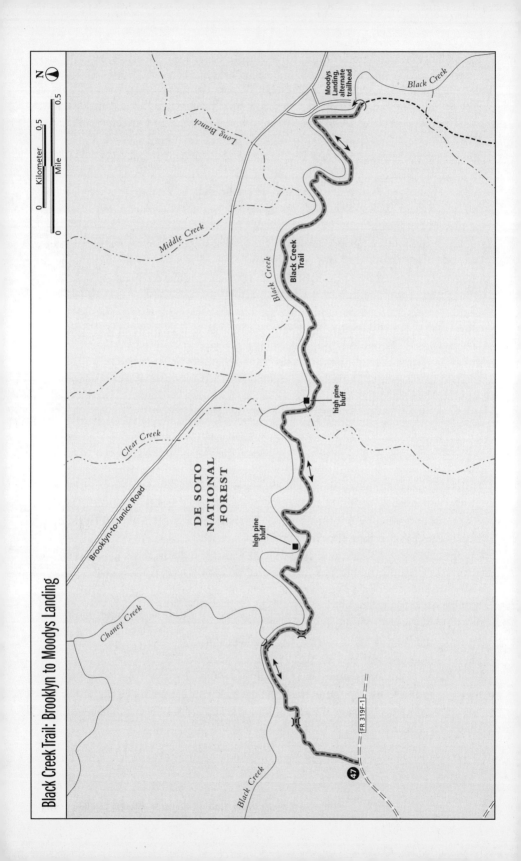

Black Creek Trail: Brooklyn to Moodys Landing

N

0   Kilometer   0.5

0   Mile   0.5

Black Creek

Moodys
Landing,
alternate
trailhead

Long Branch

Middle Creek

Black Creek

Black Creek
Trail

high pine
bluff

Clear Creek

Brooklyn-to-Janice Road

DE SOTO
NATIONAL
FOREST

high pine
bluff

Chaney Creek

Black Creek

FR 319F-1

47

Upon reaching Moodys Landing, you may change your mind about making the ford. I have seen Black Creek low and high. Go with your gut instinct concerning the ford. The river will be higher in winter and spring and lower in fall. Another alternative is to drive to Moodys Landing and assess the creek before you make your decision.

Miles and Directions

0.0 Start at FR 319 F-1. Leave the sandy road and enter woods.

0.4 Bridge a tributary of Black Creek.

0.6 Come alongside Black Creek. The trail generally stays near the creek the rest of the hike.

1.3 Reach a high pine bluff with clear streams both before and after it. This bluff saw little storm damage.

1.6 Trail makes a sharp right as a sandy forest road continues forward.

2.3 Bridge a stream, then climb to a high pine bluff with good views. Faint doubletrack forest road comes in here. Keep downstream along Black Creek.

2.6 Span a fast moving but small branch.

3.4 Sandbars come into view along the river.

4.2 Trail comes to a bluff overlooking the sandbar and boat launch at Moodys Landing. One-way hike requires a ford here. The best fording spot is upstream of the bluff across from Moodys Landing.

8.4 Arrive back at the trailhead if you opt for the out-and-back hike.

More Information

Local Information
Stone County Economic Development Partnership, P.O. Box 569, 419 S. Vardaman Street, Wiggins, MS 39577; (601) 928-5418; www.stonecounty.com.

Local Events/Attractions
Canoe Black Creek for over 40 miles through the De Soto National Forest. Black Creek Canoe Rental offers boat rentals and shuttles. They also shuttle hikers and backpackers on the Black Creek Trail. Black Creek Canoe Rental, P.O. Box 414, Brooklyn, MS 39425; (601) 582-8817; www.blackcreekcanoe.com.

48 Black Creek Trail from Janice Landing

The Black Creek Trail was the apex of hiking in the Magnolia State, but Hurricane Katrina damaged the trail. It will take a while before the reopened trail again reaches its full potential. However, the path is still a rewarding experience. It travels not only along the clear waterway and on bluffs above it, but also over side creeks and swamps spanned by boardwalks and footbridges. Open pine forests in the hill country that abut the Black Creek floodplain offer a final ecosystem to enjoy along the way.

Start: Janice Landing trailhead
Distance: 7.9 miles one way, 15.8 miles out-and-back
Approximate hiking time: 4.0 to 5.5 hours one way
Difficulty: Difficult due to distance, rugged terrain, and trailside brush
Trail surface: Leaves, needles, sand, dirt
Seasons: Winter through spring
Other trail users: Hikers only

Canine compatibility: Leashed dogs permitted
Land status: National forest
Nearest town: Brooklyn
Fees and permits: No fees or permits required
Schedule: Open year-round
Maps: Black Creek De Soto National Forest; USGS maps: Bond Pond, Janice
Trail contacts: De Soto National Forest, 654 West Frontage Road, Wiggins, MS 39577; (601) 528-6160; www.fs.fed.us/r8/mississippi

Finding the trailhead: From the junction of U.S. Highway 49 and Highway 26 at Wiggins, head east on Highway 26 for 0.9 mile to Highway 29. Head north on Highway 29 for 12.7 miles to the Black Creek trailhead parking on the left side of the road. This parking area is actually a short distance before the Janice Landing. To reach the Forest Road 319-G trailhead, head south on Highway 29 from the Black Creek trailhead for 0.8 mile to turn right on New York Road, FR 319. Follow New York Road for 4.9 miles to FR 319-G. Turn right on FR 319-G and follow it for 1.2 miles to the trail crossing. *DeLorme: Mississippi Atlas & Gazetteer:* Page 58 G2. GPS trailhead coordinates: N30 59' 16.1" / W89 3' 6.7".

The Hike

Black Creek itself is so visually appealing as to be a federally designated wild and scenic river, the only one in the state of Mississippi. It is along this creek that much of the trail travels, offering views of tea-colored waters that contrast with burning white sandbars. The Black Creek Trail, marked with white diamond blazes, initially runs in conjunction with the General Jackson Interpretive Trail. The woods are more open than not, a result of Katrina, which tore the forests apart. Where standing, the woods are rich with magnolia, beech, water oak, laurel oak, and pine.

▶ Andrew Jackson and his Tennessee Volunteer troops crossed Black Creek near Janice Landing during the War of 1812 en route to the Battle of New Orleans, decisively won by the Americans.

After Hurricane Katrina, the trailbed was widened as the Forest Service used heavy equipment to open the path. (The Black Creek Trail was closed for three years, from 2005 to 2008, after it was devastated by the hurricane.) Therefore, the woods are frequently scattered with more undergrowth because there's less tree cover. For the hiker this means the trail will be brushier on your legs, so consider wearing long pants. Winter hiking will minimize the situation. You will see fallen tree trunks, root wads, and debris pushed back from the path. This will decompose over time and the trail will once again become canopied throughout.

Overnight camping opportunities are nearly limitless on the Black Creek Trail. Water and flat spots are frequent. Many backpackers like to camp on the sandbars for scenery, breezes, and escape from the mosquitoes, which can be troublesome in late spring, early summer, and after thunderstorms. However, the shoulder seasons are ideal for trail travel, namely the months of March, April, October, and November. Winter is a very viable option. In summer, hot days, warm nights, and annoying insects keep most sane backpackers away. Hiker shuttles are available through Black Creek Canoe Rental, listed below.

Surveying hurricane damage along the trail

Black Creek Trail from Janice Landing

0   Kilometer   1

0   Mile   1

N

FR 319G

very long
boardwalk

Black Creek

hike ends at
FR 319G

multiple boardwalks
and swamps

boardwalk

bridge
sandy creek

FR 319G

boardwalk

Black Creek
Trail

Big Branch

FR 319H

FR 319N

29

FR 319

Thomas Bay Branch

New York Road

Black Creek

29

Janice
Landing

Blue Goose Branch

DE SOTO
NATIONAL
FOREST

FR 319

Janice Landing
Trailhead

P

48

Watch your footing as the terrain was made more uneven after the hurricane and the subsequent trail reopening. You'll occasionally see the old trail and white painted blazes. The path runs mostly level, except when it is near the river, where it undulates more. Watch for sandbars along Black Creek. The middle section stays along the river or bluffs above the river plain.

The final section climbs into the Red Hills. This is your first real ascent of the trip, still heading generally west. In wetter places watch for pitcher plants. The highest spots will have high pines with a yaupon understory. More pitcher plants may be seen on the long boardwalk just before arriving at FR 319-G. This is the end of this hike, but the Black Creek Trail continues westerly 15 miles to Big Creek landing.

Miles and Directions

0.0   Start at the Janice Landing trailhead, 0.3 mile south on Highway 29 of actual Janice Landing. At this point the trail is working its way back toward Black Creek from the trailhead.

0.4   Cross first of many boardwalks.

1.1   Come along Black Creek. Note the large magnolia trees. Soon reach a bluff availing a watery vista.

1.9   The trail turns westerly, eventually away from Black Creek. Pass over a couple of boardwalks.

3.2   Join a doubletrack heading north. Follow it 0.2 mile before dropping right toward Black Creek.

3.5   Bridge a deeply desiccated streambed and join a bluff.

4.3   Span a swampy tributary. Begin working around a cypress swamp, an old creek slough. Stay along river.

6.2   Begin section where you are working around swamps and over many boardwalks. Note how the cypress and tupelo trees in the swamps were not knocked over like the upland trees. Red maples grow astride these wet locales.

7.2   Bridge a clear sandy creek. Continue through the Red Hills.

7.6   Walk atop a very long boardwalk. Pitcher plants are in the area.

7.9   Reach sandy Forest Road 319-G. Turn around or have shuttle ready.

15.8   Arrive back at trailhead if you are doing the out-and-back hike.

More Information

Local Information
Stone County Economic Development Partnership, P.O. Box 569, 419 S. Vardaman Street, Wiggins, MS 39577; (601) 928-5418; www.stonecounty.com.

Local Events/Attractions
Canoe Black Creek for over 40 miles through the De Soto National Forest. Black Creek Canoe Rental offers boat rentals and shuttles. They also shuttle hikers and backpackers on the Black Creek Trail. Black Creek Canoe Rental, P.O. Box 414, Brooklyn, MS 39425; (601) 582-8817; www.blackcreekcanoe.com.

49 Tuxachanie Trail

This is simply one of the best hiking trails in Mississippi. The 13-plus-mile trek wanders through a remote section of the De Soto National Forest, along pine hills where a longleaf/wiregrass ecosystem reigns, and dipping into streams and wetlands among bay, holly, and magnolia trees. The last part sidles along Tuxachanie Creek, a secluded blackwater stream that adds yet another ecological component to the hike.

Start: U.S. Highway 49 trailhead near Saucier
Distance: 13.2 miles one way
Approximate hiking time: 5.5 to 7.5 hours one way
Difficulty: Difficult due to length
Trail surface: Pine needles, leaves, dirt, grass
Seasons: Fall through spring
Other trail users: Hikers only
Canine compatibility: Leashed dogs permitted

Land status: National forest
Nearest town: Saucier
Fees and permits: No fees or permits required
Schedule: Open year-round
Maps: Tuxachanie Trail; USGS maps: McHenry, Airey
Trail contacts: De Soto National Forest, 654 West Frontage Road, Wiggins, MS 39577; (601) 528-6160; www.fs.fed.us/r8/mississippi

Finding the trailhead: To reach the US 49 trailhead follow Highway 67 to US 49. Head north on US 49 and the trailhead will be on your right after 0.9 mile. To reach the POW Camp trailhead from the intersection of US 49 and Highway 67 just north of Saucier, take Highway 67 south for 1.3 miles, then turn left on Old Highway 67. Continue on Old Highway 67 for 4 miles to a four-way stop. Continue straight, now on Bethel Road, County Road 402. Travel for 3.9 miles, then turn left at the sign for Tuxachanie Trail/POW Camp. Turn left on Forest Road 402-E and reach the POW recreation area on your right at 0.3 mile. As you face the lake, the Tuxachanie Trail comes out on the right bank, downhill from the concrete relics of the POW Camp. *DeLorme: Mississippi Atlas & Gazetteer:* Page 61 D8. GPS trailhead coordinates: N30 40' 0.84" / W89 8' 2.7".

The Hike

Locals use the first part of the trail, near US 49, for strolls. The trail immediately heads due east, joining an old railroad grade built by Dantzler Lumber Company to reach their sawmill. Immediately bridge a small sluggish stream. Note the gum trees along the water's edge. The path leaves the grade and enters pine woods with yaupon understory, along with dogwood, hickory, and a few oaks as well.

The trail undulates in hilly pine woods, making an extended descent into the greater West Creek drainage amid bay and holly trees, bridging magnolia-heavy West Creek on a sturdy iron span. The path curves back downstream along West Creek before rising to rejoin the elevated railroad grade, occasionally bridging wet areas on planks. Cane, ferns, palmetto, titi, and sparkleberry join the other wetland trees. Note that pines and oaks in these wetlands have buttressed bases for added stabilization when these wetlands are inundated. Look for wildflowers in fall along wet margins.

The trail keeps the straight track, going slightly north of due east through longleaf/wiregrass. Cross occasional two-track forest roads that are closed to the public and utilized by Forest Service personnel to manage the forest. This remote area of the De

The Tuxachanie Trail wanders through longleaf/wiregrass woodland

Soto National Forest will emit nothing but the sounds of nature and breezes blowing through the pines.

Occasionally, the railroad grade, in an effort to keep as level as possible, will cut through a hill or travel atop a raised bed. Note how many of the trailbed tree roots run perpendicular to the trail direction. This is because these trees grew when there were railroad timbers laid down.

The Saucier Creek watershed offers floral variation as the path dips into streams and onto hills. Watch for pilings of the old railroad grade here. Keep east to cross paved Airey Tower Road and reach Airey Lake Recreation Area at 5.9 miles. It offers a restroom, parking, campground, and water. Follow old forest roads, and watch the white diamond plastic blazes as they lead to clear Copeland Spring. This structure is squared off, housing clear water. The trail continues east alternating between hills and hollows. Some of the long boardwalks cross pitcher plant habitats.

▶ James Copeland was born in Jackson County, Mississippi, in 1823 and led a life of crime until his death in 1857, when he was hung. He was a killer, a horse thief, an arsonist, a slave stealer, a counterfeiter, and an all-around bad guy. In between sprees he would hide out in this part of Mississippi, thus Copeland Spring was named after him.

Head into the Boggy Branch watershed, bridging one of its tributaries at 8.0 miles. The Tuxachanie Trail, marked with white plastic diamonds, reaches the first intersection with the Bigfoot Horse Trail—a series of equestrian loops marked with green, red, or yellow blazes. Make sure and stay with the white plastic diamond blazes, even though the trail does run in conjunction with the Bigfoot Horse Trail for the next 2 miles to reach a trail junction and rest area with a picnic table. Here the Tuxachanie Trail once again sets off on its own, angling southeast toward Tuxachanie Creek as a hiker-only trail the rest of the distance. At this point, it's a wide mown grassy track.

The final part of the hike enters the Tuxachanie Creek valley and you become enveloped in lush forest, albeit storm damaged, while traveling an irregular and sandy trailbed under bay and holly trees. Cane often crowds the trail. Tuxachanie Creek is a classic blackwater stream with sandbars on the insides of curves and fallen brush decomposing in it. The path does climb away from the stream at 12.5 miles into the storm-damaged area with many snags. After briefly returning to the creek the Tuxachanie Trail reaches a junction. Stay right here and make your way to POW Lake. The area was named for its housing captured German soldiers during World War II. Join a grassy track to shortly come out on the impoundment. Cruise past the dam spillway, completing the end-to-end hike.

Miles and Directions

0.0 Start at the US 49 trailhead. Join old railroad grade heading due east.

0.3 Trail dips and crosses a branch.

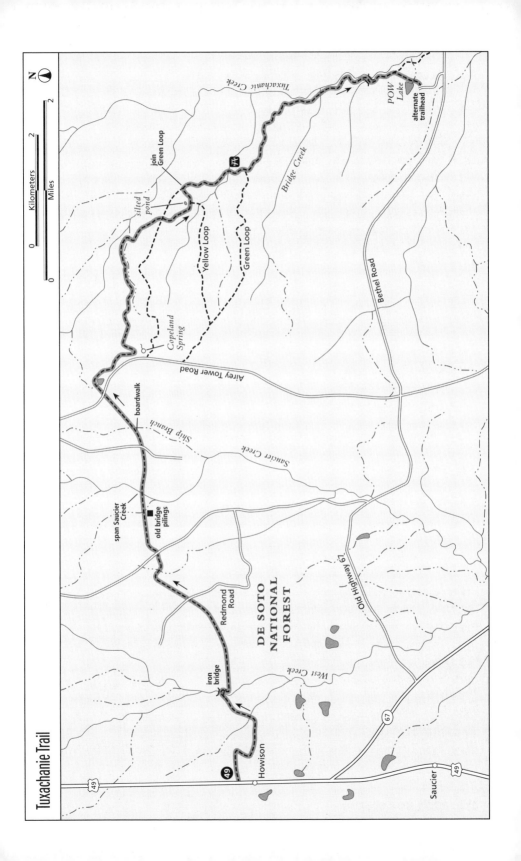

Tuxachanie Trail

N

0   Kilometers   2

0   Miles   2

Tuxachanie Creek

Bridge Creek

join Green Loop

silted pond

Yellow Loop

Green Loop

POW Lake

alternate trailhead

Bethel Road

Copeland Spring

Airey Tower Road

boardwalk

Ship Branch

Saucier Creek

span Saucier Creek

old bridge pilings

Redmond Road

DE SOTO NATIONAL FOREST

West Creek

Old Highway 67

iron bridge

Howison

49

67

49

Saucier

0.4 The Tuxachanie leaves the grade and curves south.

0.6 The path resumes easterly track in undulating pine woods.

1.0 Bridge a tributary of West Creek. Rise to pine-oaks before descending again.

1.6 The trail seemingly forks as one path keeps straight to West Creek and an old bridge site, while correct route reaches an iron bridge that replaced the old one. Potential backpack camping area on the far side of the iron bridge.

2.9 Cross gravel Redmond Road.

3.3 Extended downhill reaches a bridge spanning a feeder branch of Saucier Creek.

3.5 Cross second feeder branch of Saucier Creek. Enter longleaf/wiregrass woodland.

3.7 Cross a forest road and descend. Keep east downhill, spanning occasional boardwalks.

4.2 Bridge a feeder branch of Saucier Creek. Note old railroad pilings.

4.4 Span Saucier Creek. More railroad bridge pilings.

4.9 Cross unnamed forest road.

5.1 Boardwalk over Ship Branch.

5.7 Cross Airey Tower Road and enter Airey Lake Recreation Area, an alternate trailhead with water, restrooms, camping, and fishing. The Tuxachanie Trail splits left around the lake. Cross the dam of the lake, bridge a small streambed, and stay with the white plastic diamonds as the path half circles Airey Lake.

6.5 Pass Copeland Spring to the right of the trail. Sign states COPELAND SPRING USED BY OUTLAW JAMES COPELAND AND HIS GANG PRIOR TO THE WAR BETWEEN THE STATES.

8.0 Cross a tributary of Boggy Branch.

8.6 Cross a forest road, then intersect the Yellow Loop of the Bigfoot Horse Trail. Curve south and pass by a silted pond. Shortly reach a junction then travel in conjunction with the Yellow Loop.

9.3 Join the Green Loop after leaving the Yellow Loop at 9.1 miles. Keep south in pines and open terrain.

9.8 Descend across a long boardwalk under bay trees, then span Spike Buck Creek.

10.0 Reach a rest area and trail junction with picnic table. Green Loop leaves right while the Tuxachanie Trail continues straight.

11.3 Drift into lush woods to come alongside Tuxachanie Creek.

11.6 Cross Bridge Creek. Stay along Tuxachanie Creek.

12.5 Bridge a feeder branch then climb into storm-damaged pines.

12.7 Return to Tuxachanie Creek and continue downstream.

12.8 Reach a trail junction. Take the spur trail leading right to POW Lake. Ascend from Tuxachanie Creek. Trail continuing down Tuxachanie Creek leads to Bethel Road.

13.2 Reach POW Lake and east trailhead.

More Information

Local Information

Stone County Economic Development Partnership, P.O. Box 569, 419 S. Vardaman Street, Wiggins, MS 39577; (601) 928-5418; www.stonecounty.com.

Local Events/Attractions

Paddle Red Creek, South Mississippi Canoe Rental, 23 Old Highway 49 West, Brooklyn, MS 39425, (601) 544-4207, www.southmscanoe.com. Float over sandy shallows and beside large sandbars as Red Creek winds through Stone County just north of the Tuxachanie Trail. South Mississippi Canoe Rental can rent the boats and provide shuttles, not only on Red Creek but also the Leaf and Bowie Rivers.

50 Davis Bayou

When driving into Davis Bayou, you enter an oasis of green natural coastal woodland a few miles east of Biloxi amid the growing Mississippi coastline. Davis Bayou is part of the Mississippi Unit of Gulf Islands National Seashore. This protected part of the Magnolia State coast includes an auto–accessible mainland where you can hike amid a maritime forest and along tidal creeks with views extending toward the Gulf and alligator viewing possibilities, too.

Start: Gulf Islands National Seashore Visitor Center at Davis Bayou
Distance: 2.3 miles out-and-back, including CCC side trail
Approximate hiking time: 1.5 to 2 hours
Difficulty: Easy
Trail surface: Leaves, dirt, gravel, boardwalks
Seasons: Year-round, best late fall through spring
Other trail users: Hikers only

Canine compatibility: Leashed dogs permitted
Land status: National park
Nearest town: Ocean Springs
Fees and permits: No fees or permits required
Schedule: Open year-round
Maps: Davis Bayou Trails; USGS maps: Ocean Springs
Trail contacts: Gulf Islands National Seashore, 3500 Park Road, Ocean Springs, MS 39564; (228) 875-9057, ext. 100; www.nps.gov/guis

Finding the trailhead: From the intersection of Interstate 10 and U.S. Highway 90 in Biloxi, take US 90 east for 7.7 miles to Park Road. Turn right on Park Road and enter the national seashore. Follow the signs to the visitor center. The hike starts from the right-hand side of the parking area as you face the visitor center. *DeLorme: Mississippi Atlas & Gazetteer:* Page 62 H1. GPS trailhead coordinates: N30 23' 29.7" / W88 47' 21.6".

The Hike

The greater visitor center area includes a boardwalk that overlooks Davis Bayou and beyond. Bring a picnic, dine under the live oaks, and stop in the visitor center. This hike starts away from the water. As you face the visitor center, the trail starts in the back of the parking area to your right. Leave the parking area, heading through coastal woodland of sweetgum, pine, maple, and willow oak with a thick understory of yaupon holly and palmetto. This area was damaged by Hurricane Katrina, leaving a gap-laden tree canopy. The singletrack path is about 2 feet wide and travels generally north at this point, away from the ocean.

After reaching Park Road a pedestrian bridge and boardwalk takes you over a saltwater bayou bordered with marsh grass. Long-reaching views extend toward the Gulf. As you leave the bayou, continue on a gravel track bordering Park Road. Live oaks—those that survived Katrina—are mixed in the forest as well. Pass the CCC Trail, which leaves left 0.2 mile to an overlook of the bayou. You can take the spur now or on your return trip.

Shortly, leave the road and reach the loop portion of the hike. Head left. Note the cedars in the maritime woodland mix. The trail heads downhill, cruising along another tidal creek that feeds Stark Bayou. This is hilly terrain for the coast. Cross low areas on boardwalks. The loop ends, but take the spur trail—actually a long board-walk—that heads west over Stark Bayou. This is a good alligator-watching area, and tourists will be gathered here looking for the reptiles. Good views of the estuary open before the path rises to a picnic area. The locale has picnic tables and upright grills under shaded and non-shaded sites for you to enjoy. This is where you turn around and begin heading back toward the visitor center. Make sure and do the north side of the loop and the CCC Trail on your return trip. See the concrete relics of the Civilian Conservation Corps camp and an overlook of Stark Bayou.

DAVIS BAYOU ACTIVITIES

Beyond hiking, the Davis Bayou Unit of Gulf Island National Seashore has other recreational possibilities. A boat ramp allows those who have a boat to explore the sloughs and bayous that open to the Gulf. Canoers and kayakers ply the calmer, more protected waters in the park. Fishing is popular here, especially since Davis Bayou has its own fishing pier. Also the park puts on interpretive programs year-round on weekends.

Park visitors like to bicycle the quiet roads within Davis Bayou. For more adventurous bicyclists, the Live Oaks Bicycle Route leaves Davis Bayou and travels the back streets of Ocean Springs. You can follow the designated bicycle route signs for 15 miles past old homes, quiet beaches, and museums.

Camping is popular here as well. The campground at Davis Bayou has many ideal characteristics and makes for a quality coastal camping destination. First, the grounds are well maintained and naturally appealing. It is the right size, with only fifty-two sites. The large campsites all have water and electricity and stand on elevated terrain bordered by salt marsh creeks. The adjacent creeks are barely visible because the woods are so thick on the edge of the campground. Large live oaks draped in Spanish moss, along with pines and water oaks, shade the campsites, which are adequately spaced from one another. Grass and leaf litter cover the forest floor. A centrally located bathhouse with hot showers serves the campground. Fifty-amp and thirty-amp hookups are available for the big rigs.

RVs and trailers will mostly occupy the campground in the winter, with more tent campers during the summer. Davis Bayou fills regularly with snowbirders from January through March. It will also fill during holiday weekends such as Easter, Memorial Day, and Labor Day. Sites are generally available, but reservations are not accepted, so you must take your chances during these times. Call the park to get an idea of campground capacity if you are unsure whether to come or not. Davis Bayou is known for having many returnees coming back year after year. Fans of the national park system, birders, and many locals call Davis Bayou home for at least a few nights per year.

A trip to West Ship Island is a must for visitors. Here, you can see historic Fort Massachusetts. West Ship Island has been home to a lighthouse for over 150 years. A brick tower was first put there in 1853 to protect boats in the shallow Mississippi Sound traveling from Mobile to New Orleans. Erosion forced the erection of a second lighthouse, using the old lighthouse lens, in 1886. The new lighthouse, though built of wood, was strong enough to withstand a hurricane, as the keeper of the lighthouse, Dan McColl, and his wife found out in 1893 as they hunkered down in the tower. As dangerous as it was, the loneliness and isolation is what drove most lighthouse keepers back to the mainland. The last keeper of the light left in 1955, and later the light was relocated. But the attractive white wooden lighthouse tower remained until 1972 when campers accidentally burned it to the ground. Today the Ship Island Lighthouse has been rebuilt and has reclaimed its spot as a part of Mississippi Gulf Coast history. Rangers lead daily tours when the ferryboat is operating. Take the 0.3-mile boardwalk from the bay side of the island to the Gulf side of the island for a primitive island experience. The few island amenities, such as outdoor showers, are on the bay side of the island. A swim beach overlooks the Gulf and beachcombing can be good. For ferry schedule information, call (866) 466-7386 or visit www.msship.com.

Miles and Directions

0.0   Start at the parking area near the visitor center. Follow a singletrack trail through maritime woods. (FYI: An accompanying trail guide has numbered interpretive stops that you can enjoy. Pick up the guide at the visitor center.)

0.2   Bridge bayou along Park Road.

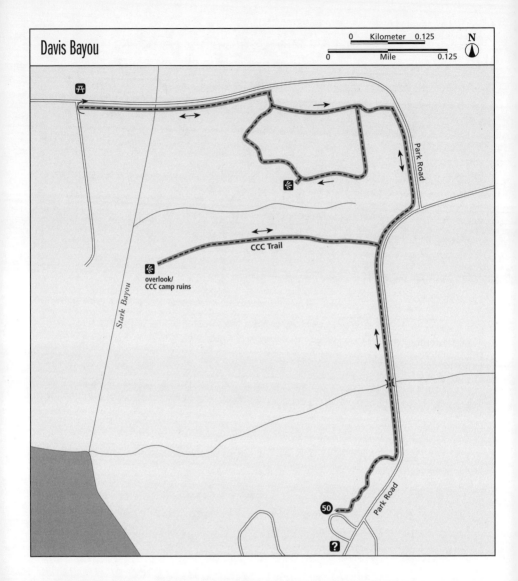

Davis Bayou

0   Kilometer   0.125

0   Mile   0.125

N

Park Road

CCC Trail

overlook/
CCC camp ruins

Stark Bayou

Park Road

50

?

0.3 Intersect the CCC Trail, which leads left 0.2 mile to an overlook and CCC camp ruins.

0.5 Reach the loop portion of the hike. Head left.

0.7 A spur trail leaves left to an overlook of the bayou.

0.9 Reach the end of the loop. A spur trail leads left toward the picnic area and over Stark Bayou.

1.1 Arrive at picnic area. Begin returning to visitor center.

1.3 Return via north end of the loop to gain new trail.

1.6 Pass the CCC Trail again. Make 0.4-mile round-trip to see CCC camp ruins.

2.3 Arrive back at the visitor center parking area.

More Information

Local Information

Ocean Springs Chamber of Commerce, 1000 Washington Avenue, Ocean Springs, MS 39564; (228) 875-4424; www.oceanspringschamber.com.

Local Events/Attractions

Peter Anderson Festival, www.oceanspringschamber.com. For this event honoring the famed potter Peter Anderson, they block off downtown Ocean Springs and make it a foot traffic only area with vendors, music, and of course plenty of potters. Held in early November, it's a good time of year to be down here.

Other Books by Johnny Molloy

50 Hikes in Alabama
50 Hikes in the North Georgia Mountains
50 Hikes in the Ozarks
50 Hikes in South Carolina
60 Hikes Within 60 Miles: San Antonio & Austin (with Tom Taylor)
60 Hikes Within 60 Miles: Nashville
A Canoeing & Kayaking Guide to the Streams of Florida
A Canoeing & Kayaking Guide to the Streams of Kentucky (with Bob Sehlinger)
A Paddler's Guide to Everglades National Park
Backcountry Fishing: A Guide for Hikers, Backpackers and Paddlers
Beach & Coastal Camping in Florida
Beach & Coastal Camping in the Southeast
The Best in Tent Camping: The Carolinas
The Best in Tent Camping: Colorado
The Best in Tent Camping: Florida
The Best in Tent Camping: Georgia
The Best in Tent Camping: Kentucky
The Best in Tent Camping: Southern Appalachian & Smoky Mountains
The Best in Tent Camping: Tennessee
The Best in Tent Camping: West Virginia
The Best in Tent Camping: Wisconsin
Day & Overnight Hikes in Great Smoky Mountains National Park
Day & Overnight Hikes in Shenandoah National Park
Day & Overnight Hikes in West Virginia's Monongahela National Forest
From the Swamp to the Keys: A Paddle through Florida History
Hiking the Florida Trail: 1,100 Miles, 78 Days and Two Pairs of Boots
The Hiking Trails of Florida's National Forests, Parks, and Preserves
Land Between the Lakes Outdoor Recreation Handbook
Long Trails of the Southeast
Mount Rogers National Recreation Area Guidebook
Paddling Georgia
Paddling Tennessee
Trial By Trail: Backpacking in the Smoky Mountains

Visit the author's Web site: www.johnnymolloy.com

About the Author

Johnny Molloy is a writer and outdoor adventurer who has spent over 500 nights backpacking in the Smoky Mountains. A graduate of the University of Tennessee, he has written more than three dozen guidebooks about hiking, camping, and paddling; outdoor adventure books; and numerous magazine articles for Web sites and blogs. He currently lives in Johnson City, Tennessee. You can visit him at www.johnny molloy.com.